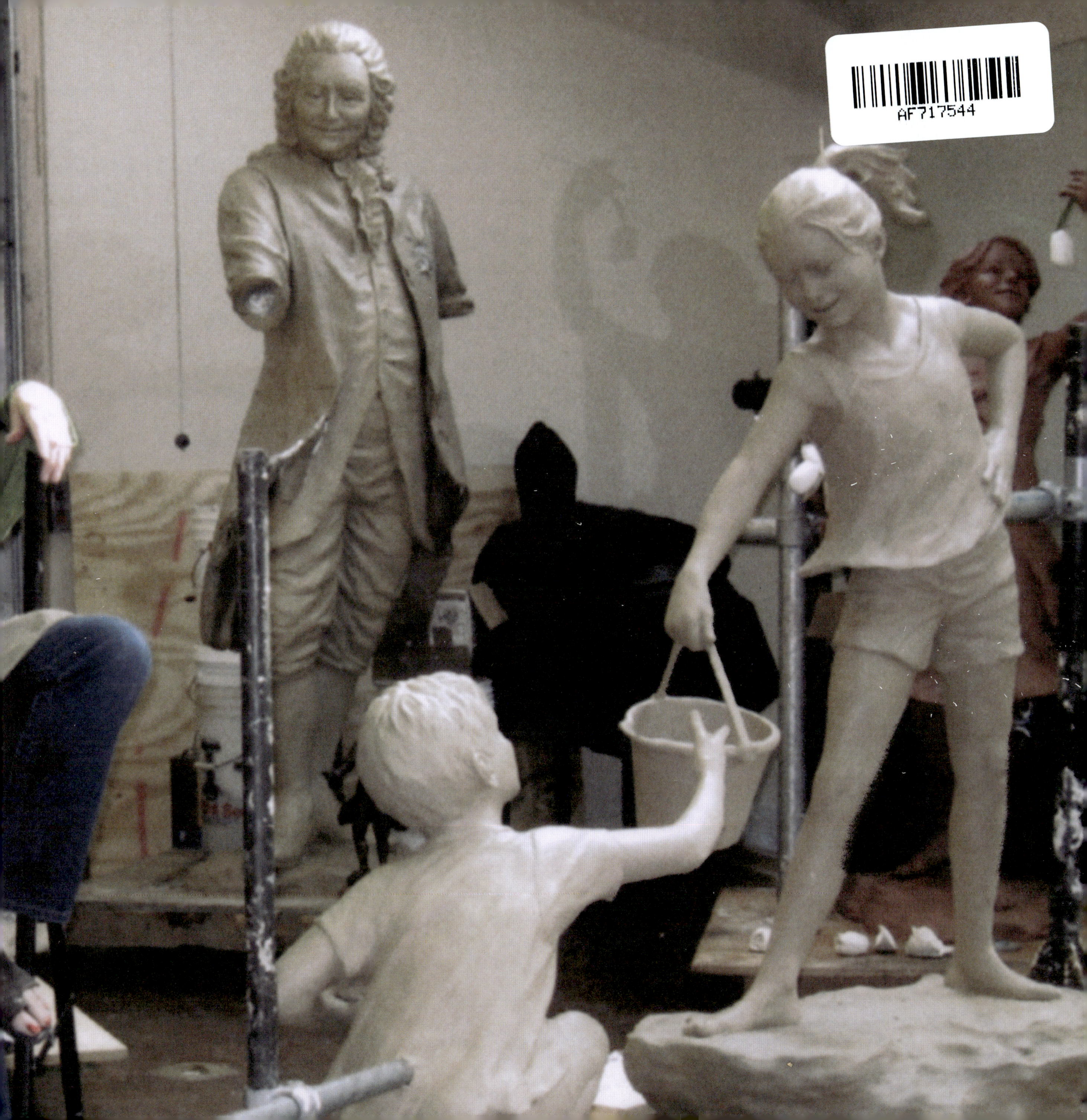

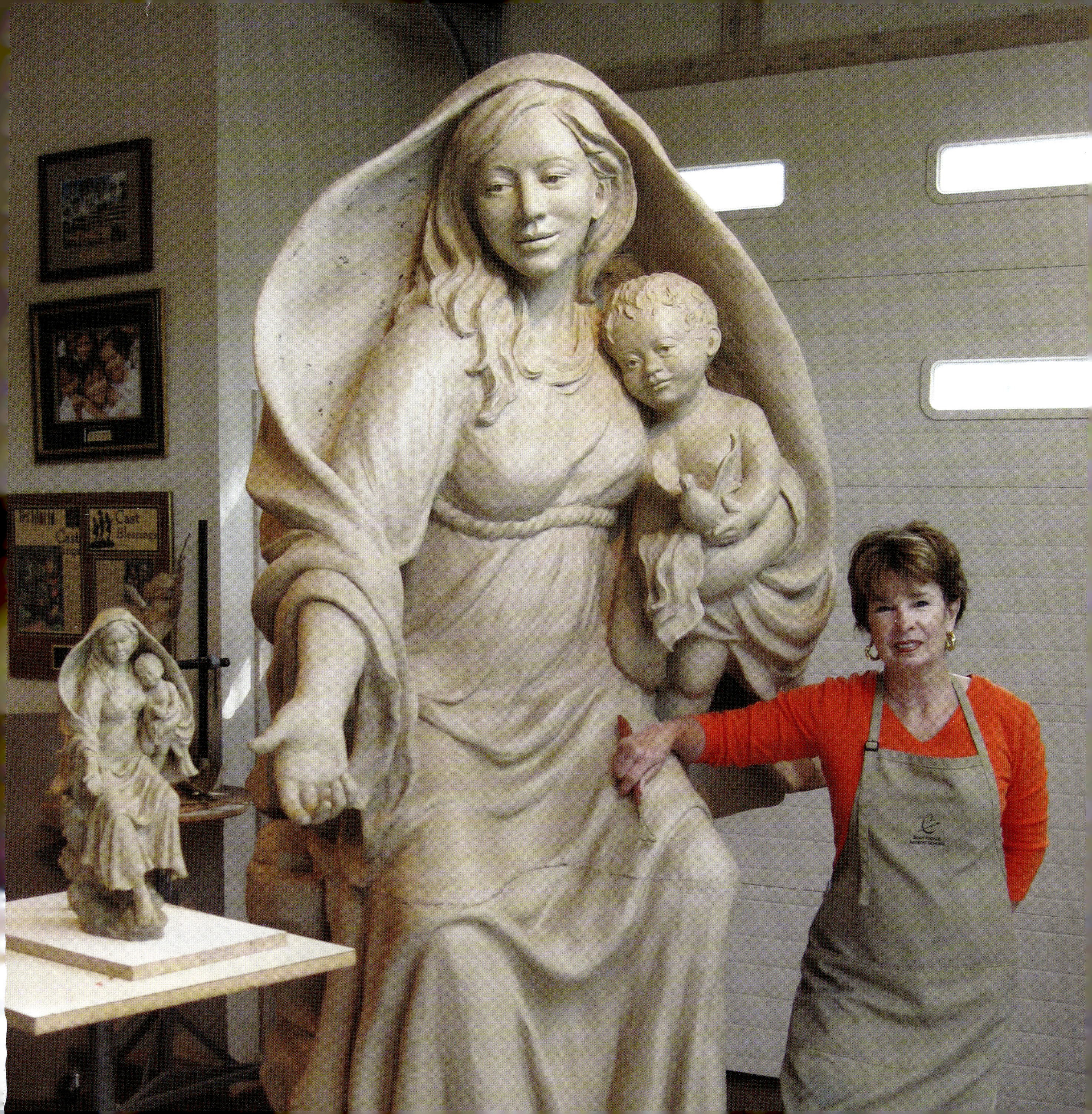
Cast Blessings

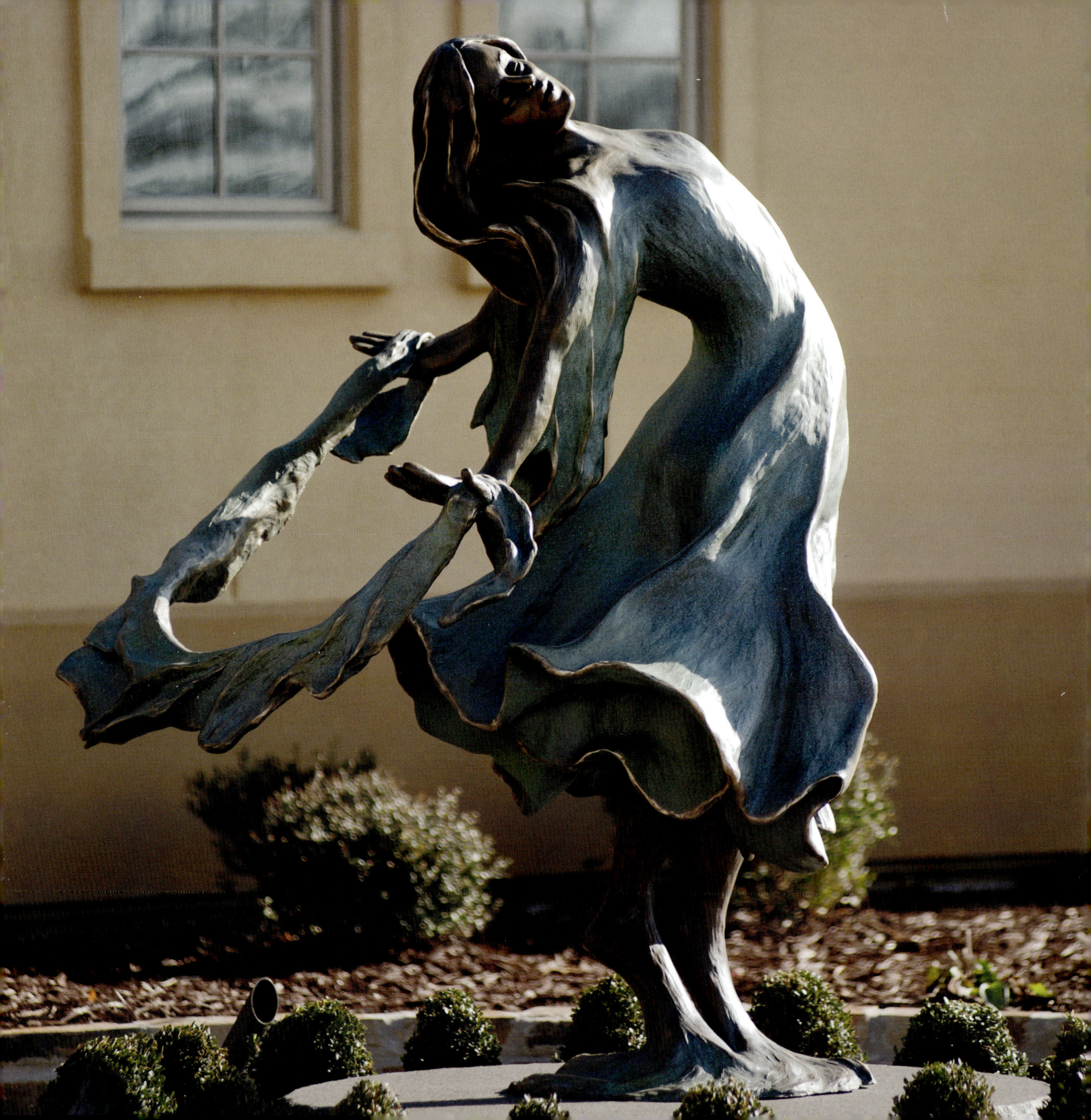

CAPTURING THE *Spirit* IN BRONZE

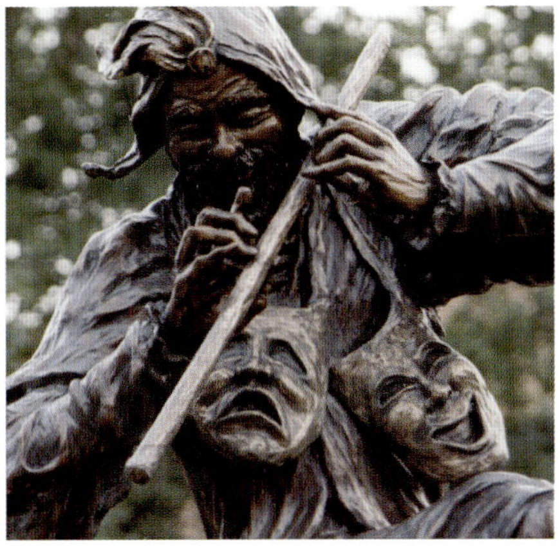

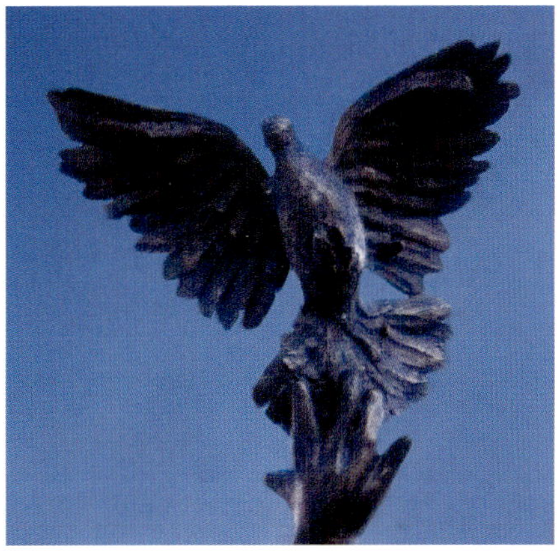

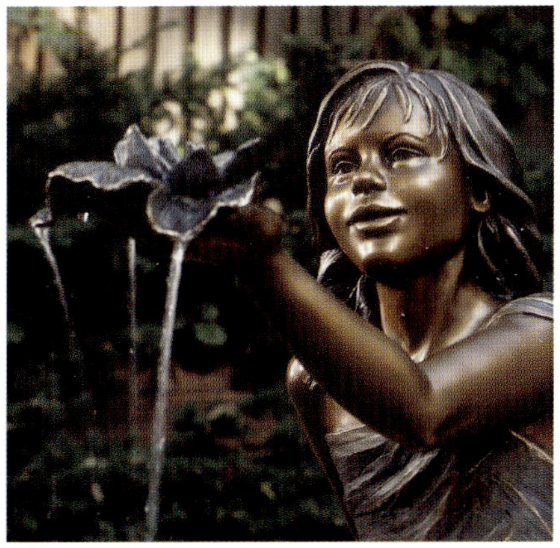

THE JOURNEY AND SCULPTURES OF

ROSALIND COOK

To Melissa

Blessings

Rosalind Cook

First Edition 2014

ISBN 978-0-9759799-2-1
JBW Publications

Printed in Hong Kong

Distributed by **Rosalind Cook Studio**
www.RosalindCook.com

Edited by **John Brooks Walton**
Designed by **Patricia Ridge Bradley**

PAGE ONE
Rosalind Cook with *The Poor Virgin of Nazareth Who Holds in Her Hands the Wealth of the World,* © 2009 Rosalind Cook. Photo by Don Kreutzweiser.

PAGE TWO
Breaking Free, © 2011 Rosalind Cook. Photo by Nathan Harmon.

PAGE THREE, LEFT TO RIGHT
Celebrating the Arts (detail), © 2000 Rosalind Cook. Photo by Andy Leitner. / *Christ's Love for the Children* (detail), © 2008 Rosalind Cook. Photo by Don Kreutzweiser. / *Water Lily* (detail), © 2002 Rosalind Cook. Photo by Bill Welch.

DEDICATION

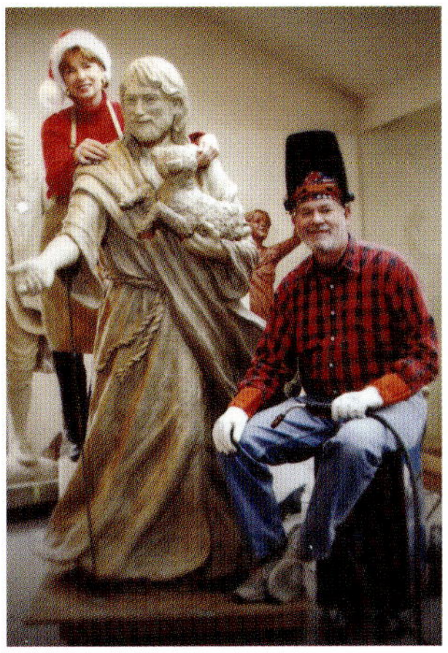

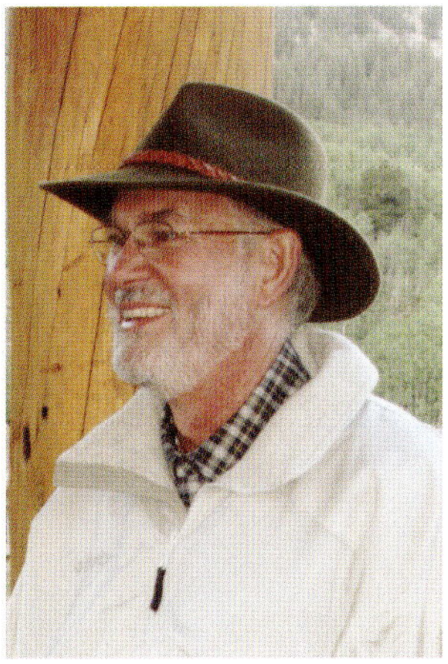

This book is dedicated to the love of my life, HAL COOK, my husband of 44 years. Hal always believed in me, even when I could not believe in myself. He supported me in every way as I pursued my dream and passion. As needed, he has been my welder, my pilot, our family cook, and part-time model. There is no one I respect more than Hal.

PSALM 112:1–9

ABOVE, LEFT TO RIGHT
Hal and Rosalind with *Christ, Our Good Shepherd,* Christmas, 2006. Photo by Don Kreutzweiser. / Hal, at our home in Crested Butte, Colorado. Photo by Sally Kull.

CONTENTS

CONTENTS

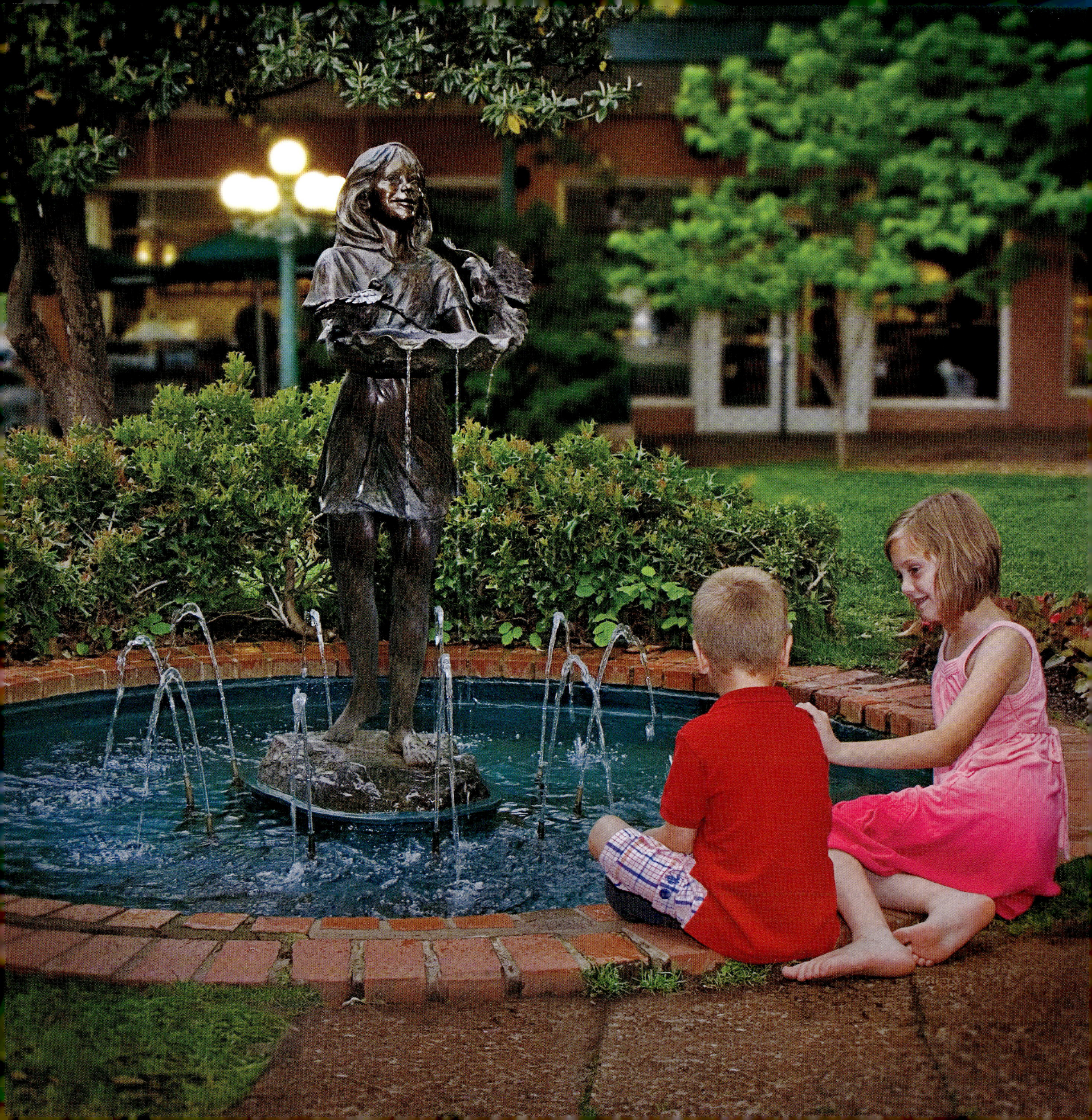

FOREWORD

What a privilege it is to share with so many the enchantment of reading Rosalind Cook's adventurous journey. This wonderfully talented lady has fulfilled her wish of writing her book to inspire others in their personal journeys. Just reading the documentation of the number of pieces of her sculptures and where they are placed in our city, state, country, and world is quite extraordinary.

Rosalind's faith is enduring, and I believe we can give Christ Jesus much of the credit. No one could have exhibited such talent unless the dear Lord had guided her hands.

It wasn't a complete surprise that my husband, Walt Helmerich, was so taken with the sculptures Rosalind produced so beautifully. They fulfilled the purpose of bringing to life his gift of Utica Square. The Square was not just a shopping center to him; it was his way of giving the best to Tulsa and Tulsa families. Trees, gardens, shops, and entertainment were chosen carefully. Walt was not easy to please, but it did please him that the public could see and enjoy the gardens. We walked there, dined there, and literally used it as an extension of our home. Joyfully, we found many doing the same, and Rosalind's art in the Square made the gardens come alive.

I was interested in Rosalind's undergraduate work in Special Education for the visually impaired and blind at the University of Texas. In my acting career, I played the role of Judy Greene in the movie *Bright Victory*, a true story about a young veteran who had been blinded in World War II and overcame many obstacles to become a trial lawyer. Filmed at the Philadelphia Hospital for Blind Veterans, I learned how important the sense of touch can be for someone unsighted. Rosalind's talent lies not only in the viewing of her sculptures, but also in the hands-on experience of "seeing" by touching.

This book is truly a thanksgiving to the many people who have been a part of Rosalind Cook's life journey. She is an inspiration to all who aspire to fulfill their own dreams.

PEGGY V. HELMERICH

OPPOSITE
Welcome, Friends, ©1995 Rosalind Cook.
Photo by Don Kreutzweiser.

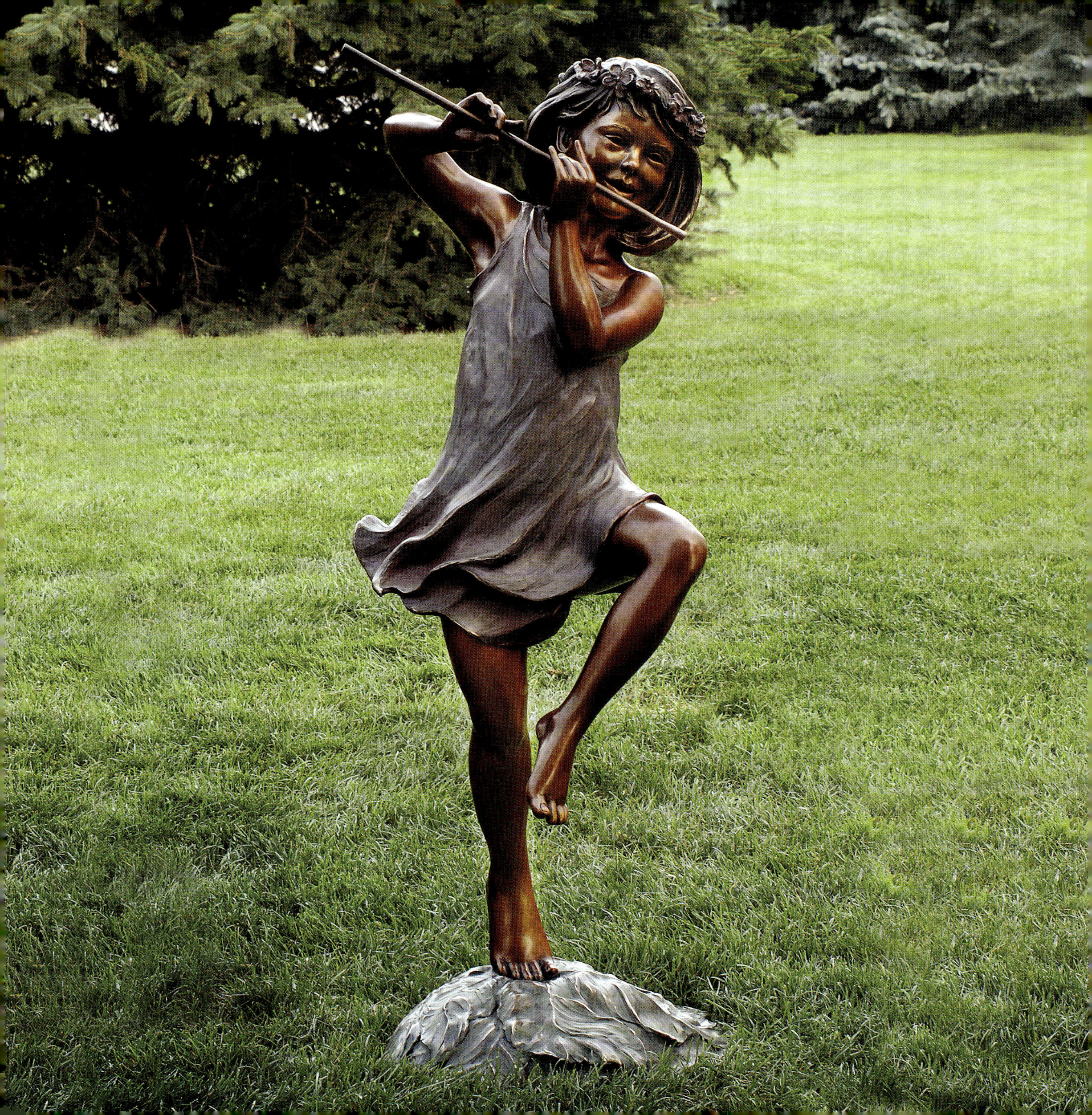

FOREWORD

A work of art is capable of doing many different things.

It can teach and inspire. It can disturb and confound. It can celebrate accomplishment and commemorate loss.

But perhaps the most important thing a work of art can do is evoke a sense of joy.

Joy has been the defining characteristic of Rosalind Cook's sculpture from the very beginning of her career. It goes beyond the smiling, serene faces of the figures she has crafted, be they images of happy children or dancing minstrels. It is a joy that one can tell has infused the entire process of creating a given sculpture, from the first spark of an idea to the installation of the finished bronze.

Another important aspect of Cook's art is one of community. Even when the sculpture is of a single individual, Cook composes the image so that the figure appears aware not just of its surroundings but of the viewer as well. Her art is designed to draw one in, to share in the joy.

In a world that focuses too much on what is ugly and dark, Rosalind Cook in her art attempts to embody the words of the Apostle Paul in his letter to the Philippians: "Whatever is true, whatever is honorable, whatever is just, whatever is pure, whatever is lovely, whatever is commendable, if there is any excellence, if there is anything worthy of praise, think about these things."

JAMES D. WATTS JR.
Art critic for the *Tulsa World*

OPPOSITE
Melody, © 2001 Rosalind Cook.
Photo by Jim Digby.

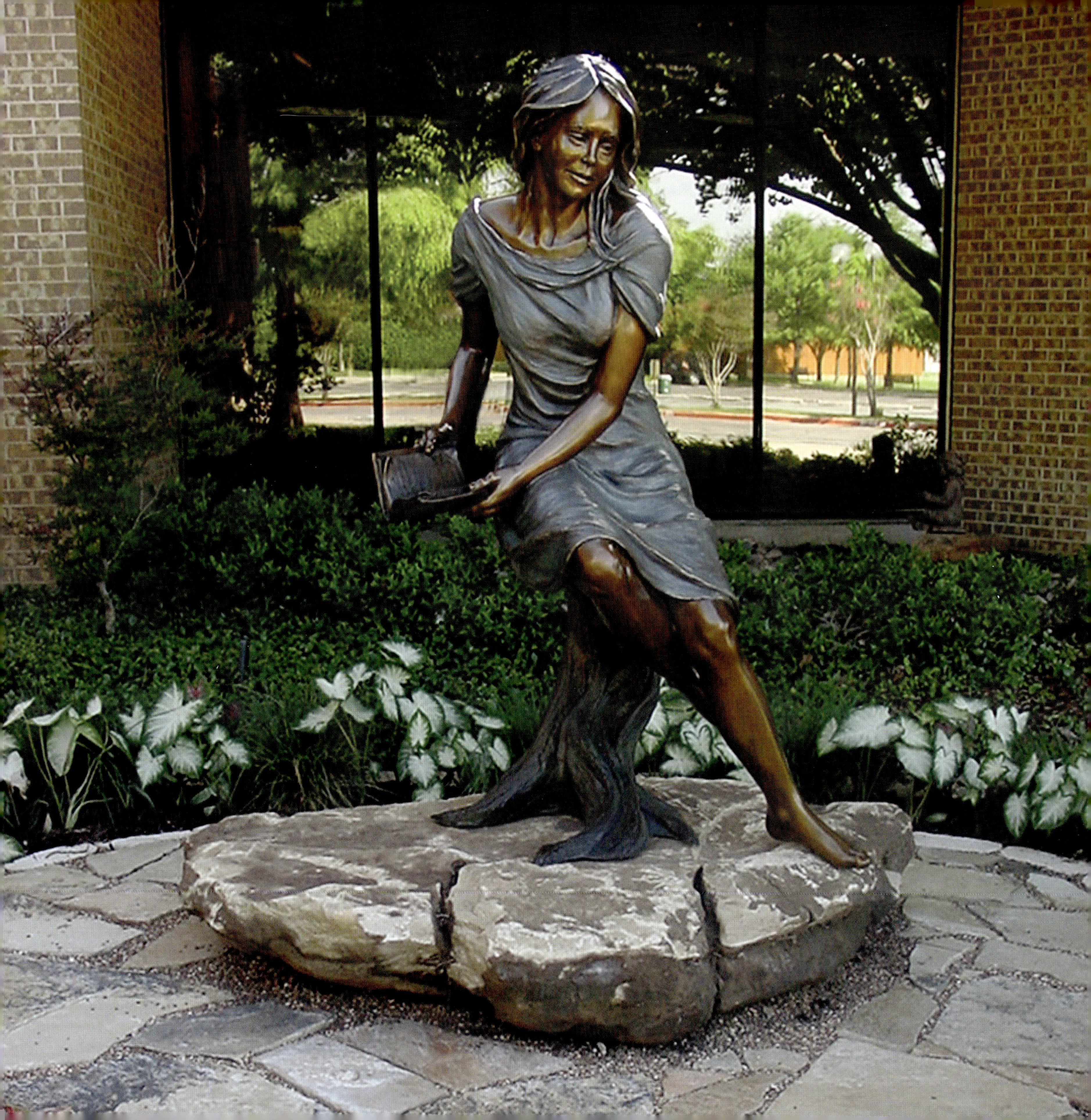

PREFACE

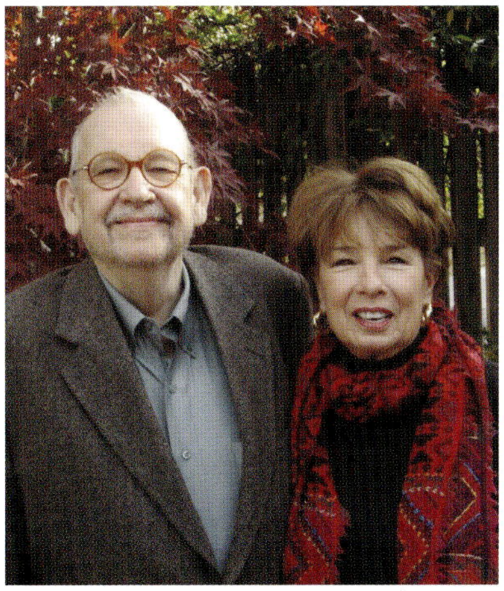

My first meeting with Rosalind Cook was during the writing of my book *The Artwork of Tulsa*. I was featuring five of her sculptures in my book. We met in her studio to discuss the creation of these sculptures.

Upon meeting Rosalind, it was "love at first sight," for she was not only a talented sculptor, but also a lovely lady. Through the years, we would meet at social affairs, and I always enjoyed our conversations.

In the fall of 2012, I received a call from Rosalind saying, "John, I want to document the stories about my sculptures and my journey, but I have no idea where to begin. Will you help me?"

My quick reply was, "When do we start?"

JOHN BROOKS WALTON

OPPOSITE
Poems and Promises, © 2003 Rosalind Cook. Photo courtesy of Hurst Library.

ABOVE
John and Rosalind

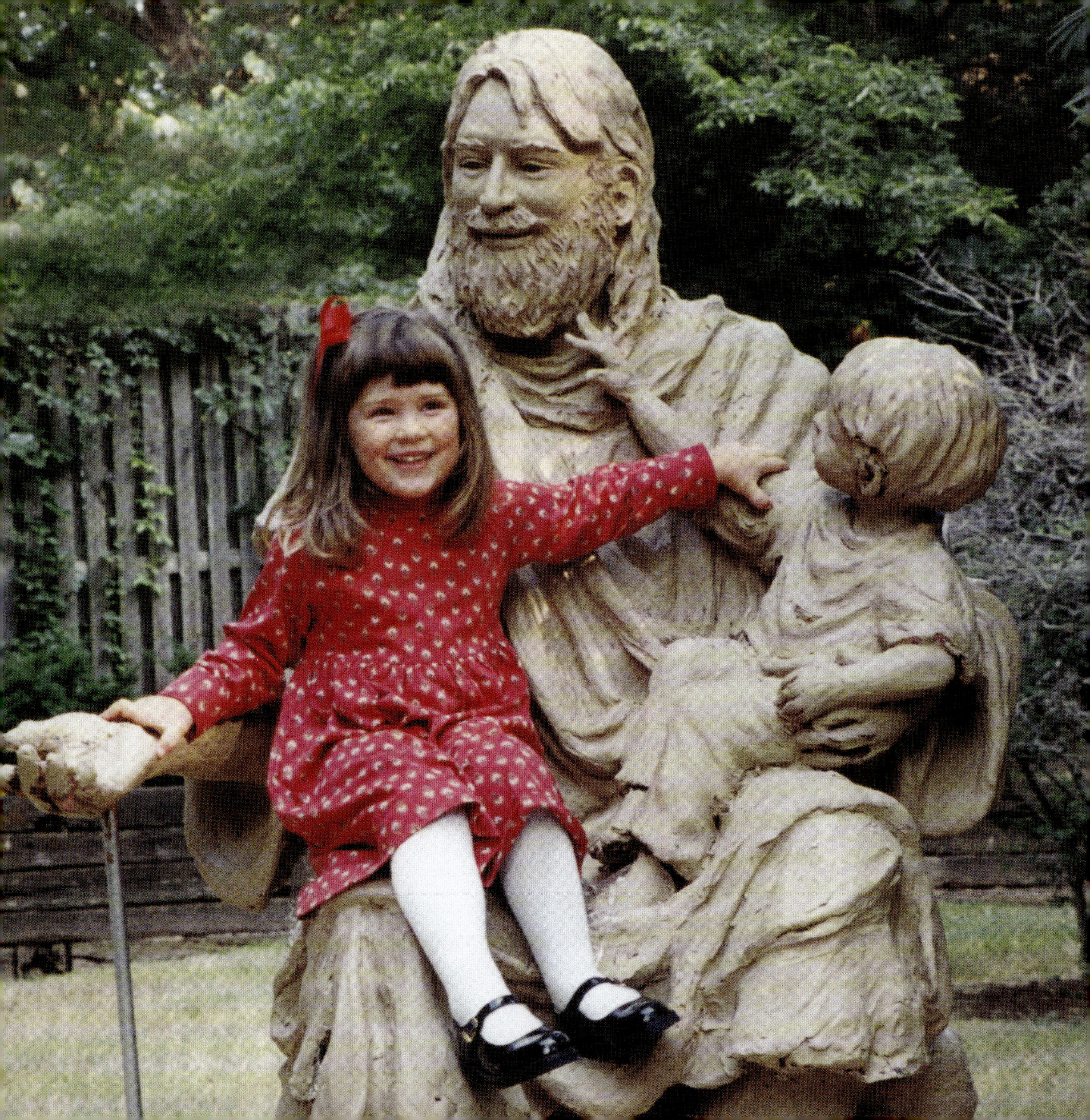

ARTIST'S PERSPECTIVE

In my studio is a small abstract-shaped rock under a glass dome. My mother, Dorlene Wright, returned this rock to me when I flew my family to Seattle, Washington, in 1995, for the dedication of my monument for the World Vision Headquarters.

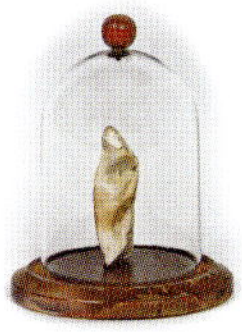

Upon presenting it to me, she told me that, as a toddler, I had found this rock in the loose gravel of our driveway in Peru and had run into the house exclaiming, "Look, Mama! This is Mary holding Baby Jesus!" My mother had kept this little rock in her jewelry box all these years thinking it might be a promise of what God would do in my life. This small, natural sculpture was actually the beginning of my career!

Along with creating many smaller works, there are over 30 life-size and larger sculptures of mine in public places in the Tulsa area, and over 90 significant large works across the United States. The story behind each sculpture is inseparable from the sculpture itself.

In this book, I am leaving a printed record so that you, the viewer, and future generations to come, might have the full story behind each sculpture. It is also my heart's desire to inspire others in their personal journey to fulfill their passion and their dreams.

Sculpting has been a joyful and deeply meaningful discovery of God's calling for my life. I have been stretched to go far beyond what I could accomplish on my own. I have been guided through the agonies of hard work, doubts, and fears. Some of my most disappointing times have led me into brighter new directions. Through distilling the strengths of natural forms and incorporating principles of design, I seek to "Capture the Spirit in Bronze."

ROSALIND COOK

OPPOSITE
My four-year-old granddaughter, McKenna Cook, with *Come Unto Me.*

ABOVE
The rock from the driveway.

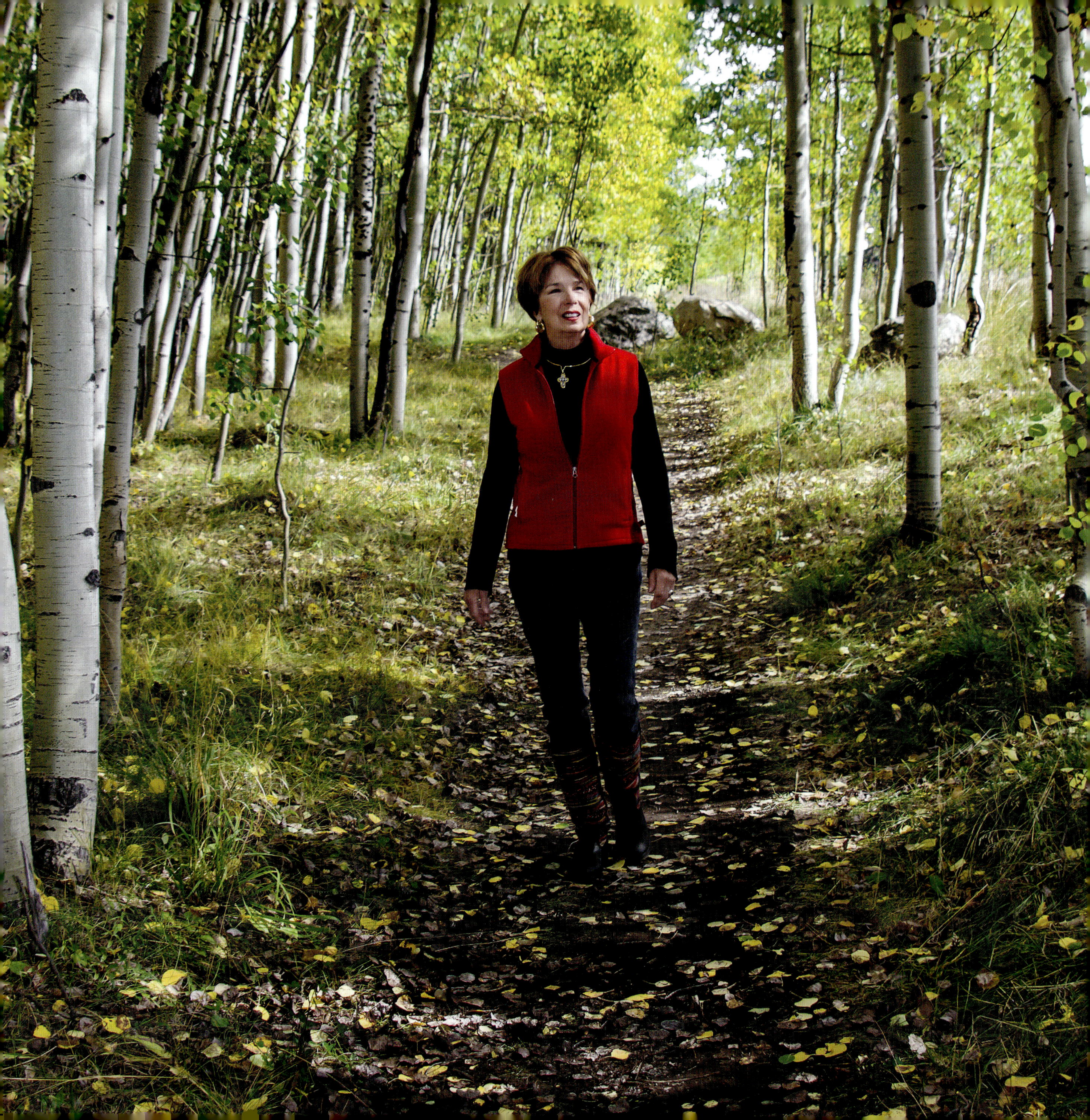

MY JOURNEY

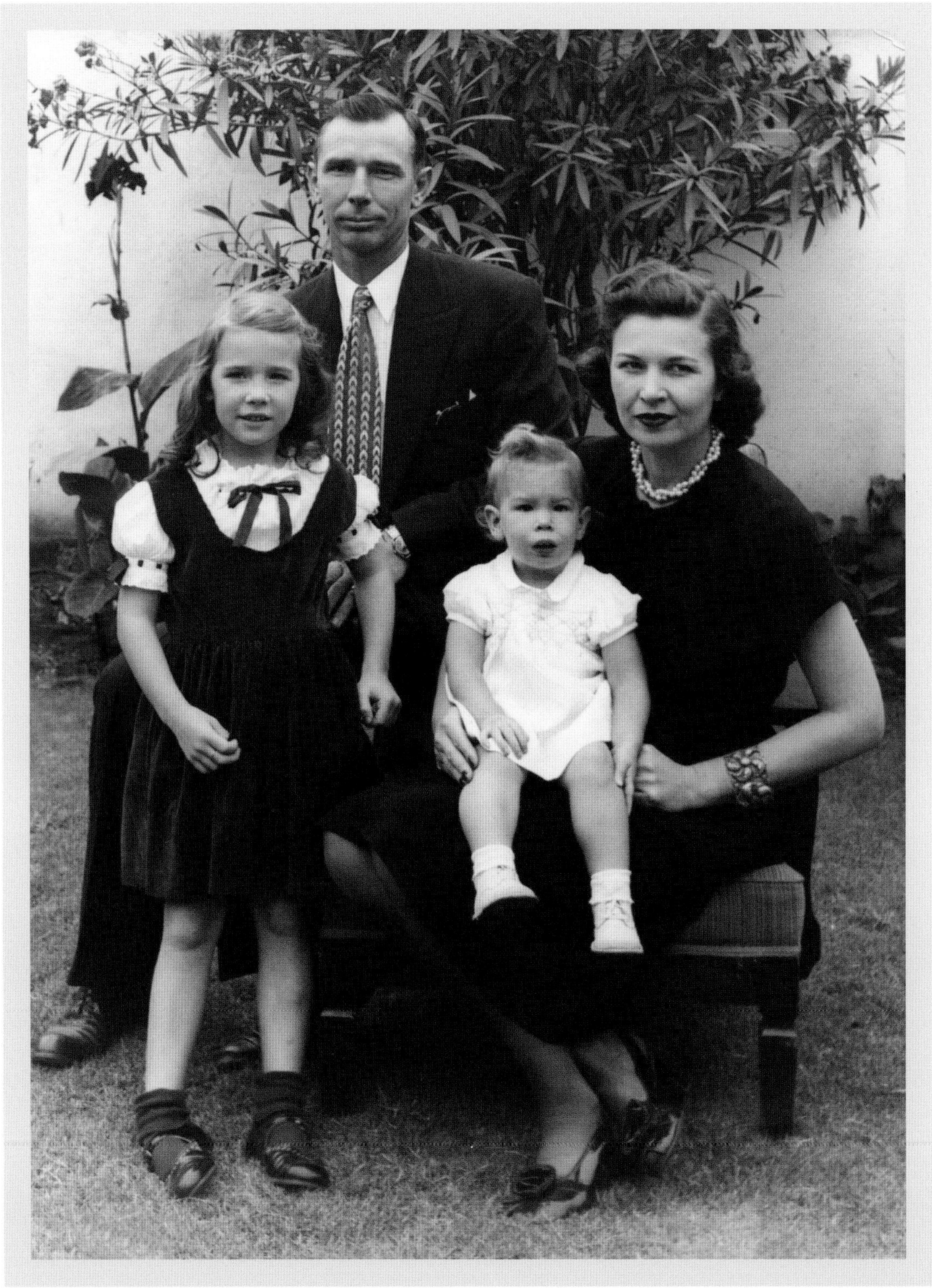

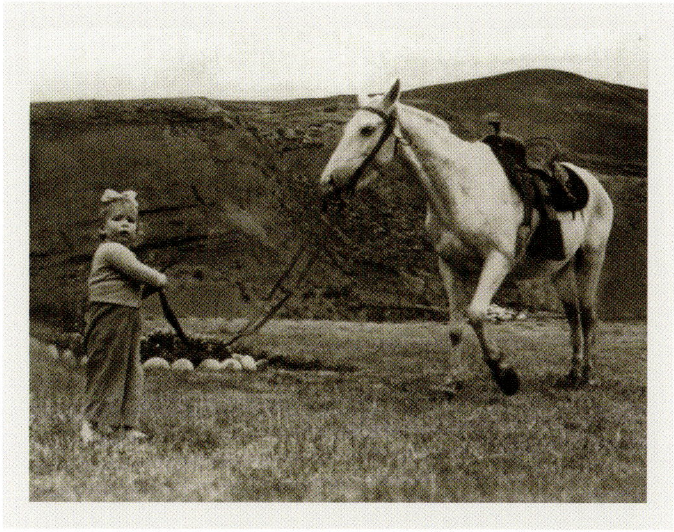

My Peruvian birth certificate from 1946 proclaimed me as "legitimate" My father, Richard H. Wright, a former Texas Aggie football player and animal husbandry major, had been offered a job to manage a million-acre ranch in Peru for the Cerro de Pasco Mining Corporation, a copper-mining operation out of New York. In area, it was larger than the state of Rhode Island, and was composed of 26 separate ranches spread from Peru's coastal plains to the eastern slope of the Andes Mountains.

Many of the ranches were connected by a narrow-gauge railroad on which all of the ranch children loved to ride. My adventurous mother, who was three months pregnant with me, her five-year-old daughter, Pamela, and my father boarded a four-engine DC-4, and we flew off to what was to be my home for the first seven years of my life. We lived in La Oroya, a small town on the eastern slope of the Andes Mountains.

The village was comprised of expatriates from Europe and America, as well as Peruvians. We spent our time between the ranch and town, living at 12,200 feet above sea level, which is above the timber line. Llamas grazed the hillsides as cattle do in the United States. My grandmother back in Texas protested saying, "If you can't grow trees there, how do you expect to grow children?"

PAGE 17
Rosalind in Colorado. Photo by John Miller.

OPPOSITE
My family in 1947: parents Richard and Dorlene Wright; my sister, Pamela; and me on my mother's lap.

ABOVE
With my father's horse in the mountains of Peru.

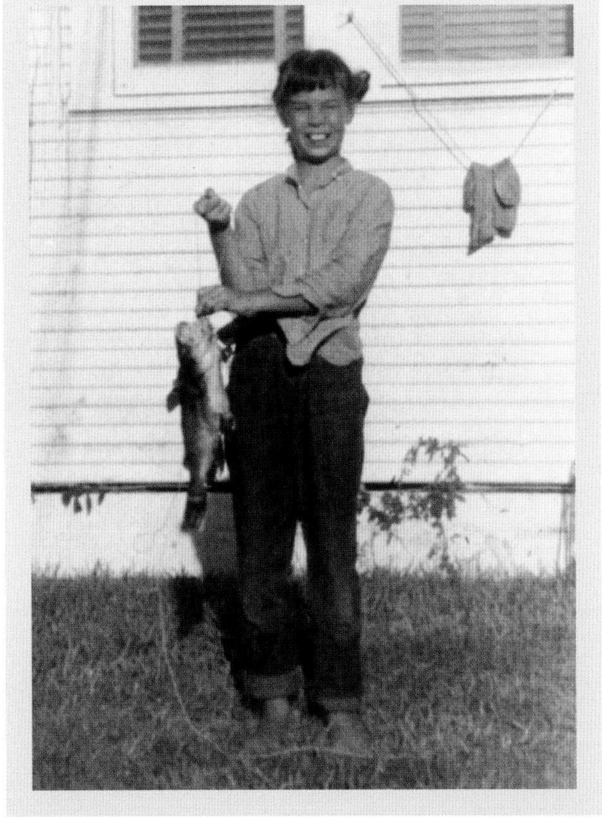

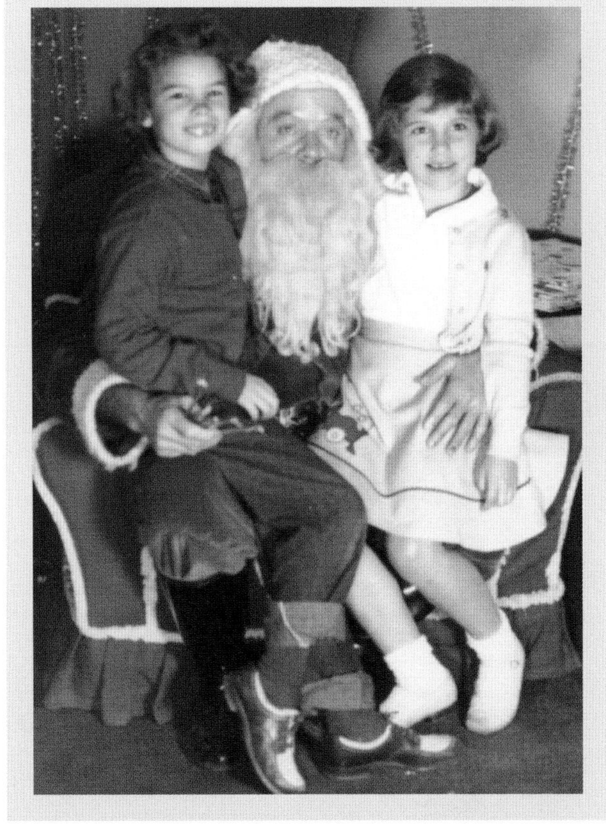

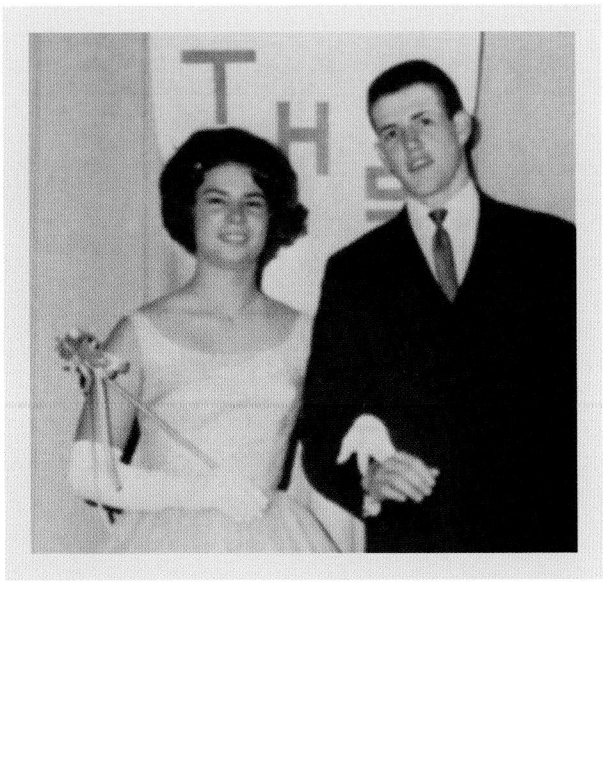

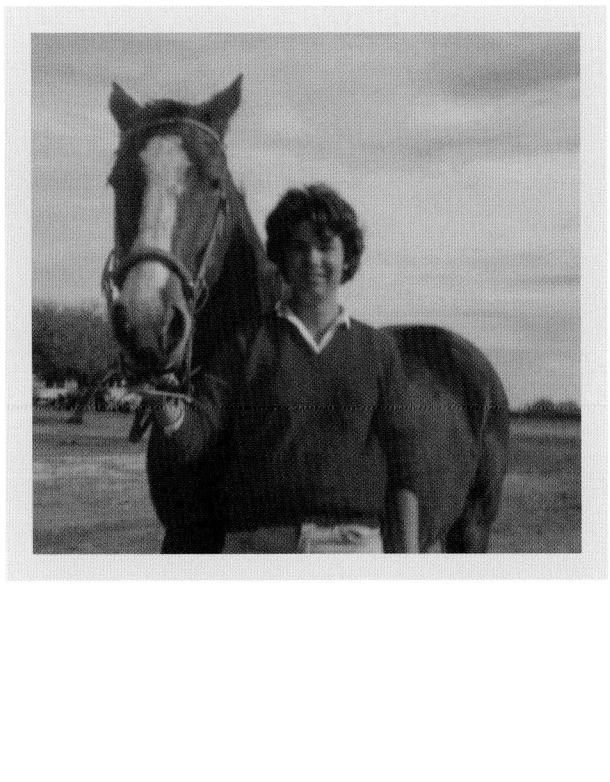

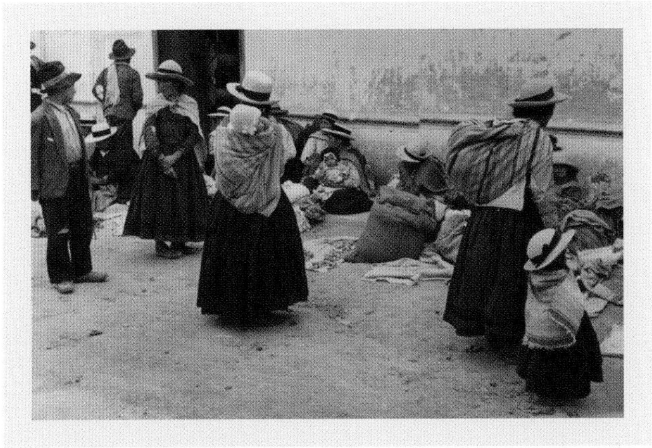

In La Oroya, there were no stores as we know them in the States—only street markets, where the Inca descendants sold their produce and handmade items. We often made many of our own toys and decorations, using cans, string, and bars of soap, along with whatever else we could find. Perhaps my creativity had its roots in this environment. It was a glorious and fun childhood!

OPPOSITE, CLOCKWISE FROM UPPER LEFT
Caught a big catfish in Texas. / A friend and I visit with Santa. / My horse, "Buck," in high school. / Queen and King nominees of Taft High.

ABOVE
The market in La Oroya, Peru, 1940s.

RIGHT
With Mother, on a shopping trip to the mall.

In the 1950s, the Peruvian government began nationalization, taking the large ranches, breaking them up into small parcels, and giving them to the native people. It was a dangerous time for American and European landowners, so the Wright family returned to the United States and settled in Taft, a small town in south Texas with a population of 5,000.

Beginning at age eight, I enjoyed living in this close-knit community, where we rode bikes to school and played freely out-of-doors with complete safety. High school was much like the old TV show, "Happy Days," but with absolutely *no* art classes. My mother and grandmother both painted as a hobby, and they encouraged my creativity, often taking me to their art classes.

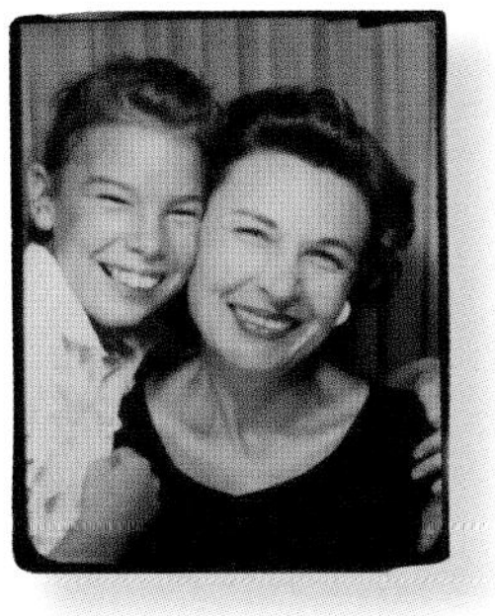

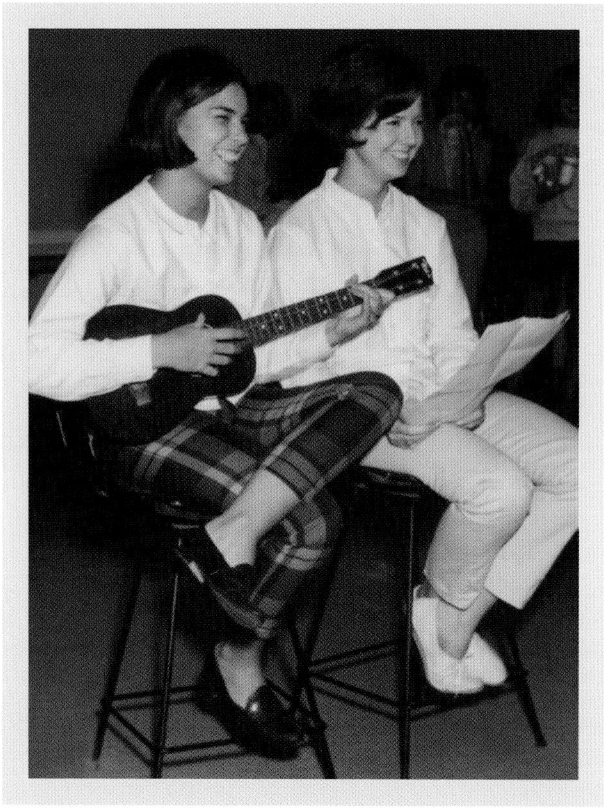
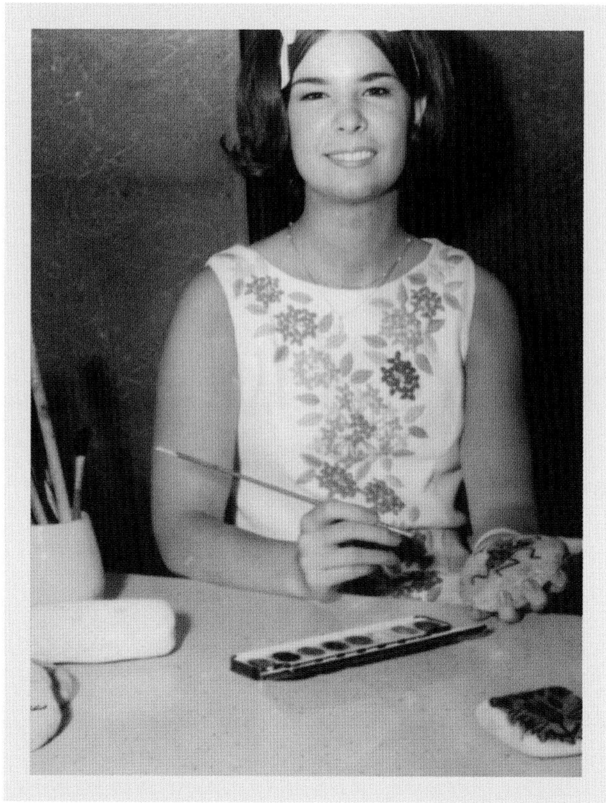
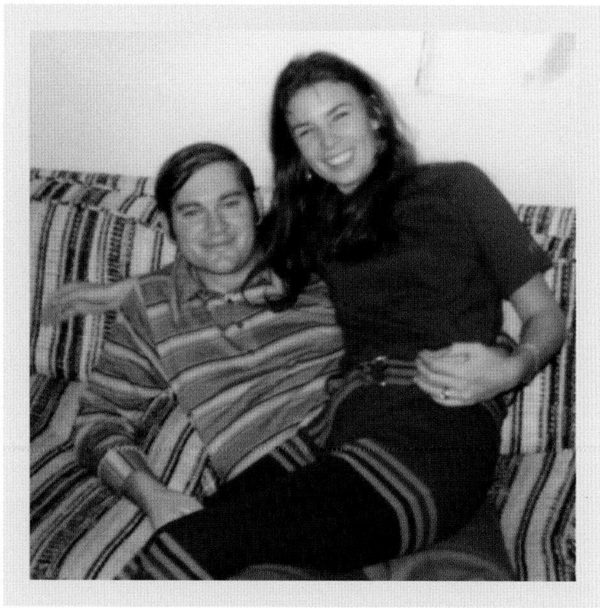
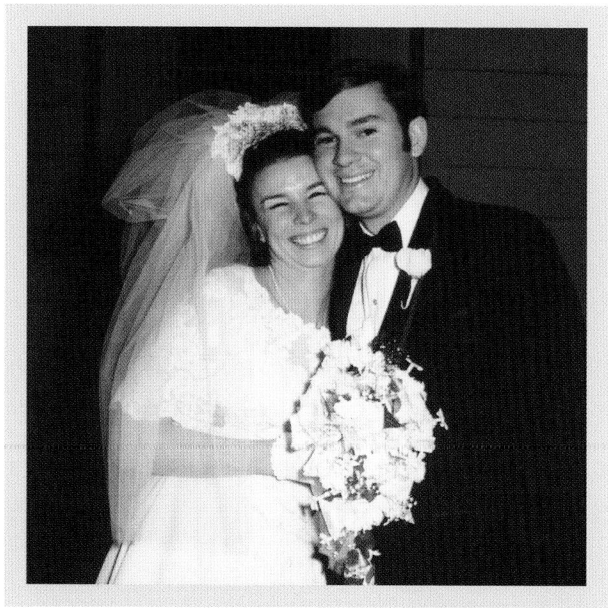

When it came time for me to go to college, my father, being a practical man, refused to let me major in my true love—art. He told me, "I will pay for you to attend college, but you need to choose a major that will allow you to support yourself." Since I had such a love for children with special needs, I majored in Special Education for blind and visually impaired children. This field of study drew on my creativity and increased my awareness of texture, shape, and form.

For spending money, I painted river rocks with sorority/fraternity logos, animals, and local scenes, and sold them through the college bookstore as paperweights and doorstops. It was quite a successful little enterprise. After graduating from the University of Texas, I was hired as an itinerate teacher for the visually impaired in the Dallas public school system.

Dallas was an exciting place for a young adult to begin a career. I roomed with some friends from college and greatly enjoyed my job. After I had taken a vow to never again go on a blind date, a friend talked me into "just one more time… Pleeeze?" When I opened the door, there stood Hal Cook. Hal was an engineer, very practical, and steady in his emotions. Not only was he handsome, but most important, he had the strong character and the integrity I had seen in my father.

I fell madly in love with Hal, and we were married in my little church in Taft, Texas, in 1970. It is absolutely true that opposites attract. Hal carefully thinks things through and is very self-assured. I am impulsive, emotional, and full of energy. Hal is what I am not, and I am what he is not, so together we make a whole. It takes years together to recognize the benefits that opposites bring into a relationship, and the rewards are rich. Our marriage is going on 45 years now, and these are the sweetest years ever!

During our early marriage, Hal and I came to know that God was not some distant cosmic existence, but rather our Creator who longed for a personal relationship with us. This relationship became real through accepting Christ, His Holy Spirit, and His words to us in the scriptures.

OPPOSITE, CLOCKWISE FROM UPPER LEFT
Sorority skit at the University of Texas. / Painting river rocks for spending money. / Mr. and Mrs. Hal Cook. / Happily married in the 1970s.

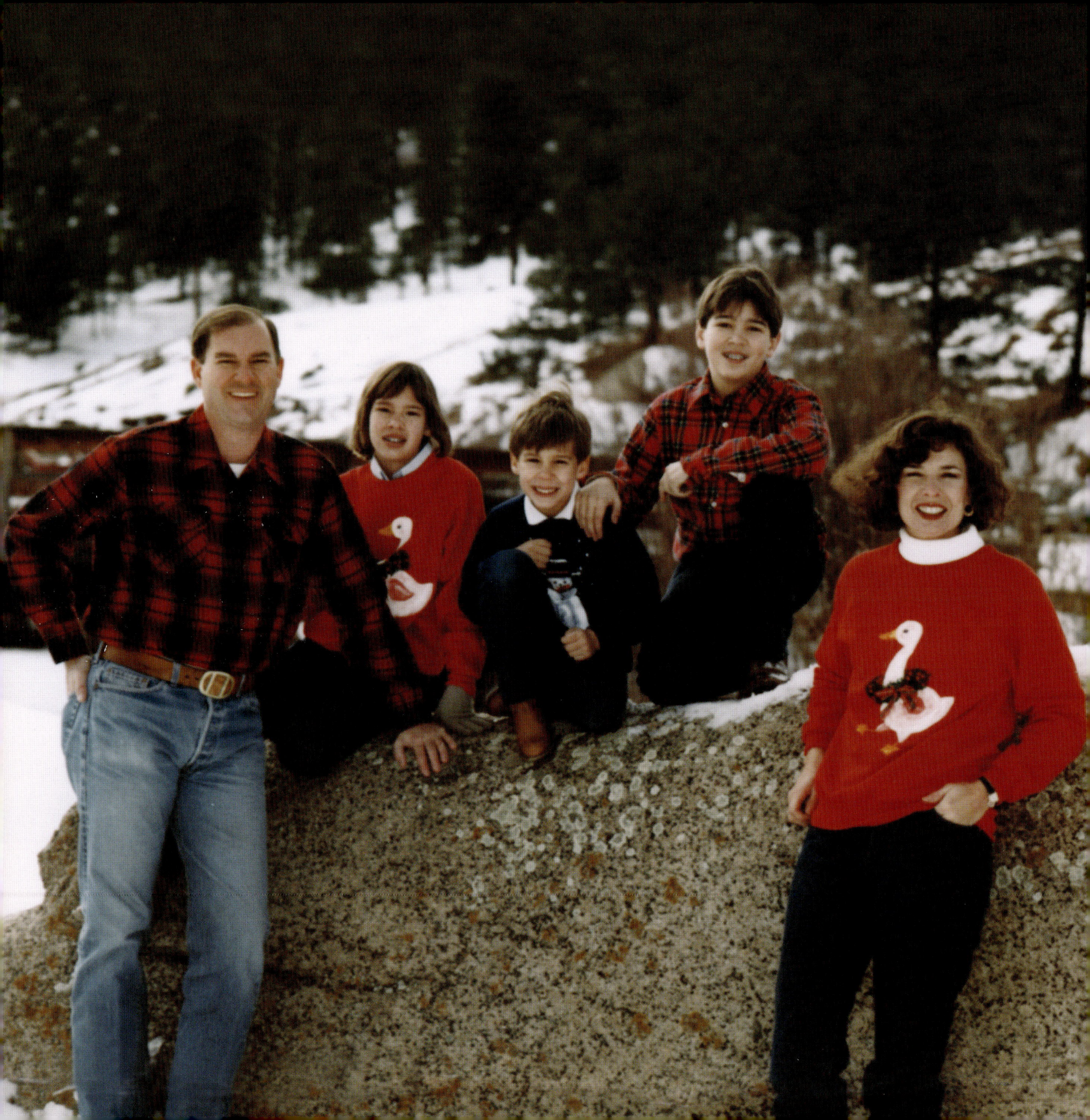

MY "AHA MOMENT"

In 1972, Hal took a job with Atlantic Richfield Company in Dallas, Texas. I was pregnant with our first child and retired from teaching so I could be a full-time mom. I soon became terribly bored awaiting the birth. A friend introduced me to a little sculpture studio tucked away in a wooded old neighborhood in the Oak Cliff section of Dallas. This studio was run by an older man named Octavio Medellin, who was a master artist. He taught me the technique of hand building in terra-cotta clay and the basic foundations of sculpture. Octavio had built a foundry behind his studio, where students learned to pour bronzes.

I describe this time as the "Aha moment" of my life. There was something so deeply satisfying and nourishing to my soul to move clay into meaningful forms. I knew that somehow sculpting was what God had intended for me to do. I worked in Octavio's studio on a daily basis until the week before delivering our son Mark. Soon afterward, we were transferred to Ardmore, Oklahoma, where our daughter, Amy, was born in 1974. Two months after her birth, Atlantic Richfield moved us to Tulsa, Oklahoma, and we purchased a ranch-style home on East 26th Place between Harvard and Lewis avenues.

I soon made my first friend in Tulsa, Melanie Sutton, who lived right next door with her husband and three small children. We baby-sat for each other and played in our big backyards. Little did I know that, years later, Melanie would become my business manager, and I would have a new career! I am amazed how God brings the threads of our lives together to make a beautiful tapestry.

Life was busy with raising two children, church activities, and school activities. I also volunteered at The Little Light House, a Christian developmental center for children with special needs. We relocated once again to the Maple Ridge Historic District, where our third child, Clint, was born in 1979. I happily devoted these years of my life to Hal and our three young children, who needed me. In 1978, Hal joined Kaiser-Francis Oil Company as manager of acquisitions.

OPPOSITE
Our young family in Colorado.

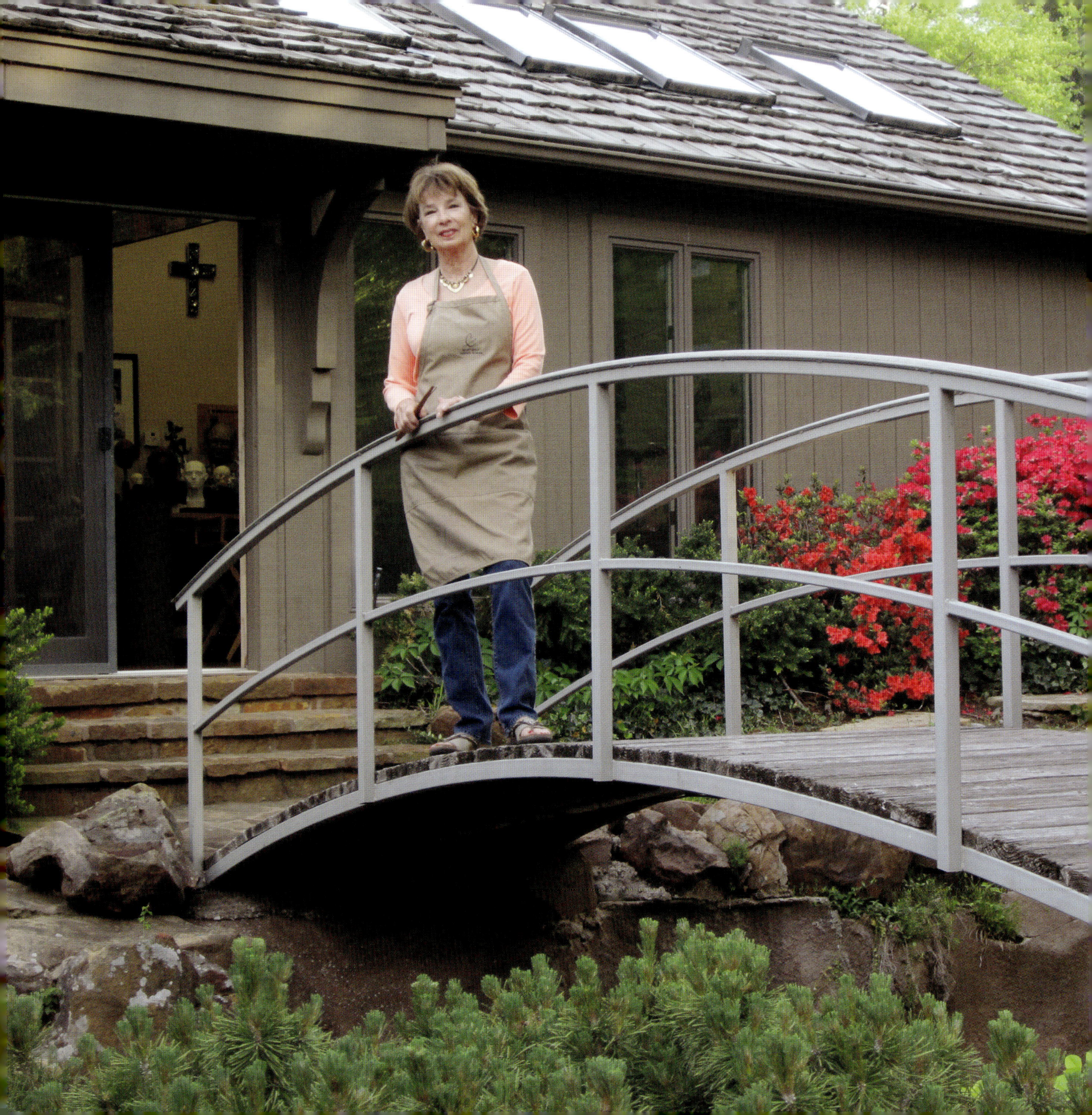

LIFE CHANGES

In 1983, we moved to the Creek House in Bolewood Acres, where we live today. The house is named for the fact that a connecting wing of the house spans a creek that cuts through the property.

As the children grew into junior high school, my hunger and yearning to sculpt began to grow stronger. Hal bought me a used Paragon kiln and installed a 220-volt outlet for it in our garage. During any spare time I could find, I created terra-cotta sculptures and fired them. My first commission came from Tom and Lindsey Berry, who wanted a sculpture of their three children and their dog in fired clay. I was thrilled, and actually, there was quite a likeness to their children in the 15-inch-high sculpture. From this small success, I began sculpting children and dogs for my friends.

After improving my skills with water-based clay, I longed to move forward into a more serious medium of plastilene, an oil-based clay used with an armature. It lends itself to much more detail and variety of design and composition. My friend Janie Brady introduced me to a retired metallurgist named Claude Hixson, who worked in this medium and cast his work in bronze. One day in 1986, I bravely called on this gentleman and asked if he would work with me on a weekly basis and teach me all he knew. He agreed to a weekly class and charged me $10 an hour. Mr. Hixson did not need the money, but he did want to be sure I would value his time with me.

My understanding of sculpture continued to grow, and I loved it! Hal built a small studio connected to our house, where I could work and keep my books and sculpting materials. As I turned 40, my inner life was in great conflict. I wanted to spend more and more time sculpting, but it seemed selfish, because sculpting did not benefit anyone else. Sculpting could not be found among the list of "good works," such as volunteering, teaching, and feeding the poor. God well knew this conflict in my heart. I sculpted in my spare time, all the while feeling guilty.

OPPOSITE
At home in the Creek House.

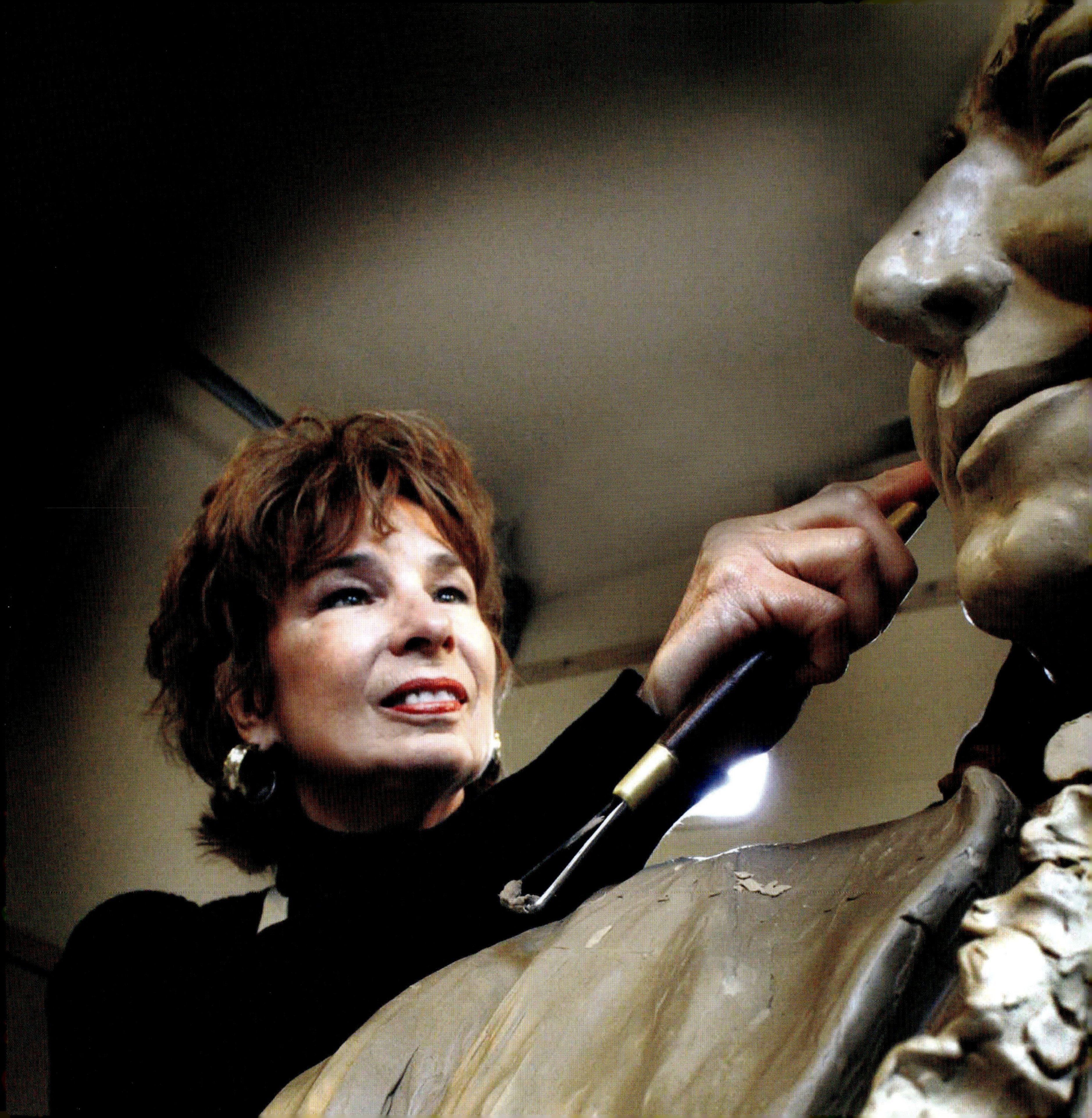

A NEW PURPOSE

I firmly believe that our God always meets us right where we are, and what happened next was amazing! For years Hal and I have helped support the Morse family, which is comprised of three generations of missionaries working in Burma, Thailand, and China. Robert Morse, who was in the midst of devising a written language and translating the Bible for the illiterate hill tribes of Burma, came to spend a week's furlough with us. One night when I was working in my studio, Robert came in and asked me what I was working on. I soon began to cry as I told him of the conflict within me. "Why would God give me this hunger to sculpt when it does no good for anyone else?"

Robert actually laughed as he said, "Rosalind, don't you know that you were created in God's image, and the first thing He did was to create! You are His child, and it is He that has given you this strong passion. As for how He will use it, leave that up to Him." With those words coming from this holy man, I felt a huge burden being replaced with great joy and freedom. Maybe, just maybe, sculpting was part of His plan for my life.

Another confirmation came from my dear friend Janet Young. Her words hit me like a bolt of lightning when she said, "Rosalind, all of these many things you are busy doing are good things, but you might be missing out on God's best purpose for you."

So, there it was. I knew I was being led toward a new path for my life. It was then that I began to pursue my passion for sculpting. Knowing it would take discipline and commitment, I crossed off three days a week to study and work on sculpture. Inevitably, I would get a phone call requesting my attention somewhere else. Swallowing hard, I would say, "I am sorry, but I already have a commitment." And that commitment was to me!

OPPOSITE
Working on *Carolus Linnaeus*.
Photo by Jimmy Bloyed.

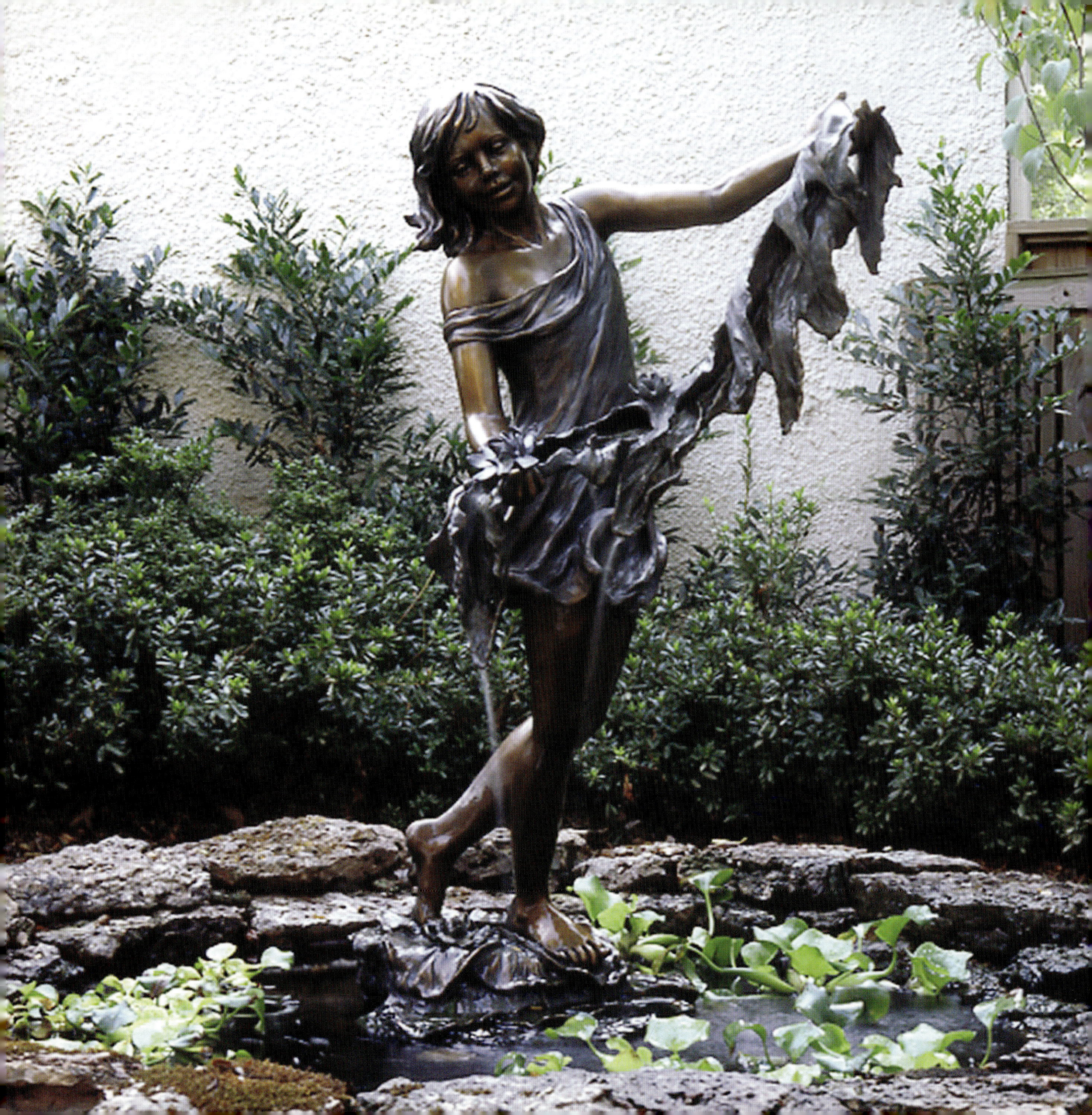

DREAMS AND PASSIONS

Over the years, I have had many studio tours and speaking engagements. I feel compelled to share the importance of making time for dreams and passions. Women, by nature, are great nurturers and supporters, and we often neglect our own dreams. In reality, we are stronger, happier, and better at supporting others when we are feeding our own souls as well. So whatever you have a desire to do, and no matter your age, make a plan and do it.

It was blatantly obvious that I had many empty holes in my sculpting education. Rather than give up my dreams, I began to take serious steps to fill those holes. My knowledge of anatomy was slim-to-none, so I bought a 24-inch skeleton. Next, I hired a darling girl who taught exercise and was a certified massage therapist. She came to my studio weekly for two years. Using an anatomy book, each week we took a section of the body, created the muscles in clay, and applied them correctly to the skeleton. Using this multisensory technique, I learned the attachments and functions of every muscle in the body. I was even given tests each week! This knowledge began to be reflected in my work.

With the support of my precious husband, Hal, who kept our children on schedule, I began to take week-long courses from sculptors whose work I admired. In 1988, I went to Scottsdale Artists School to study with Glenna Goodacre, perhaps one of the most famous women sculptors of our day. On the last day of class, Glenna pulled me aside and said, "Rosalind, you have a gift. You need to take it more seriously." I thought, "*Wow!* Are you talking to *Me?*" Right then I realized perhaps I could consider sculpture as more than a hobby. I thought, "Maybe I will..." and so I did.

OPPOSITE
Lillith, © 1998 Rosalind Cook.
Photo by Andy Leitner.

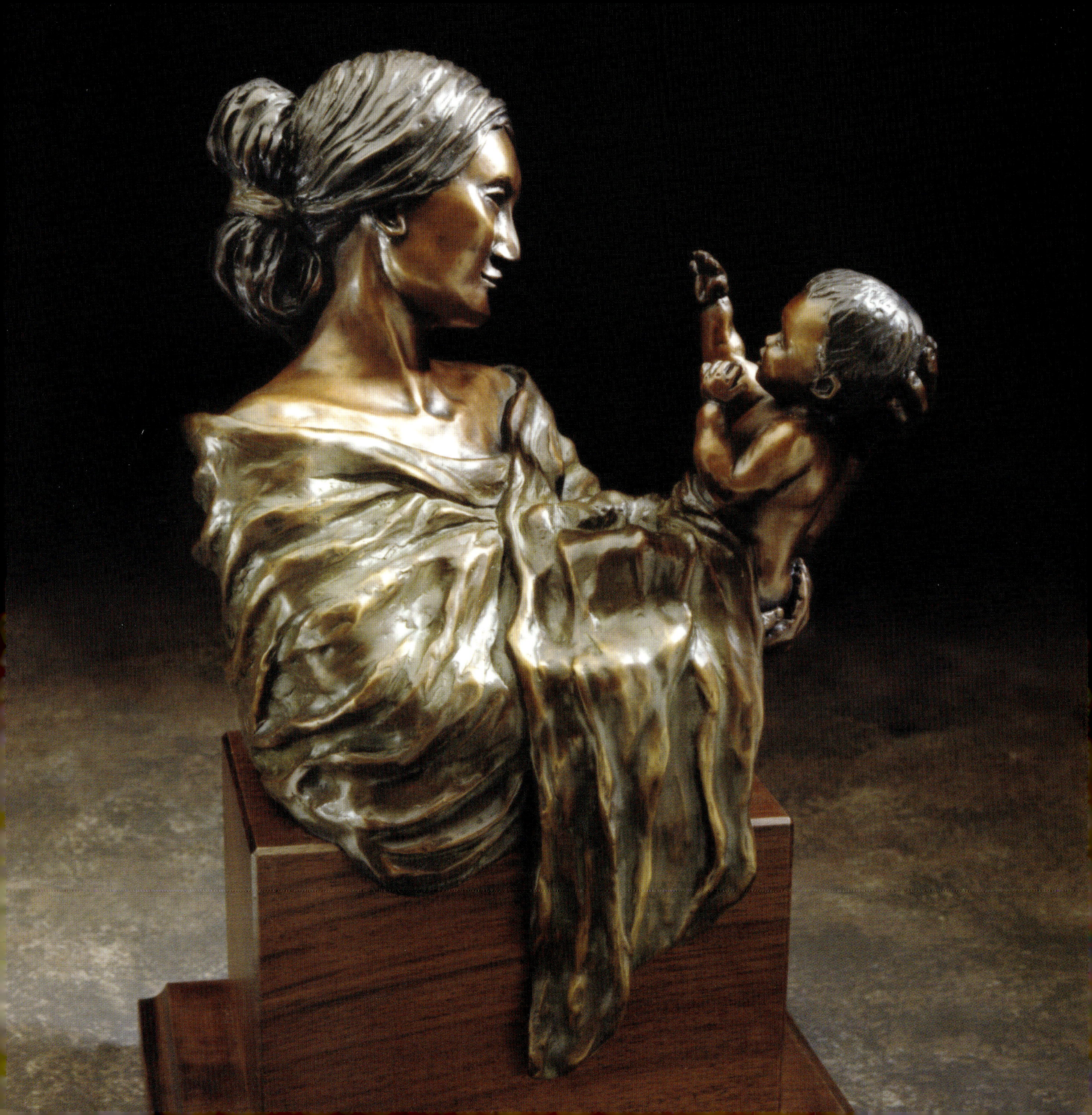

A LEAP OF FAITH

I soon began working on a piece called *Adoration*. A young mother from my Sunday School class, Cindy Evans, was my model. Cindy has beautiful high cheek bones, which reflect that of a Navajo mother. She held up her baby adoringly, and I took photographs to use for my work. What joy I was experiencing!

I also created a little girl running with her arms reaching up, as if into the arms of her father. I titled this piece *Abba, Father.* Both of these pieces were cast into bronze using a small local foundry run by a friend and fellow sculptor, Gary Hale.

In 1989, the Bank of Oklahoma was sponsoring a show titled "Of Women, By Women" to be held in the lobby of the BOK building. Have you ever experienced a leap of faith? I took the leap and entered both of these bronzes into the show, having very little confidence in doing so. *Adoration* sold almost immediately, and *Abba, Father* an hour later. It was thrilling to have created a piece of sculpture that someone else wanted to purchase! I clearly remember calling my parents that night and shouting my joy to them.

The next morning I received a call from Joe Dodson, owner of Dodson Gallery in Nichols Hills, Oklahoma City. Joe informed me that he had attended the show, was impressed with my work, and would like to represent me in his gallery. The Dodson Gallery represented many highly regarded artists.

This was my first gallery and it was a fine, reputable gallery at that. With this invitation, I dared to believe that, just maybe, I could become a successful professional sculptor. My heart was filled with gratitude.

OPPOSITE
My first bronze sculpture, *Adoration*,
© 1989 Rosalind Cook. Photo by Gary Hale.

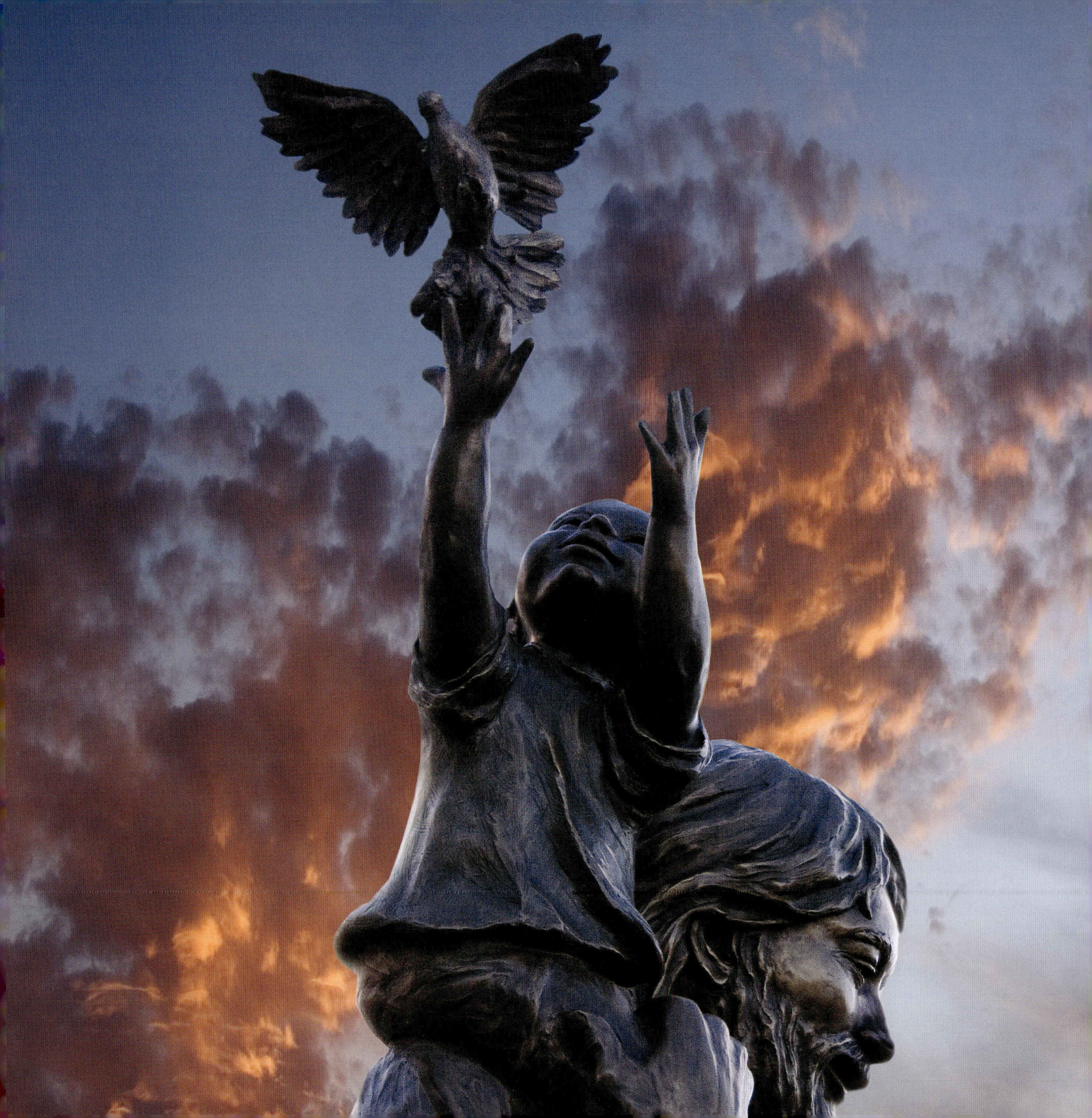

A CAREER TAKES FLIGHT

Opportunities during the next fifteen years reminded me of watching popcorn pop! Acceptances into nationally acclaimed art shows, sales, and gallery solicitations began to come frequently. I continued to study with sculptors whose works challenged me. The next big leap in my education was a trip to Florence and Pietrasanta, Italy, to study the works of the Renaissance masters and sculpt in a studio built in the 1500s. *Magnifico!*

As a result of my success, the business of art was taking up more time than the production of art, and the need for a business/office manager became urgent. Recognizing the many gifts of my long-time friend Melanie Sutton, I asked her to work for me two days a week. Since 1994, it has been a perfect arrangement, and our friendship has only grown stronger.

During this same growth period, I built a 1,000-square-foot studio with 12-foot ceilings, office, gallery, study areas, and a large work space with windows overlooking my creek. A tall garage door allows equipment and trucks access to my studio. Hal installed a surround-sound system, and I was in heaven!

By then I was working with three foundries: Art Castings of Colorado and Bronze Services, both of Loveland, Colorado, and the Bronze Horse of Pawhuska, Oklahoma. A sculptor must have a close working relationship with the foundries, as there are so many details to attend to during the casting and patina process of each and every sculpture. The foundry owners and workers became my friends as we worked together.

The late Jim Pendergast, a retired builder and master woodworker, made pedestals and studio work platforms with casters for each of my life-size and monumental works. He even designed a clay warmer with tool drawers measured exactly for my needs. In 2002, Denise Rinkovsky, a former student with great talent, became my studio assistant on large works. I never could have met my deadlines without her skilled help. I am glad to see Denise now creating her own magnificent large works.

OPPOSITE
Christ's Love for the Children, © 2008 Rosalind Cook. Photo by Don Kreutzweiser.

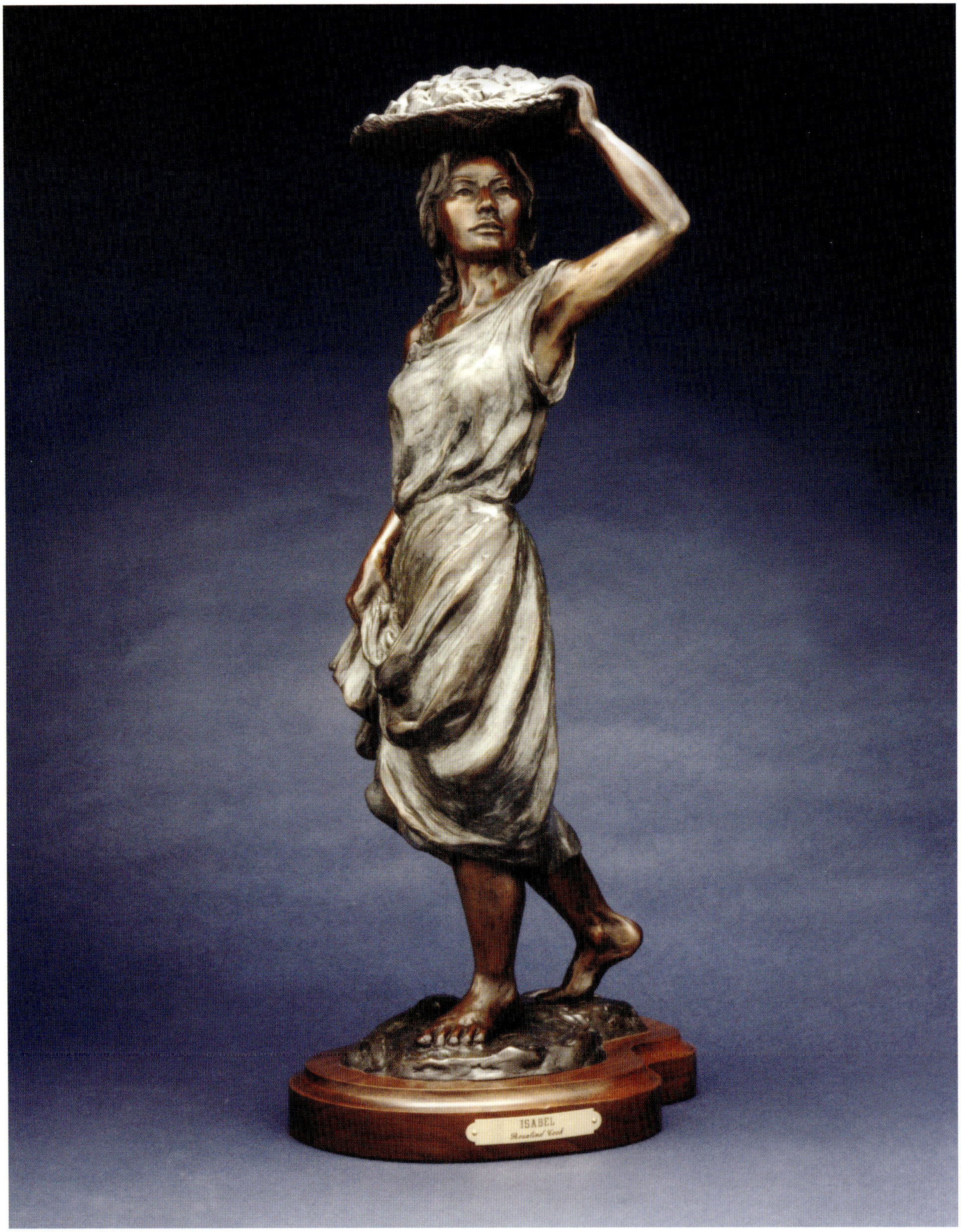
ISABEL

LOOKING BACK

Along with great success came great challenges. My greatest challenge was that of keeping my priorities straight and in alignment with what was truly important in my life. My family and my relationship with God and with my friends have always been the most important things to me. As work and public demands increased, I realized how easily my priorities could slip, allowing my life to tilt out of balance. I knew that I had to be very intentional and disciplined about setting aside work in order to give attention to my children and have quality time with Hal. Work, notoriety, and success can never compare to the importance of relationships. I remember my mother saying, "Notoriety is just like chewing gum. It is to be enjoyed, but never swallowed."

It has been my joy and privilege to have taught at prestigious art schools and museums. I always tell my students, "Never preconceive the final outcome of your sculpture, but allow it to evolve, always exploring aspects and possibilities to make your work stronger and more dynamic so that it may take on its own message." Looking back on my career, that is exactly the path I have taken, for I never could have imagined all that has taken place in my life.

OPPOSITE
Isabel, © 1992 Rosalind Cook.
Photo by Gary Hale.

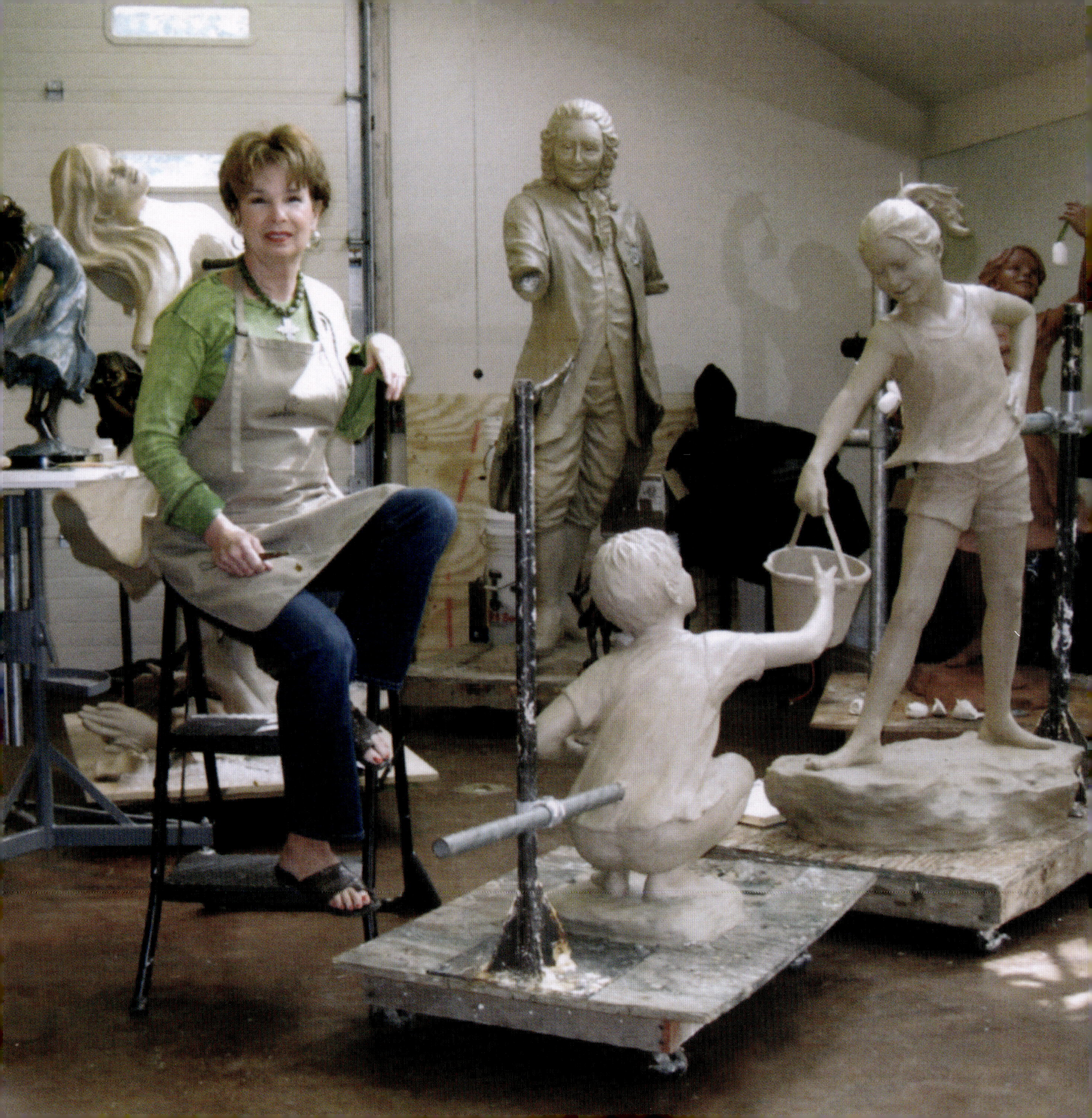

EACH SCULPTURE
HAS A STORY TO TELL

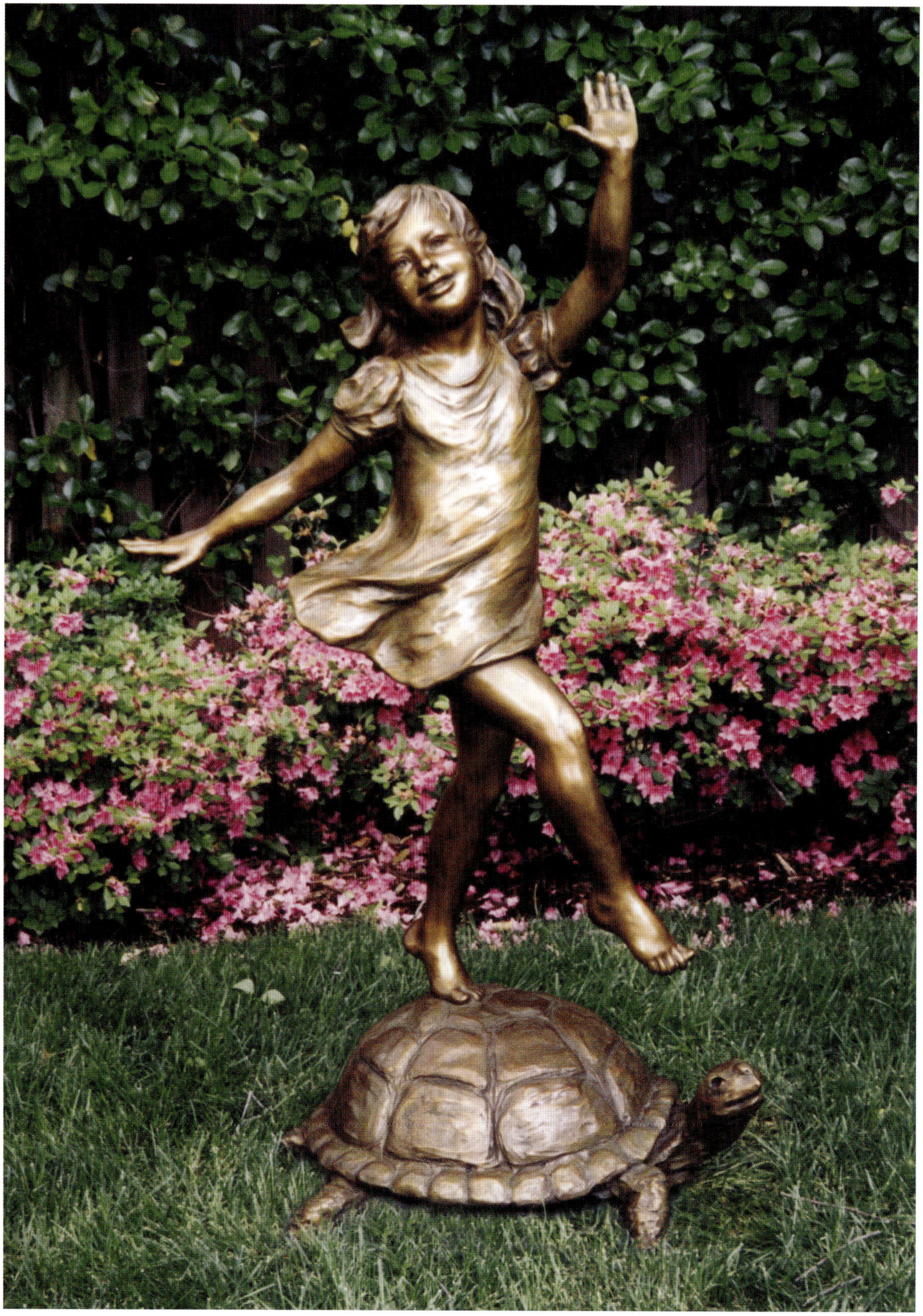

IMAGINATION AND INSPIRATION

One of my favorite authors, Oswald Chambers, says that one of the greatest gifts God gives to man is the gift of imagination. It is the wellspring of all creativity and is without limitation. I can honestly say that I feel God's pleasure when I am sculpting in my studio, using the gifts He has given me.

People often ask me where I get the inspiration for a sculpture. I think they expect that I will respond with some amazing experience or a cause that I want to champion. In reality, it is the small, everyday happenings that find themselves captured in my bronzes.

Sometimes the inspiration comes from researching a topic, such as the significance of a person's life or a principle of living. In my imagination, I begin to visualize how to instill the character, values, and feelings of the subject into a sculpture while integrating strong elements of design and composition. If the experience can be creatively frozen into bronze and executed well, then the same feelings of that moment can be felt over and over again as the sculpture is viewed.

I am grateful to have more than 30 large sculptures in public locations in the Tulsa area, as well as 90 significant installations in public places across the United States. Since these sculptures will be viewed in my lifetime as well as by following generations, I cannot leave this world without sharing the stories that lie behind some of the better-known works.

OPPOSITE
Turtle Dancer, ©1997 Rosalind Cook.

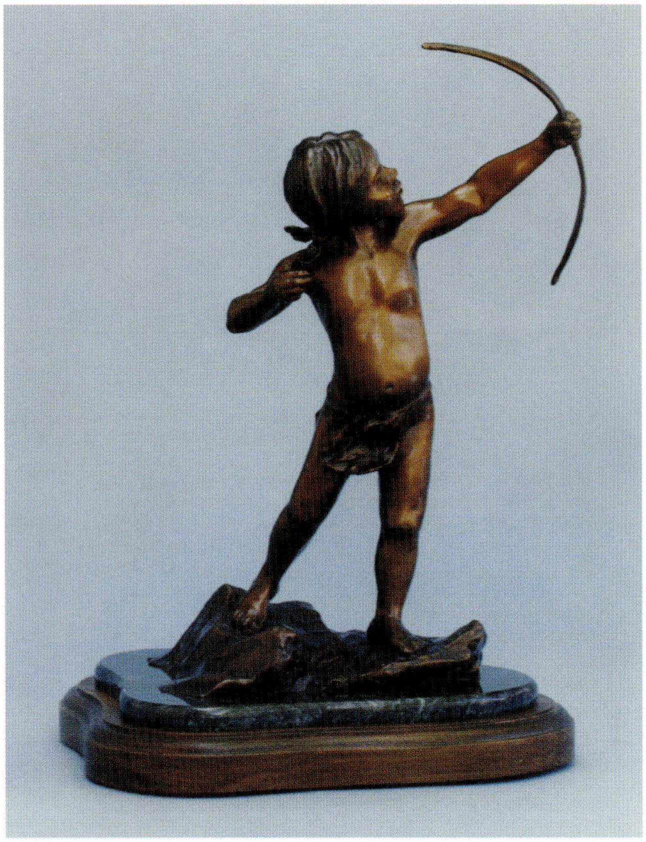
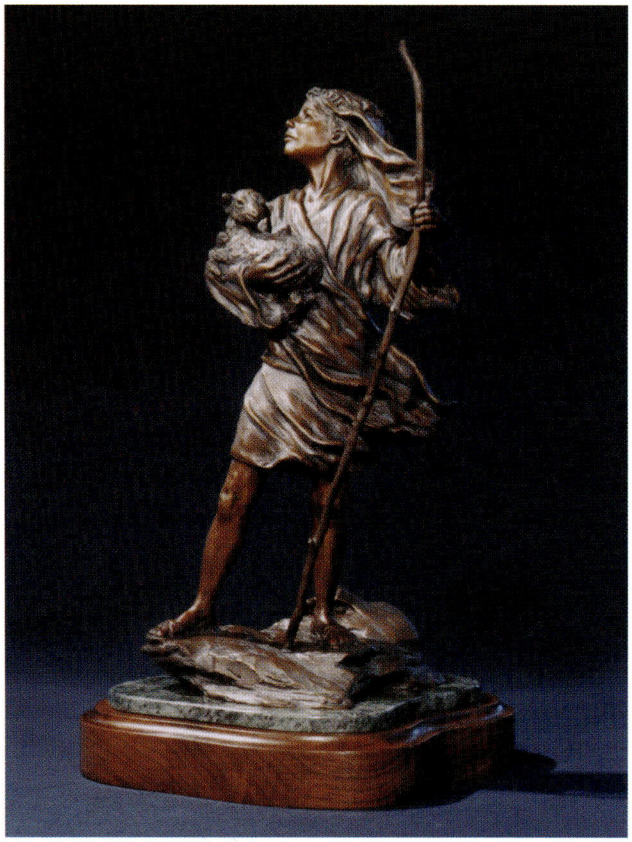
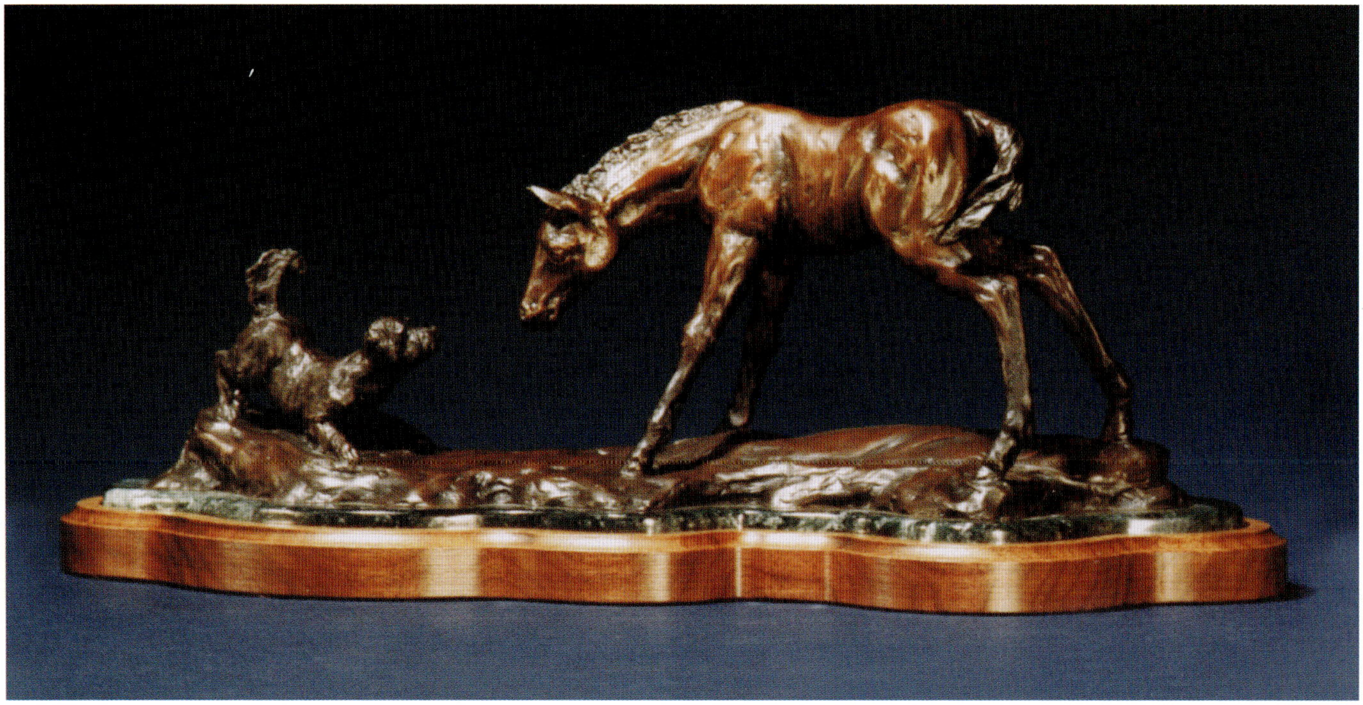

THREE SCULPTURES FOR MY THREE CHILDREN

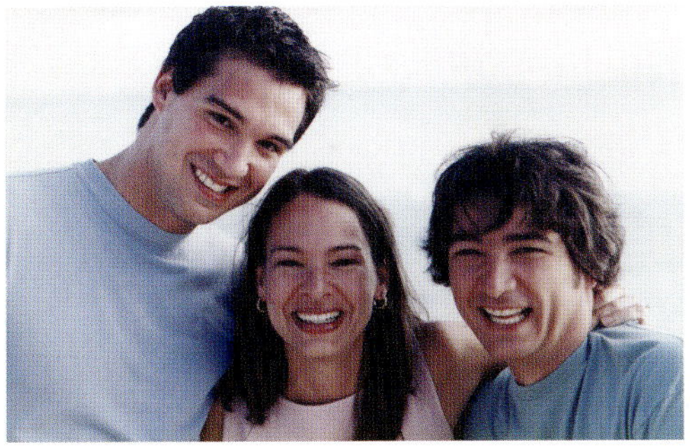

My greatest accomplishment is being the mother of our three wonderful children, Mark, Amy, and Clint. Upon their graduation from high school, I created a special commemorative sculpture for each of them.

Hope was for Mark, the first born. In the culture of the American Plains Indians, a grandfather would make the first bow and arrow for his grandson. In this sculpture, the grandson has just released an arrow. We always encouraged Mark to choose worthy goals and aim for them. He was the first grandchild for both sets of grandparents, so this sculpture was very relevant.

OPPOSITE, CLOCKWISE FROM UPPER LEFT
Hope, ©1990 Rosalind Cook. Photo by Gary Hale. / *Christmas Night,* © 1991 Rosalind Cook. Photo by Mel Schockner. / *Getting Acquainted,* © 1992 Rosalind Cook. Photo by Mel Schockner.

ABOVE, LEFT TO RIGHT
Clint, Amy, and Mark

Getting Acquainted was created for our only daughter, Amy, who was on her way to Colorado State University and was to be on the equestrian team. In this sculpture, Josh, our family dog, is acquainting himself with a new colt. Amy would be doing the same in a whole new world when she left home.

Christmas Night was for Clint, our youngest child. I had been inspired by a Christmas card of a young shepherd full of awe and wonder. I wanted to capture Clint within that scenario. When Clint was eleven, I put a pillowcase on his head, had him hold a sheepskin rug and broomstick, and pose for photos. It captures the wonder of a young boy as he sees the Christmas star. My prayer was that life would hold wonder for him all the days of his life. This became one of my most-loved sculptures, and I gave Clint a casting upon his graduation.

Each of our children has married a wonderful partner and is living a significant life. Our grandchildren are truly a blessing. We are so very proud of our family and cherish our time together.

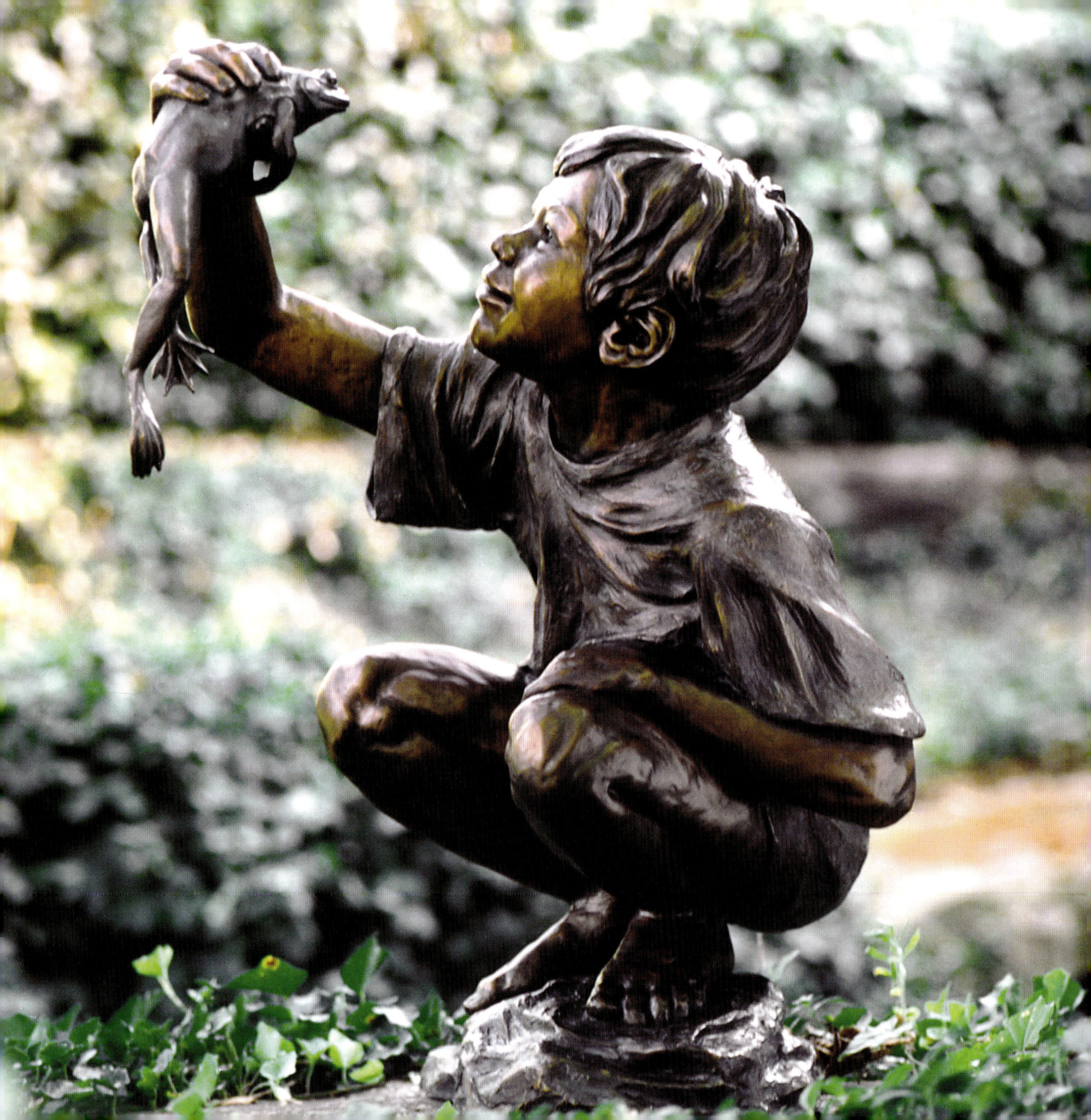

FINDERS KEEPERS

Ronald McDonald House, 6102 South Hudson Avenue, Tulsa, Oklahoma

Finders Keepers was given to The Ronald McDonald House, which provides "a home away from home" for families who have children with serious injuries or illnesses in Tulsa hospitals.

In 1990, I was challenged to move into creating life-size work. Again it was a step in faith. I borrowed the cost of casting, with a strong feeling that this first life-size sculpture would sell well because the subject matter was appealing.

When our children were growing up, we often took camping trips with other families, and the boys would typically end up in the rivers, ponds, and creeks where they would catch frogs and other creeping creatures. This sculpture depicts a magical moment in time, when a little boy is discovering the wonders of a bullfrog and vice versa. The first castings sold well, and I repaid my loan with a big smile.

One of my collectors, Mr. Red Hudson, of Hudson Foods (now Tyson Foods), told me why he *had* to have a casting of this particular sculpture. "When I was a boy, I would gig frogs and sell them to the local restaurants, and that is how my future in food was established." Nothing gives me more satisfaction in my career than when someone makes a personal connection with one of my sculptures!

OPPOSITE
Finders Keepers, © 1993 Rosalind Cook.
Photograph by Gary Hale.

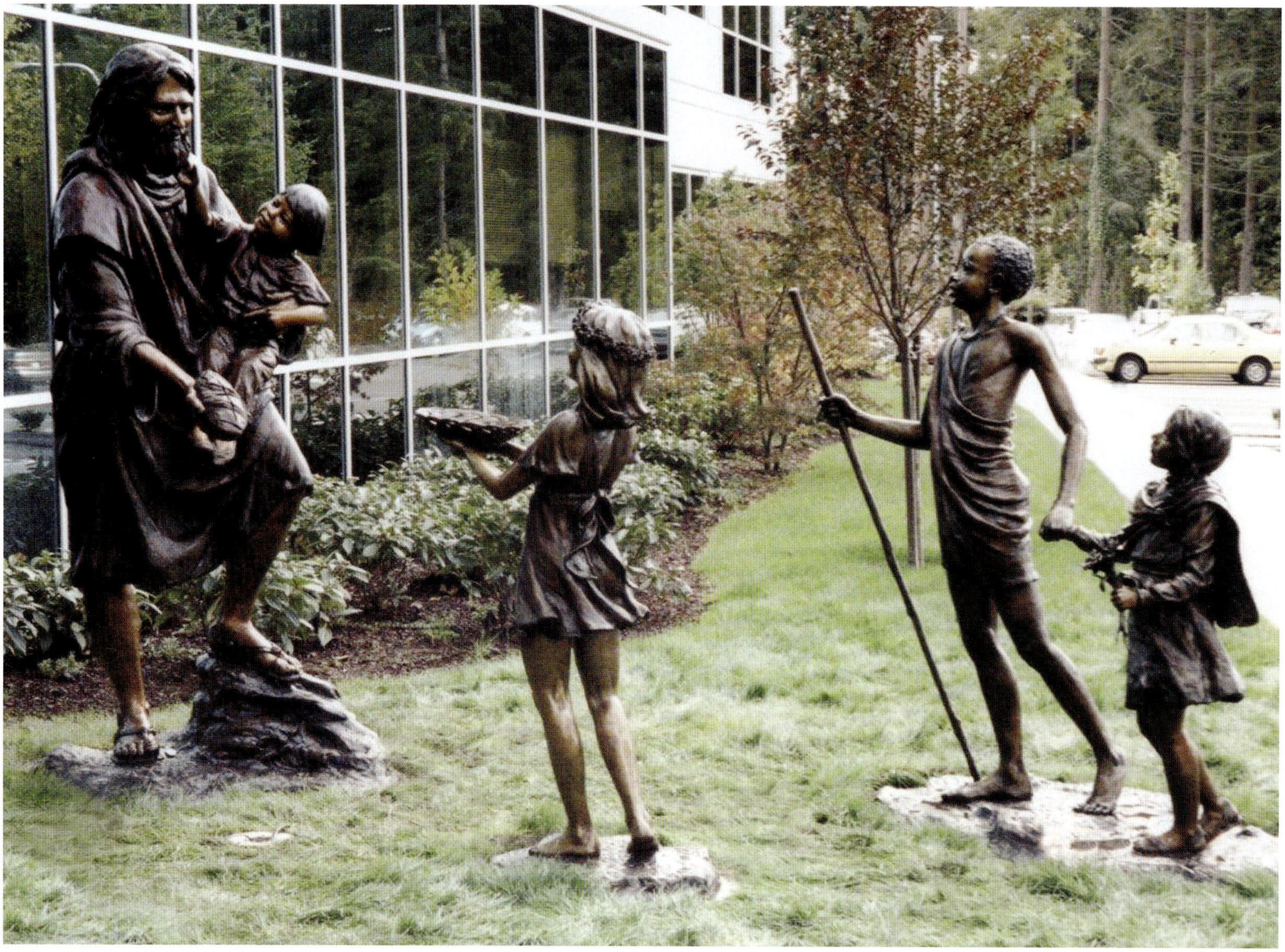

THE SCULPTURES OF WORLD VISION

World Vision Headquarters, 34834 Weyerhaeuser Way, Federal Way, Washington

A "DIVINE APPOINTMENT"

In 1994, I was in the midst of building a new 1,000-square-foot studio and also participating in a highly juried show in Colorado. Terry Madison, editor of *World Vision Magazine*, came to see my work in the show, pored over my portfolio, and said he would be in touch. I knew in my spirit that this had been "a divine appointment."

World Vision is the largest Christian relief, development, and advocacy agency in the world, working in nearly 100 countries. World Vision was building new headquarters in Federal Way, Washington, near Seattle.

The president of World Vision at the time, Bob Sieple, asked if I would study their mission statement and design a sculpture for the entrance to their new building. I immediately thought, "They have made a mistake and think I am someone I am not." This project was far beyond my experience at the time in size, scope, and significance, but I did not voice my fears. Instead, I excitedly agreed, sensing this was something I had been chosen to do. I knew that this would be a walk of faith and I had to depend on God in the process.

I flew to Federal Way and spent two days at the site wearing a hard hat, talking to engineers, looking over plans, and taking measurements to determine the size of the sculpture in relation to the building and its exterior spaces. Upon returning home and spending time in thought, prayer, and the study of their mission statement, I visualized a strong and loving Christ holding out the bread of life to children from all over the world. The bread of life would symbolize not just food, but also help of every kind: the spiritual food and new life given by Christ through World Vision. As visitors approached the building, they would be looking into the face of Christ. As they left the building, they would be looking into the faces of the children who would represent people of all ages served by the ministry.

OPPOSITE
Christ, The Bread of Life, © 1995 Rosalind Cook.

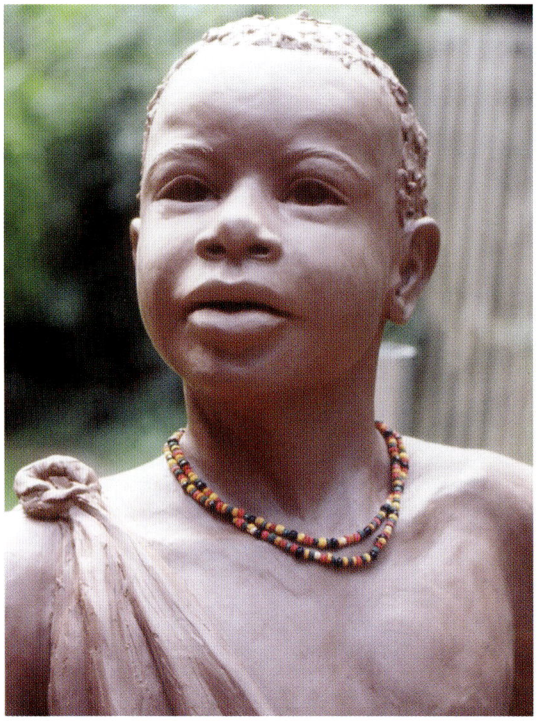
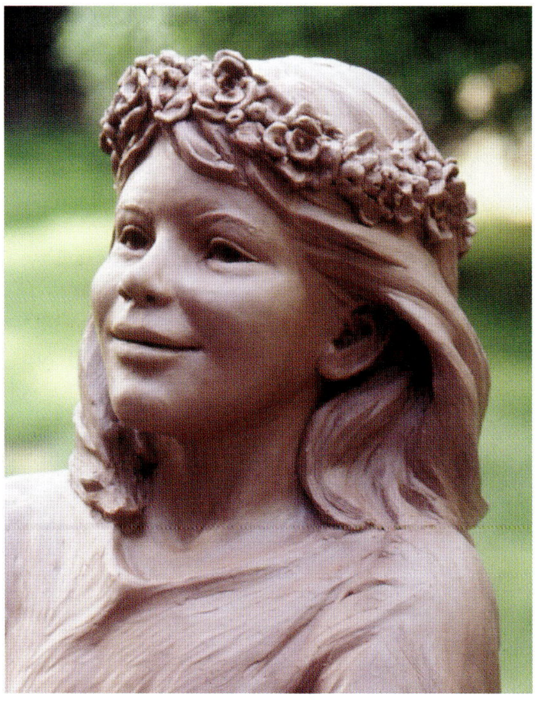
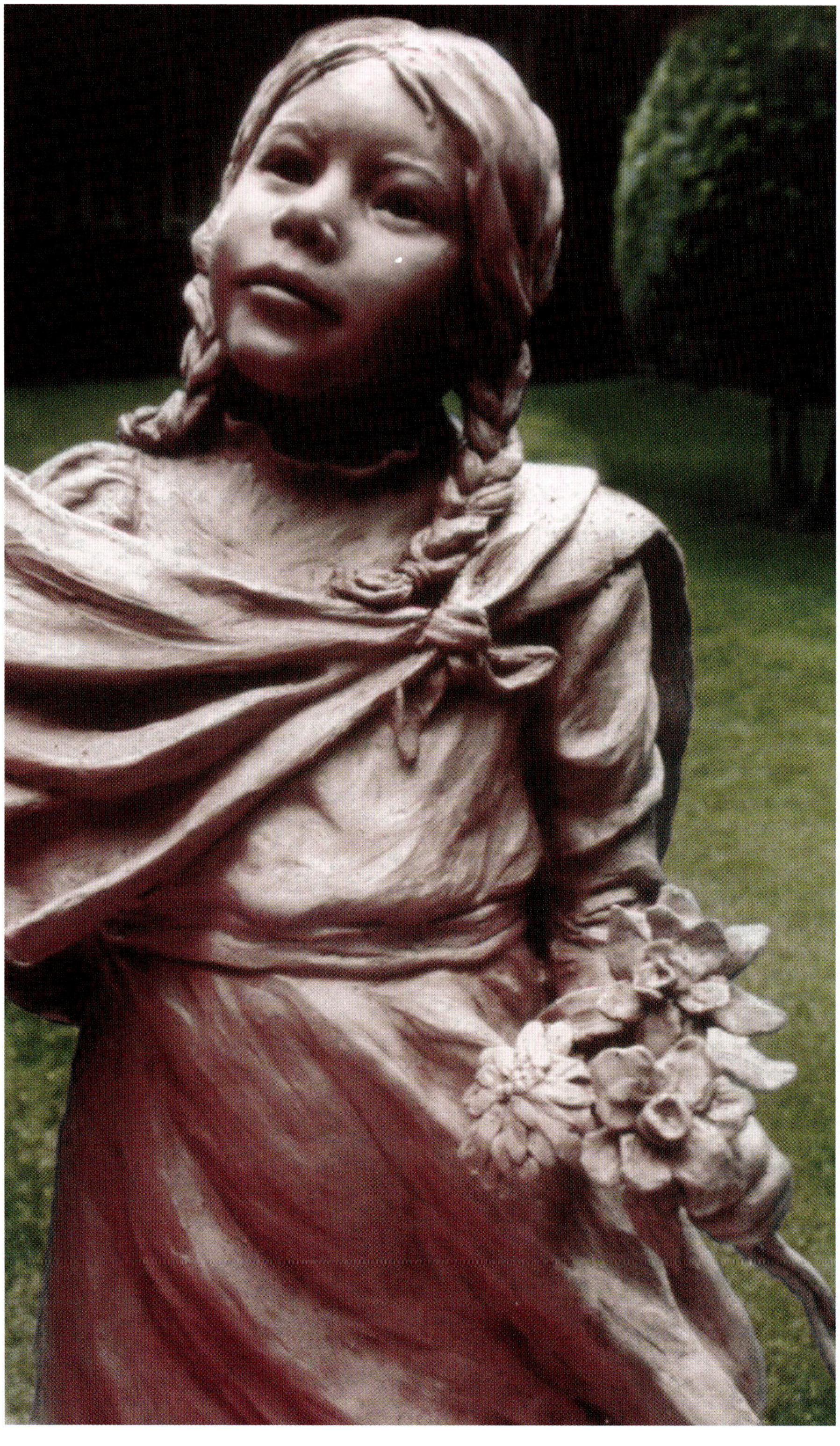

THE AGONY AND ECSTASY

I sent the preliminary sketches of my idea to World Vision, and the concept was approved. It was now 1995, and I had only five short months to complete this monument of five figures. I spent 10 to 12 hours a day in the studio. Hal took over much of the cooking and responsibilities for the children. Every day began with prayer and supplication for wisdom, strength, and the skill to create the sculptures. I battled the voices in my head that said, "Who do you think you are? You are going to fall flat on your face." However, I knew that if God wanted me to do this, He would help me complete the sculptures and do them well.

The interior of my new studio was being completed by Keith Winfrey, a gifted carpenter and old friend. He had a strong body, a beard, loving, twinkling eyes, and was a mighty believer in God. Right in front of me was the perfect model for my Christ figure! I told Keith, "Put on these sandals and this tunic and pose for pictures. You are going to be my Jesus."

OPPOSITE, CLOCKWISE FROM UPPER LEFT
The African, Peruvian, and Caucasian children in red clay.

Then I needed models for the children. One night I was at a restaurant with my son Clint and saw a couple walk in with a young Cantonese girl. She was the perfect age and size for the Asian child in my sculpture. I told Clint, "There is my model!" I approached the mother and her child, introduced myself, and explained my project. The woman told me that she and her husband were missionaries and had found this abandoned baby girl under a bridge during a mission. She agreed to let her daughter model for me, so I set up an appointment for photos with Keith holding her on his knee. After that, I found models for the African, Peruvian, and Caucasian children. Everything I needed was being provided for me.

Then, on the morning of April 19th, a terrorist's bomb destroyed the Alfred P. Murrah Federal Building in Oklahoma City, killing 168 people, 19 of whom were children. As I was sculpting the children, the rescuers were finding bodies of the victims. My heart was heavy with grief and horror. I had new motivation to capture life in the bodies, and especially the faces, of the children that I was working on in clay.

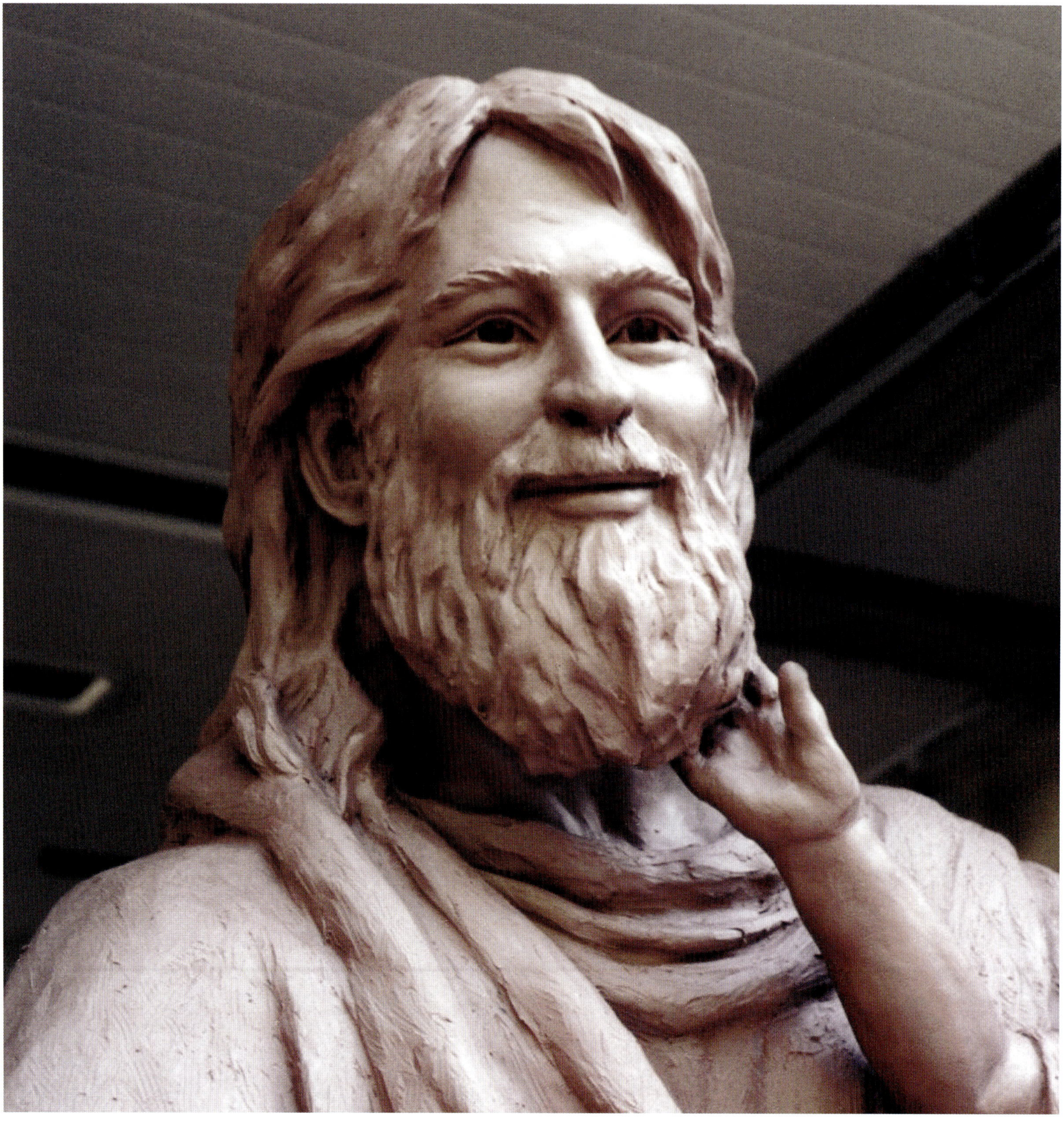

THE FACE OF CHRIST

The focal point of the entire sculpture group was to be the face of Christ. I felt the heavy responsibility of the awesome task of depicting Jesus Christ. Though I had scaffolding around the large figure, I had taken the head off the clay figure and was working it on a pedestal that was at eye level. The face was not what I wanted it to be, appearing either too sweet or too stern. Over and over, I took the clay back to the bone structure and began again. Finally, late one night, after another attempt, I created the face of Christ that I thought captured all of His character qualities: love, compassion, strength, and justice. I felt satisfied and exhausted as I climbed into bed. My last thought was a prayer, "Lord, I am pleased with this face, but I need to know that *You* are pleased," and fell into a deep sleep.

The next morning I had climbed onto the scaffolding and was attaching the head to the body when the phone rang. The caller was a doctor and client of mine from Louisiana. "Roz, I'm in Tulsa at a medical convention and I was wondering if I could bring some doctors to your studio during our lunch break." Every fiber of my being wanted to tell him, "Not possible," but I found myself saying, "Sure, come on over, but I cannot stop working on my current project as I am on a tight deadline."

Soon, eight doctors were milling around my studio while I worked. I kept noticing that one doctor would not leave the Christ figure and was staring at the face. Finally, I put my tools down and asked him if I could answer any questions. He said, "All my life I have only seen the emaciated, suffering Christ that I could not relate to. I think I could go fishing with this guy." I assured him that Jesus would love to fish with him. God sent the answer to my prayer through a visitor to my studio, whom I almost turned away.

OPPOSITE
The face of Christ in clay.

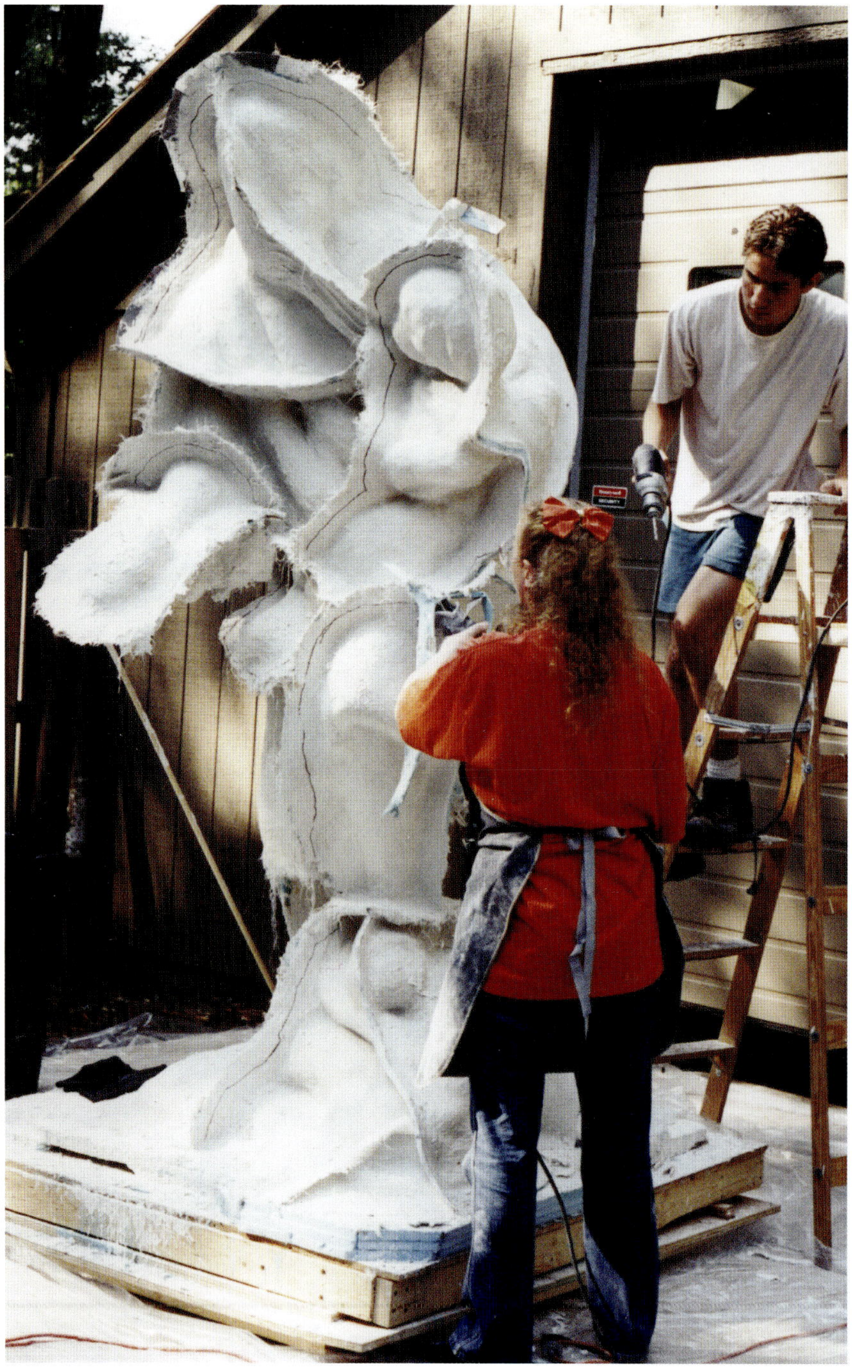

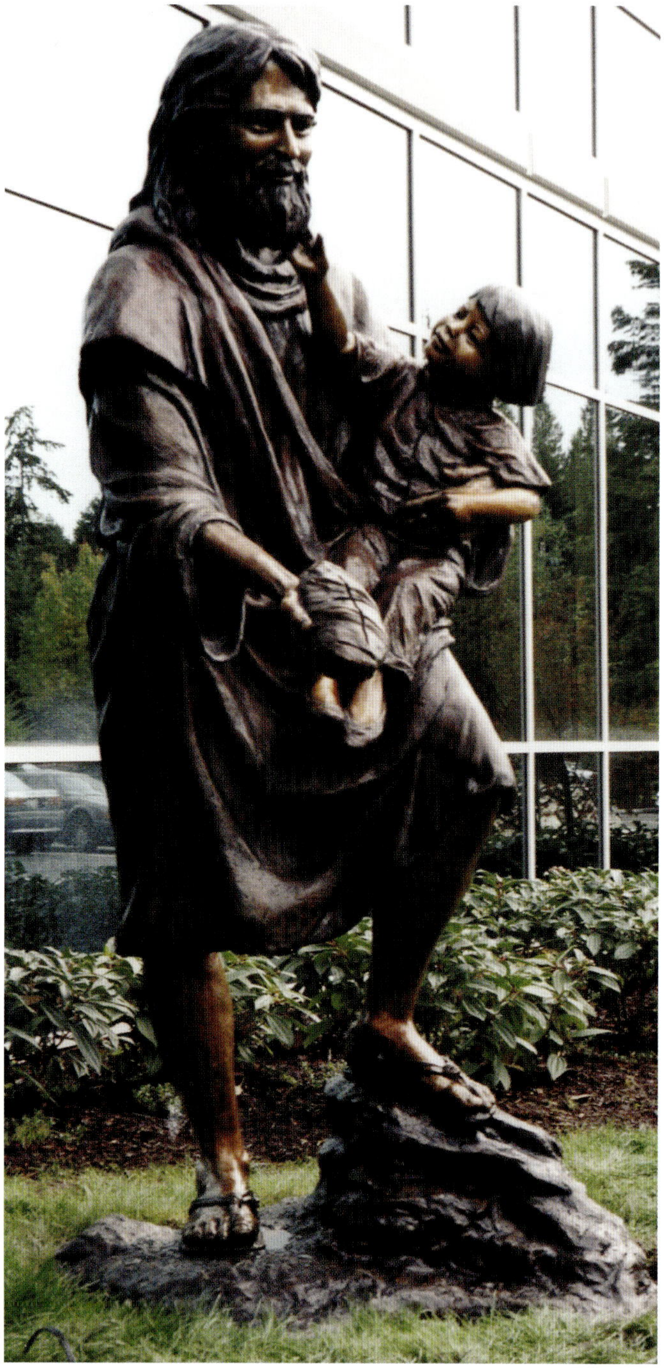

FINISHED AT LAST

After five long and emotional months, the clay sculptures were completed. The officials from World Vision and many supporters of their organization flew into Tulsa. World Vision had a catered dinner on our patio and an unveiling in my studio for 40 people. The sculpture was celebrated and approved. I shared the amazing stories that took place during its creation.

A week later mold makers from the Bronze Horse foundry in Pawhuska, Oklahoma, and one from California, arrived in my studio and began to section off the figures and create the silicone rubber molds. Then, a plaster mother mold was formed over each section of rubber. After a week of daily work, we pulled the cured molds off of the original clay and were thrilled to see that the rubber had captured every detail, which would insure a good casting. The molds were trucked to the foundry in Pawhuska.

OPPOSITE, LEFT TO RIGHT
Workers created molds to cast the Christ figure holding the Asian child. / The finished bronze.

The ancient lost-wax casting began, resulting in a bronze sculpture exactly as the original clay piece was created.

I made many trips to the Bronze Horse foundry to oversee each step of the process. Finally, the day arrived when the bronze sculptures were loaded onto a large moving truck and driven to Federal Way, Washington. I flew commercially, along with John Free, owner of the Bronze Horse, and we installed the sculptures on the entrance lawn of the new Word Vision headquarters.

Two weeks later, on November 1,1995, I flew back with Hal, our parents, and family for the grand dedication of the building and sculptures. Dignitaries and officials came from all over the world. As I spoke from the podium about the sculptures, I had a deep sense of completion and fulfillment. To this day, I am grateful that God worked a miracle through me; conquering my doubts, and giving me confidence and ability to create life-size and monumental works. This experience taught me how to truly "capture the spirit in bronze."

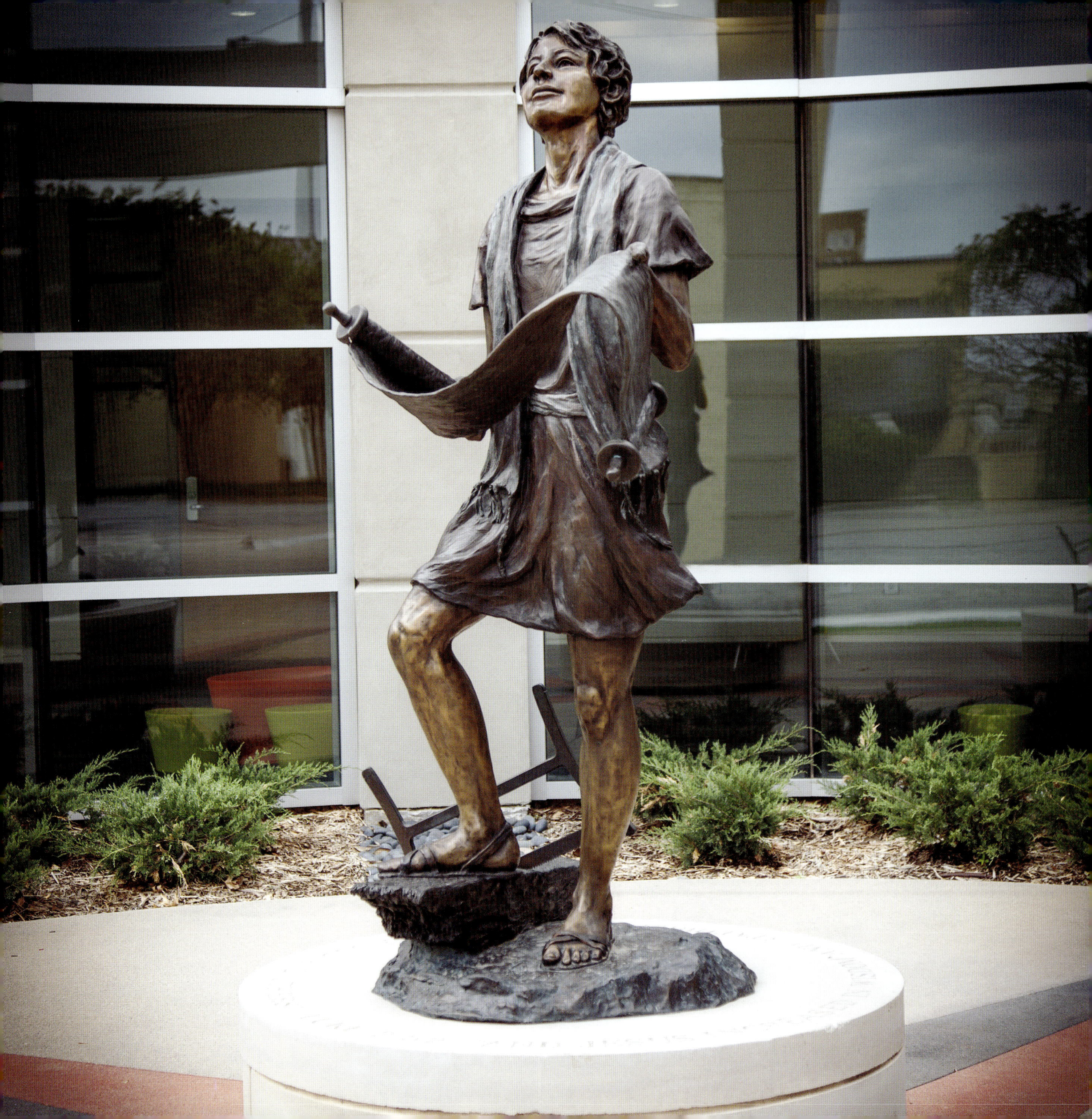

THE SCULPTURES OF FIRST UNITED METHODIST CHURCH

1115 South Boulder Avenue, Tulsa, Oklahoma

In 1886, Tulsa was a rowdy frontier cattle town in Indian Territory. A hardy group of settlers started a Methodist Episcopal Church, with 21 charter members in an open-air brush arbor. Today, First United Methodist Church, with more than 6,000 members, holds services in a large Gothic cathedral and has associated buildings covering two city blocks.

TURNING POINT

One day in 1995, I received a call from my son Mark, who was taking a religion class in college. At the end of our conversation, he asked, "What was Christ like as a boy?" That very week, Dr. James Buskirk, senior pastor of First United Methodist Church, called and asked me to create a sculpture of Christ as a youth for the new Youth and Family Life Building. I soon began my research.

Luke 2:40 tells us, "And Jesus grew in wisdom and stature and in favor with God and man." He also assisted Joseph in the carpentry shop. I wanted to be historically accurate, spiritually inspiring, and to create a sculpture relatable to the youth of today.

OPPOSITE
Turning Point, © 1996 Rosalind Cook.
Photograph by David Miller.

My model was Zachary Winters, a young boy who was lanky and curly-headed. At age 13, a Jewish boy passes from boyhood to manhood, so my Jesus figure wears a ceremonial prayer shawl over his tunic. His right foot rests on an old log crossed by a carpenter's bow saw. These two juxtaposed items symbolize the cross that lies ahead for Jesus. His torso is turned, holding the scroll and looking up toward heaven, as if He understands the scripture in Isaiah 61:1-3 that foretells his destiny.

Every youth has a turning point. In this sculpture, Jesus is turning from his earthly father's work in the carpentry shop to his heavenly Father's call; thus the name *Turning Point*. Today, it has been relocated outside the church on 12th Street.

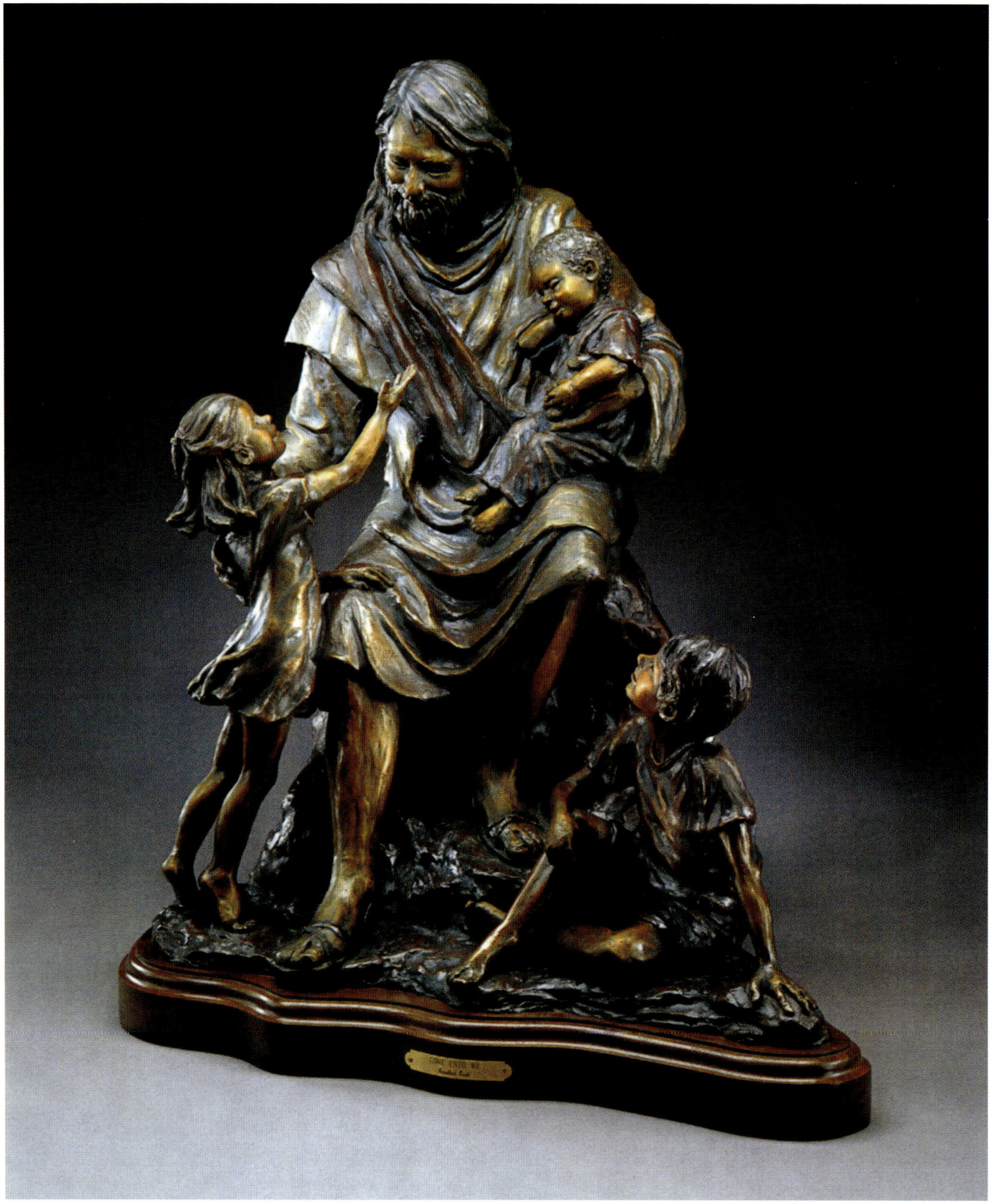

COME UNTO ME

Because First United Methodist Church is our family church, a church that has loved us, spiritually fed us, and nurtured our children, Hal and I gave *Come Unto Me* to the church as a token of our gratitude. The three children portrayed in this sculpture not only represent my three children, but also portray the various ways one can respond to Jesus. The young preadolescent boy is not sure who Jesus is, but he's interested and wants to know more. The young girl is imploring and reaching out to Him, while the littlest one is resting with complete trust in His arms.

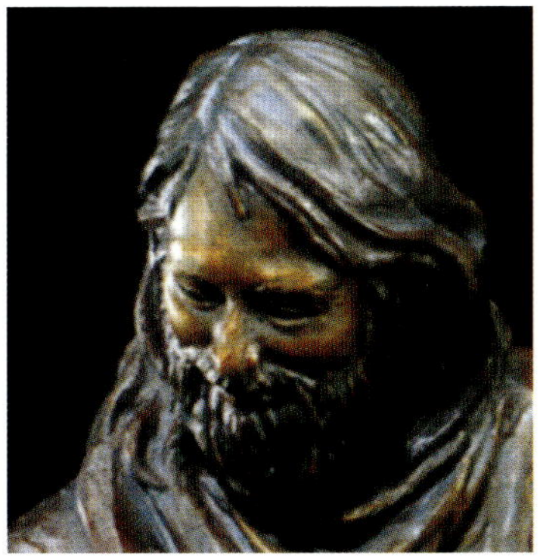

With a strong triangular composition, the main lines direct the viewer's eyes to the kindly face of Christ. Christ's foot extends beyond the base, making Him accessible and welcoming rather than unreachable. As with other sculptures, I incorporated the many lessons of design I learned from studying works of the early European master sculptors.

OPPOSITE
Come Unto Me, © 1998 Rosalind Cook.
Photograph by Mel Schockner.

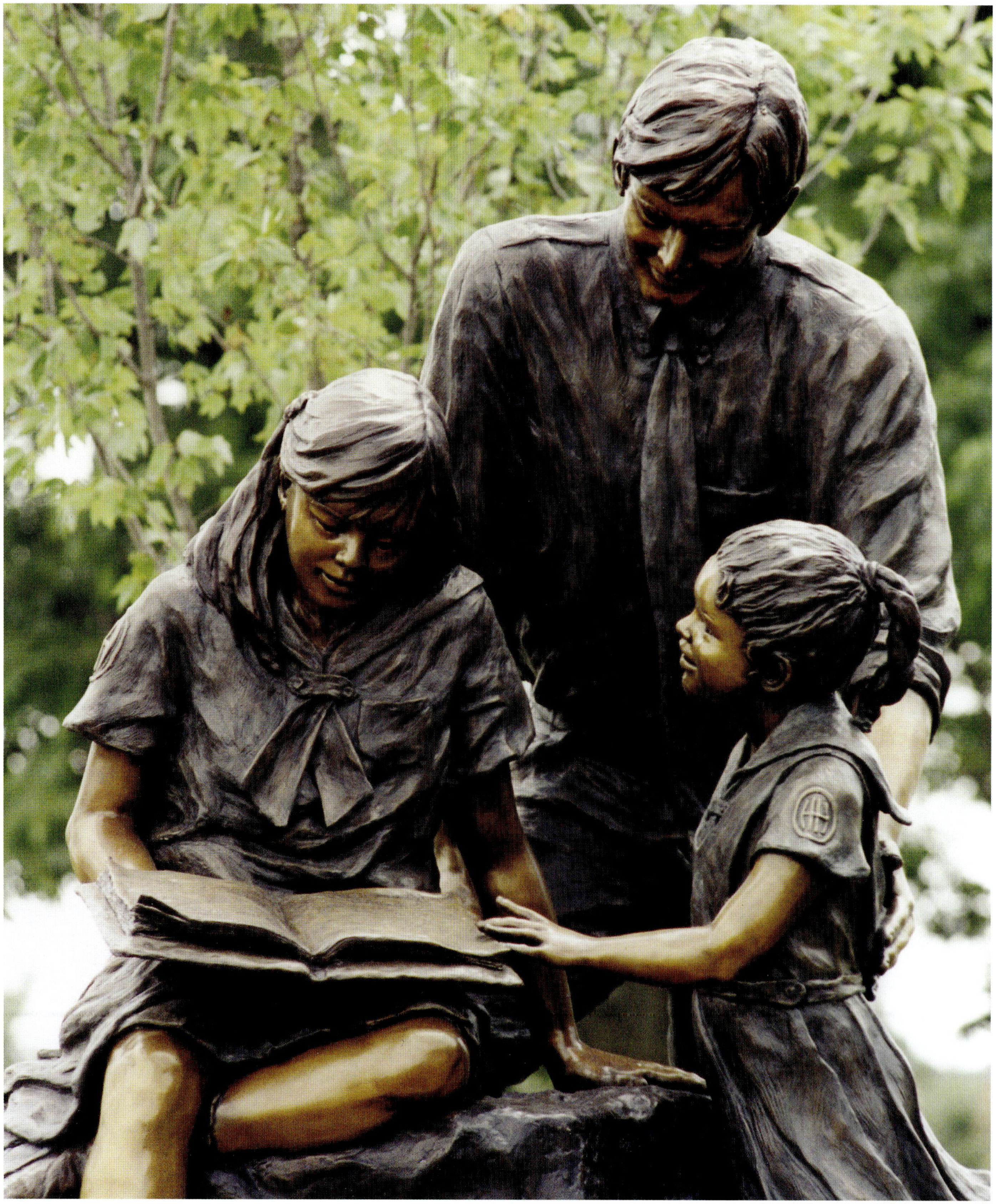

BELONGING AND BECOMING

Holland Hall, 5666 East 81st Street, Tulsa, Oklahoma

Holland Hall is an independent college preparatory Episcopal school. Founded in 1922 by nine prominent Tulsa citizens, the school was named to honor its first headmistress, Winnifred Schureman, who was of Dutch ancestry. Today, Holland Hall's large campus educates over 1,000 students from preschool through grade 12.

In 1997, I was approached by Holland Hall to create a life-size sculpture to be placed in the center of the circular entrance to the school. My guidelines were to depict a senior high student, a junior high student, and an elementary student wearing their school uniforms, and to incorporate the ideas of both academia and sports.

Among the many strengths of the school is that of the older students mentoring the younger students. This became my springboard for the triangularly composed sculpture. The three students of varied grades are gathered around a single book, and in body positions typical of their ages, with heads on different levels. I incorporated a basketball and a field hockey stick at the base of the sculpture. The major lines take the viewers' eyes to the center focus, which is the relationship of the three students. The title, *Belonging and Becoming,* is appropriate in that they all belong to the same school, yet each student is becoming a unique and individual person.

OPPOSITE
Belonging and Becoming, © 1998 Rosalind Cook.

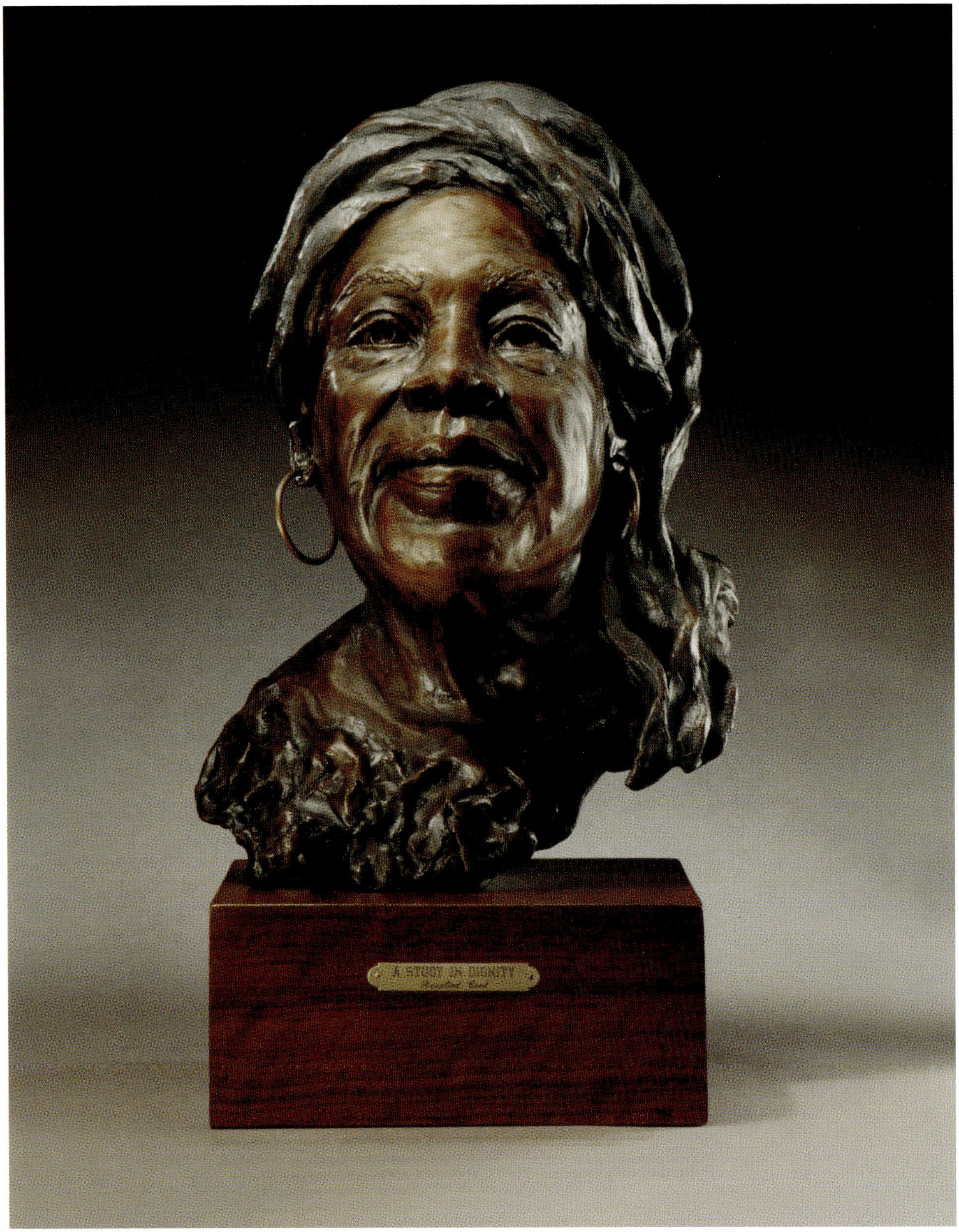
A STUDY IN DIGNITY

A STUDY IN DIGNITY

Alexandre Hogue Gallery, The University of Tulsa, 2930 East 5th Street, Tulsa, Oklahoma

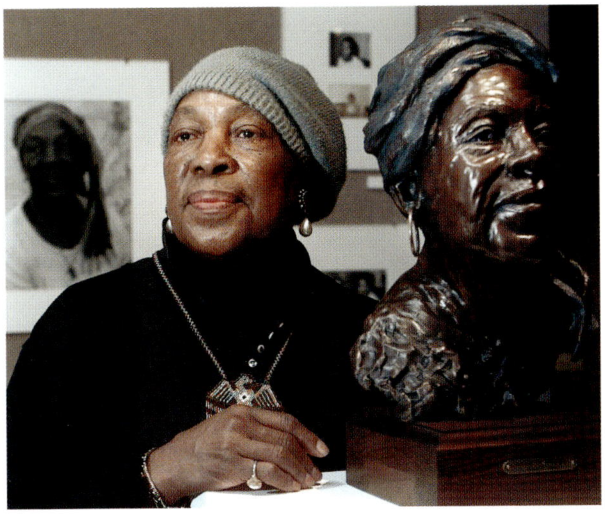

Most artists who have taken a life drawing class in Tulsa are familiar with this lovely lady, Helen Hines. In 1964, Helen was working in a laundry in downtown Tulsa. One day, walking down First Street, she stopped to watch Delbert Jackson, a professional artist, who was painting a huge mural about oil production in Oklahoma. The mural was commissioned by the Pan American Oil Company for the Smithsonian Institution in Washington, D.C. Mr. Jackson noticed Helen and asked her to pose for the mural, which became her first job as a professional model. She has since modeled for Philbrook, The University of Tulsa, The Bartlesville Artists' Association, Okmulgee Technical School, and for many art classes taught by Tulsa's figurative art teachers.

Helen modeled for a sculpting class I taught at Philbrook in 1996. I was immediately taken with her poise and countenance, and how she kept her chin tipped up. As a model, Helen can be wearing nothing but earrings and she is as elegant as royalty. My purpose in sculpting a bust of Helen was to capture the essence of this beautiful person. She truly is a *Study in Dignity*.

OPPOSITE
A Study in Dignity, © 1999 Rosalind Cook.
Photo by Mel Schockner.

ABOVE
Helen, by the image of herself.
Photo by Stephen Pingry, *Tulsa World*.

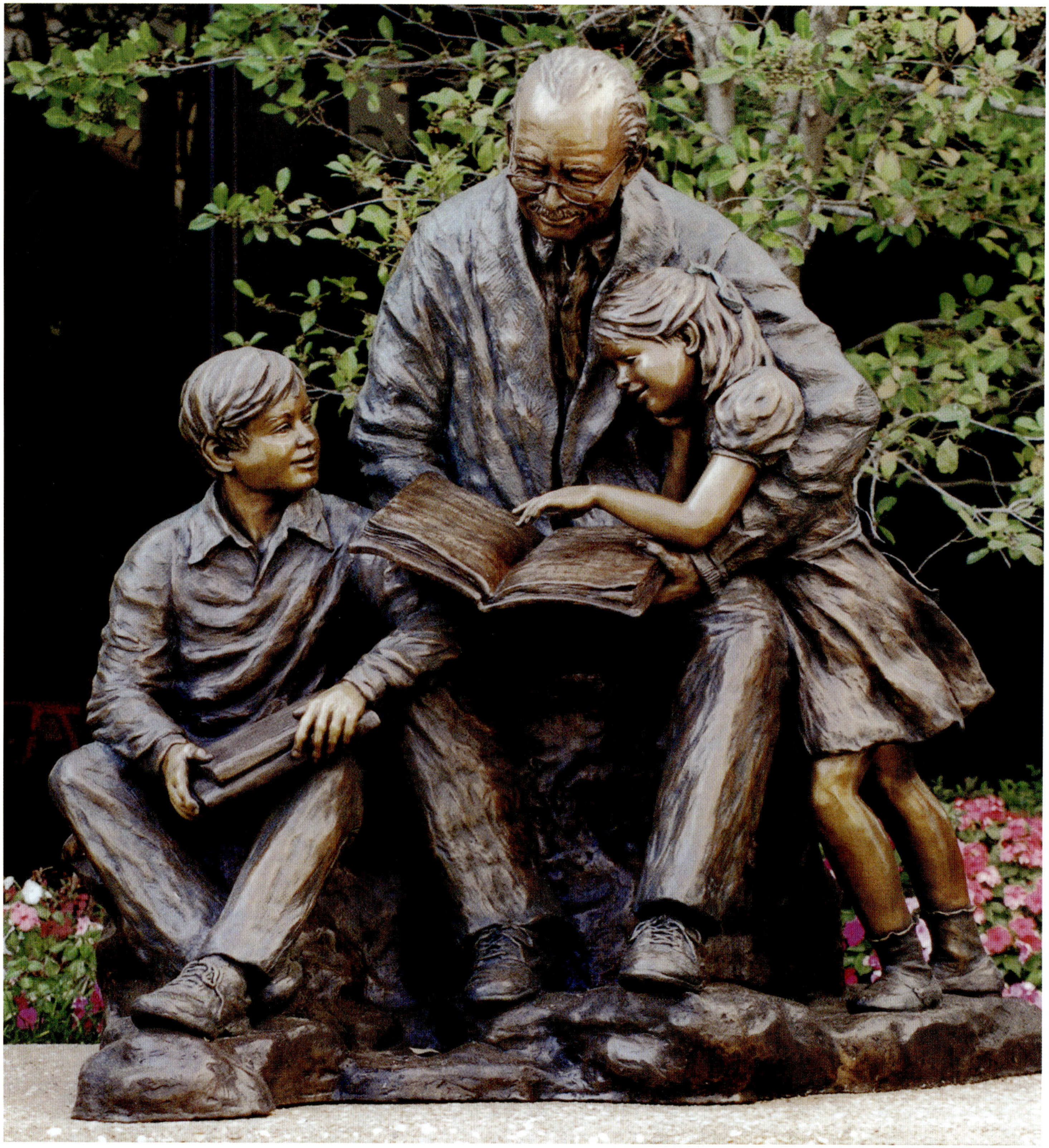

LEGACY OF LITERATURE

Peggy V. Helmerich Branch Library, 5131 East 91st Street, Tulsa, Oklahoma

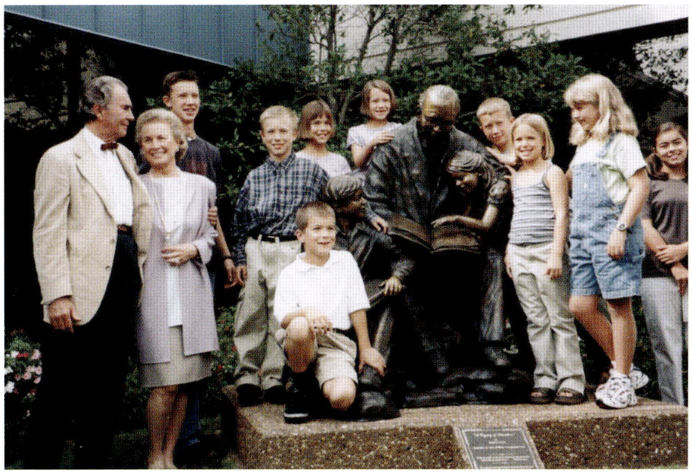

In 1998, Walt and Peggy Helmerich called me about creating a life-size sculpture to be placed outside the entrance to the Peggy V. Helmerich Branch Library. Prior to creating the maquette (a small preliminary model), I researched neighborhood library statistics and discovered that the two age groups that most use branch libraries are senior citizens and young children.

For this sculpture, I created three figures: a grandfather, an adolescent boy, and a young girl, using a strong triangular composition. A maquette is the sculptor's laboratory, allowing the exploration of various options of line and form to create the strongest design that communicates the artist's ideas before the work is created life-size. If one follows all of the main lines of this sculpture, they lead to the faces of the three subjects. The heads are all on different levels. The girl has many "S" curves and the man and boy are very angular, but without any of the 90-degree angles that can kill a composition.

Peggy Helmerich chose the scripture from Proverbs 22:6 to be inscribed on the pages of the book. The sculpture is appropriately named *Legacy of Literature*.

OPPOSITE
Legacy of Literature, © 1999 Rosalind Cook.

ABOVE
Walt and Peggy Helmerich with *Legacy of Literature* and many young readers.

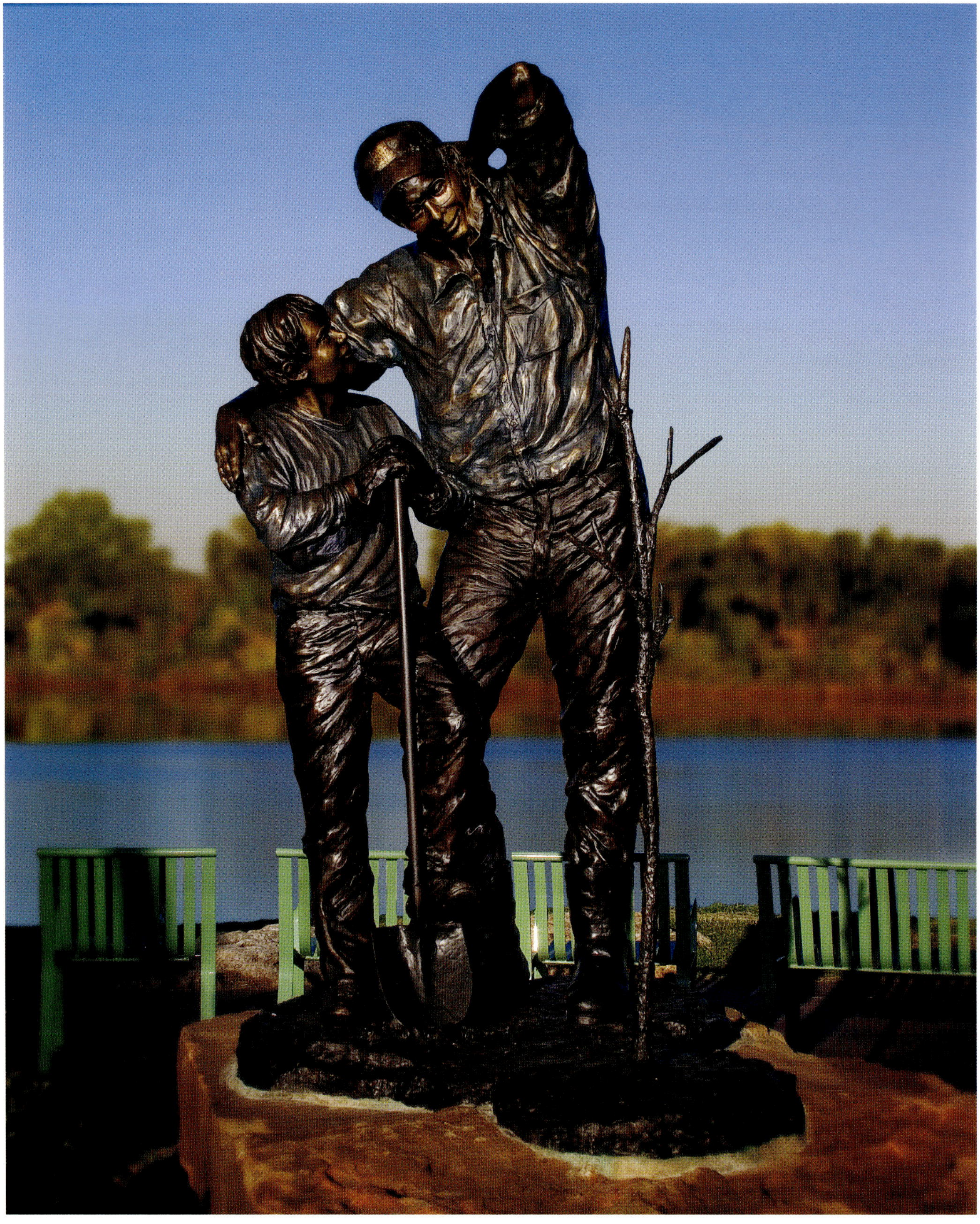

PLANTING FOR THE FUTURE

Tulsa River Parks, North of 31st Street and Riverside Drive, Tulsa, Oklahoma

In 1976, Tulsa faced a crisis: the urban forest was seriously shrinking as a result of development, storm, and disease and was an estimated 200,000 trees short. With this report, Street Commissioner Sid Patterson became very concerned. One day he received a phone call from a young teenager asking him what the city intended to do to replace the loss of so many trees in our beautiful city. Sid's concern then became ignited into a vision to "plant for the future." Through the support and funding of many Tulsa organizations, private citizens, and volunteers, "Up With Trees" was formulated, grown, and remains a vibrant example of the results of one man's dream.

Len Eaton, the first board chairman of the River Parks Authority, approached me in 2007 about creating a sculpture to commemorate Sid Patterson, then 86 years old, and Sid's mission of Up With Trees. The sculpture was to be placed in River Parks just North of 31st Street, alongside the American flag.

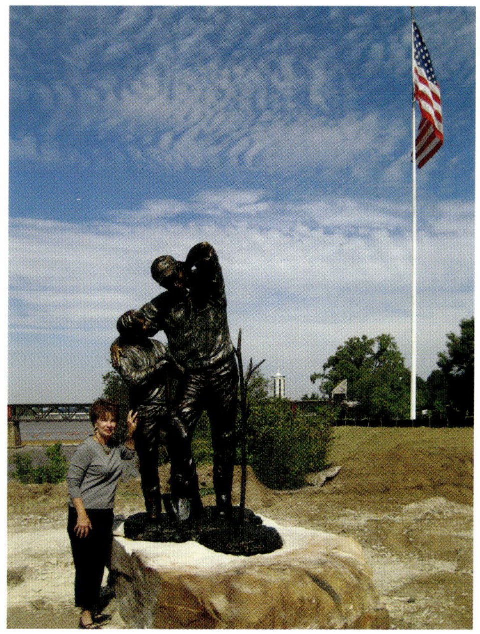

OPPOSITE
Planting for the Future, © 2000 Rosalind Cook. All photos by Don Kreutzweiser.

RIGHT
Just installed at Tulsa River Parks.

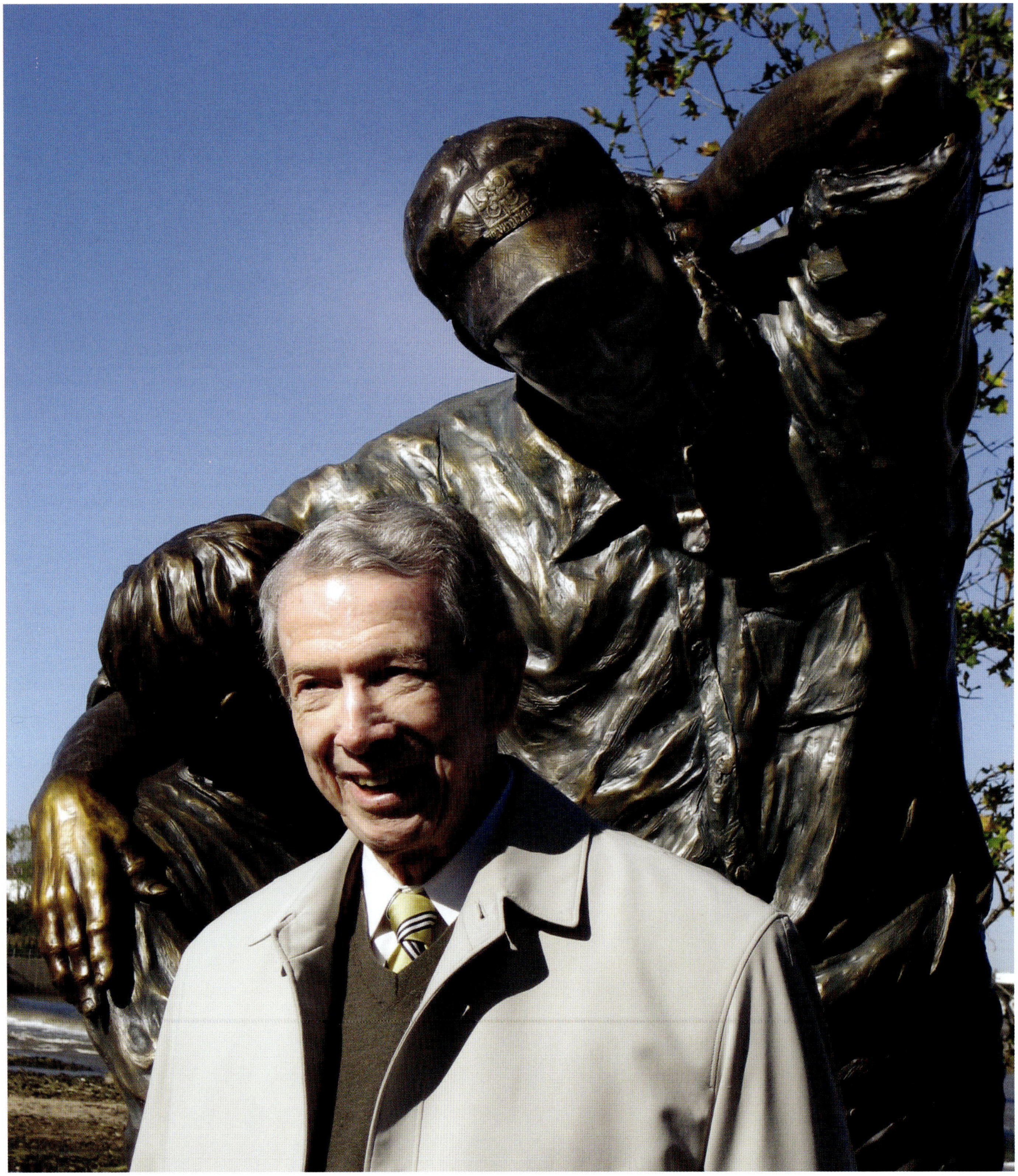

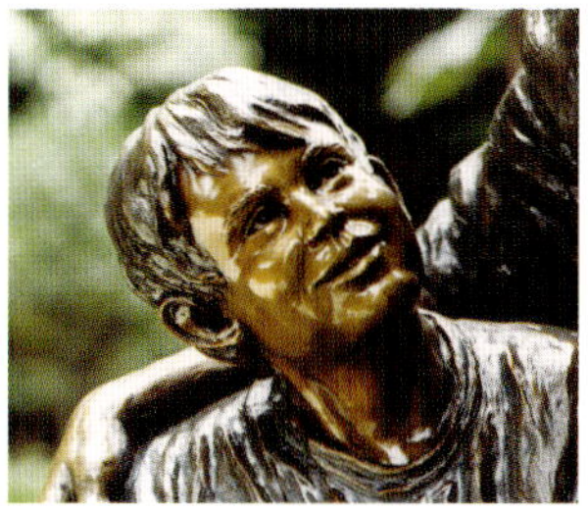

Coincidentally, I recently had installed a sculpture of a man and young boy planting a tree together for the entrance to the Kilohana Hardwood Plantation on the island of Kauai, Hawaii. This was the perfect sculpture to honor Sid, but the face had to be changed to resemble him as a younger man. A depiction of the young teenager who inspired Sid is also part of the sculpture, representing the future. After a wax was poured from the existing molds, I reworked the face, put the Up With Trees logo on his hat, and added eye glasses. *Voilà!* There was Sid!

I was so grateful that Sid was alive for the unveiling and dedication of this

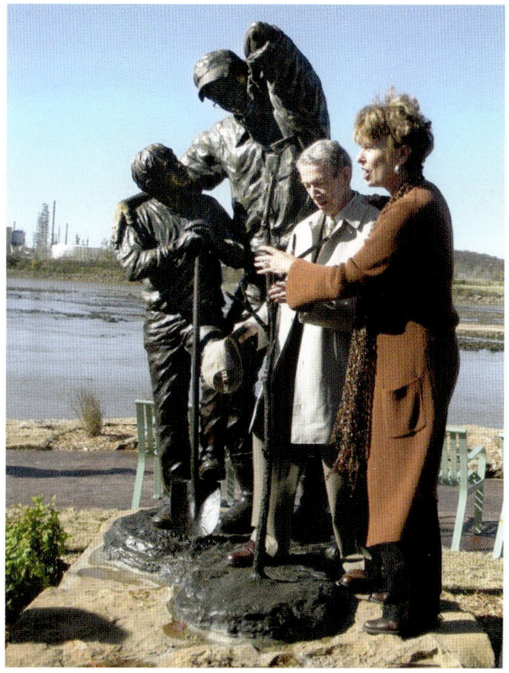

sculpture, *Planting for the Future*. The ceremony was held November 6, 2008, led by Mayor Kathy Taylor and attended by a large group of supporters of both Sid Patterson and Up With Trees. Sid passed away in 2012, leaving a significant legacy that continues to benefit Tulsa.

OPPOSITE
Sid Patterson with *Planting for the Future*.
Photos by Don Kreutzweiser.

ABOVE LEFT
The face of the young teenager.

ABOVE RIGHT
Sid and I spoke to the crowd at the dedication day ceremony.

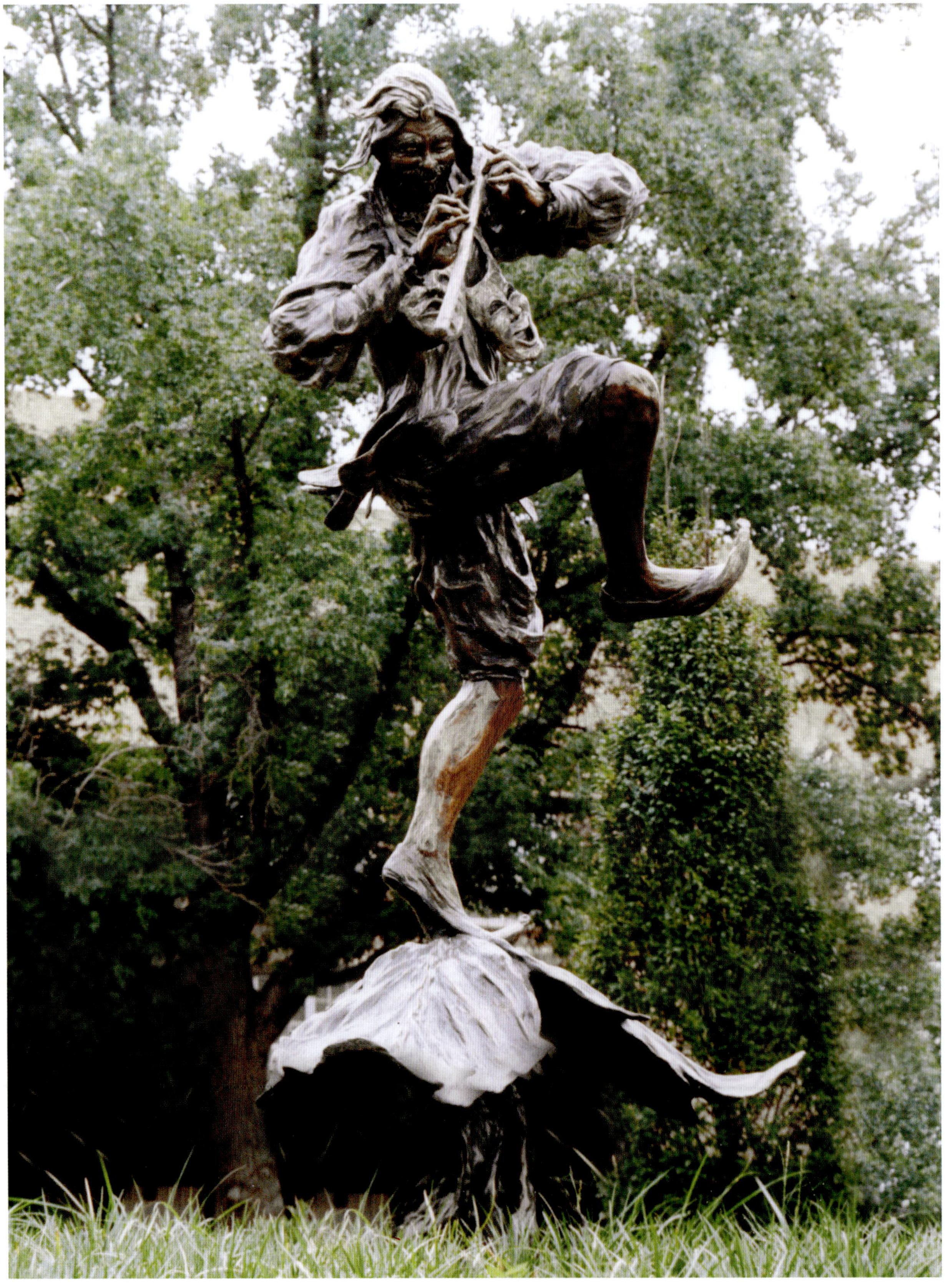

CELEBRATING THE ARTS

Harwelden Mansion, 2210 South Main Street, Tulsa, Oklahoma

Earl and Mary Harwell completed their oil-baron mansion in 1928. It was designed in the Gothic style of architecture by Biollot and Lauch Architects of Kansas City. Upon her death in 1976, Mrs. Harwell bequeathed the mansion to the Arts and Humanities Council of Tulsa.

When the Arts and Humanities Council approached me in 1999 about creating a sculpture for the front of Harwelden, I immediately began to brainstorm and do research for the piece. Since the mission statement of the council is to promote the arts and humanities, I was drawn to the minstrel, a character of medieval times who had the same purpose.

This historic figure would also be in keeping with the Gothic architecture of Harwelden. The minstrel, symbolically and historically, has played a major role in the development of arts and humanities, for it was the poet-musician who traveled around the countryside entertaining with dance, songs, musical instruments, stories, and dramas. Minstrels brought the arts not only to the royalty and nobility but to the common people as well. The ballads, folk tales, and stories were preserved and handed down to the next generation with every performance. With this concept and history of the minstrel in mind, I began to sculpt this significant symbol.

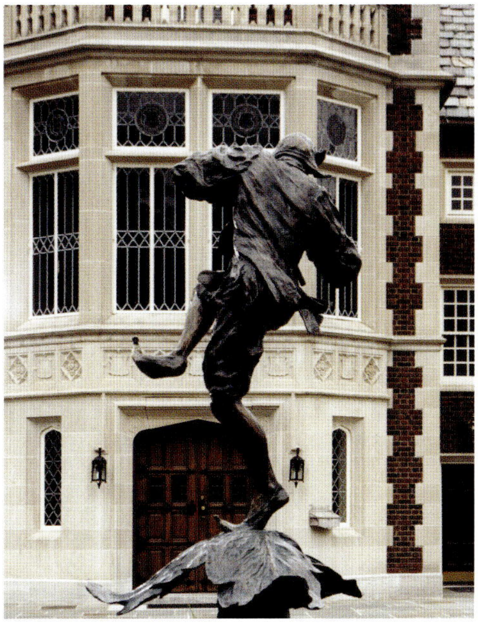

OPPOSITE AND RIGHT
Celebrating the Arts, © 2000 Rosalind Cook.
Photos by Andy Leithner.

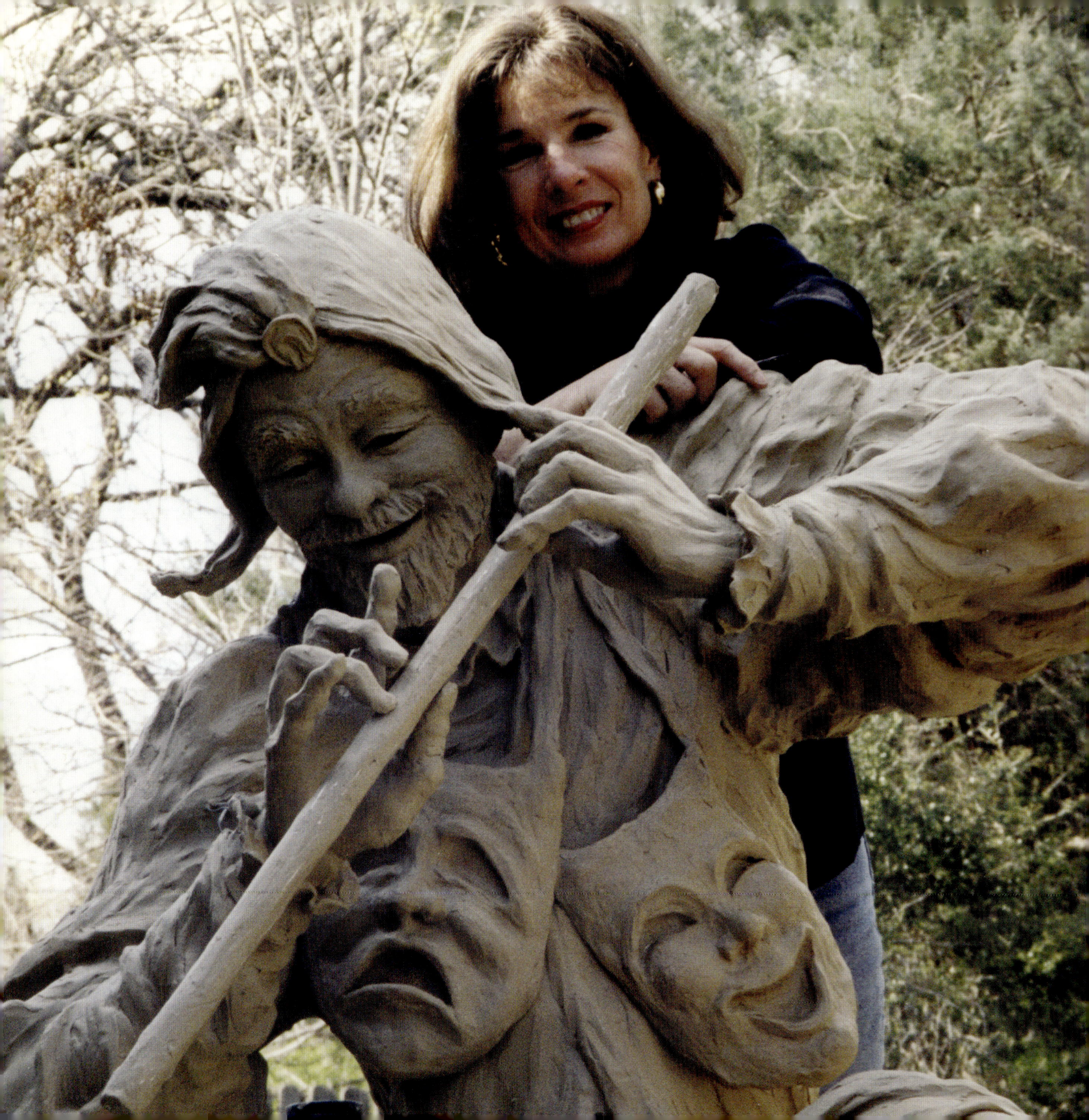

My minstrel is a very lively and exaggerated entertainer. All the arts are represented in this character: he is dancing, he is playing a musical instrument, masks of comedy and tragedy swing from his chest, and he, as a sculpture, is a part of the visual arts as well. As an artist, I wanted the sculpture to become airborne in some way, so I created a form made of a twisted tree trunk with three huge leaves upon which he is dancing, symbolic of how our lives flourish through the arts. The three leaves represent the body, mind, and spirit.

Sometimes, the unexpected happens in my studio. My husband, Hal, walked in as I was finishing the minstrel's face and remarked, "He looks just like my father" Hal's father, usually a very somber person, had passed away several years earlier. Now Hal Cook, Sr. is captured in bronze, dancing and forever smiling.

OPPOSITE
Rosalind with the clay version of *Celebrating the Arts*.

ABOVE RIGHT
The minstrel's shoe.

AN ODE TO KATIE

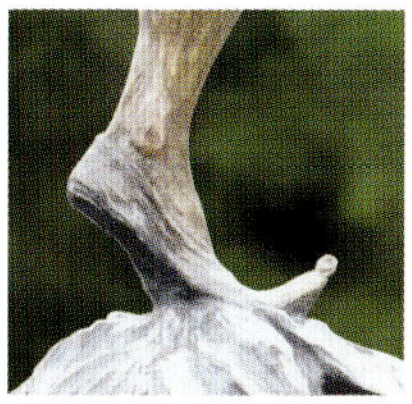

Tulsa's beloved Katie Westby, patron of the arts, who was still very much involved with the arts in her 80s, graciously wanted to fund this sculpture project. Katie came several times to my studio in her wheelchair and watched me create the original minstrel in clay. With this connection, I became very fond of her amazing spirit. One day, when I was adding balls on the end of the minstrel's long, pointed shoes, it occurred to me that this sculpture would outlive Katie and me. I had Katie press her thumbs into each of the shoe's balls so that her very own thumb prints would be cast forever in bronze.

I was privileged to create a bust of Katie Westby for Harwelden Mansion. Katie brought me an earlier photograph of herself and said, "I was always noted for my friendly smile and would like for you to capture it." So I did. Dear Katie passed away in 2000.

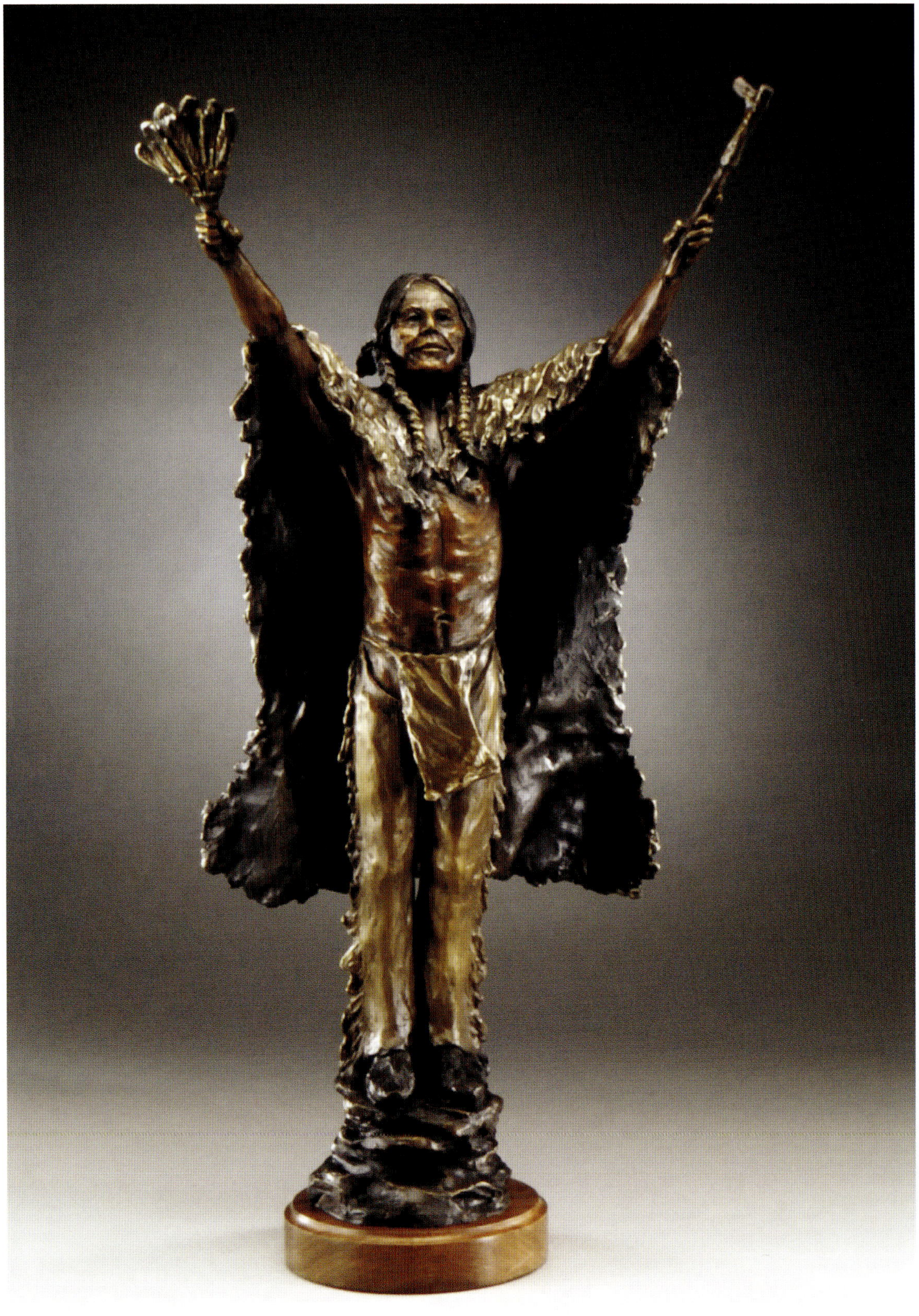

SOARING SPIRIT

Oklahoma State Capitol, 2300 North Lincoln Boulevard, Oklahoma City, Oklahoma

In 2000, I was one of six Oklahoma sculptors invited to submit a clay maquette of a sculpture for the new Oklahoma State Capitol dome. Though Senator Enoch Kelly Haney's sculpture, *The Guardian,* won the competition, *Soaring Spirit* was a finalist. A casting of this sculpture is now placed on permanent exhibit in the Oklahoma State Capitol building.

This sculpture depicts an older, wiser Native American, with uplifted arms showing dignity and pride. He is blessing the land. Upon his back is a buffalo hide, symbolizing great endurance and lending a sense of nobility. The relationships of the Native American to the Great Spirit and to mankind are symbolically depicted. His right hand holds out a prayer fan commonly used throughout all tribes. The feathers of the prayer fan are thought to carry the prayers of the people to the Creator. The uplifted left hand holds a calumet, or peace pipe, symbolic of his relationship with mankind. The calumet is used to ceremonially seal agreements.

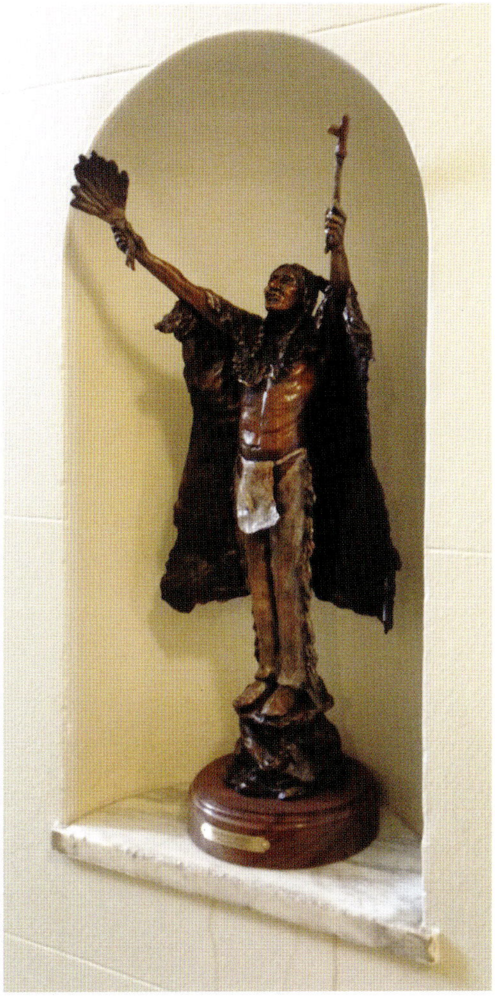

OPPOSITE
Soaring Spirit, © 2000 Rosalind Cook.
Photo by Mel Schockner.

ABOVE RIGHT
Soaring Spirit was installed in the Oklahoma State Capitol in 2014.

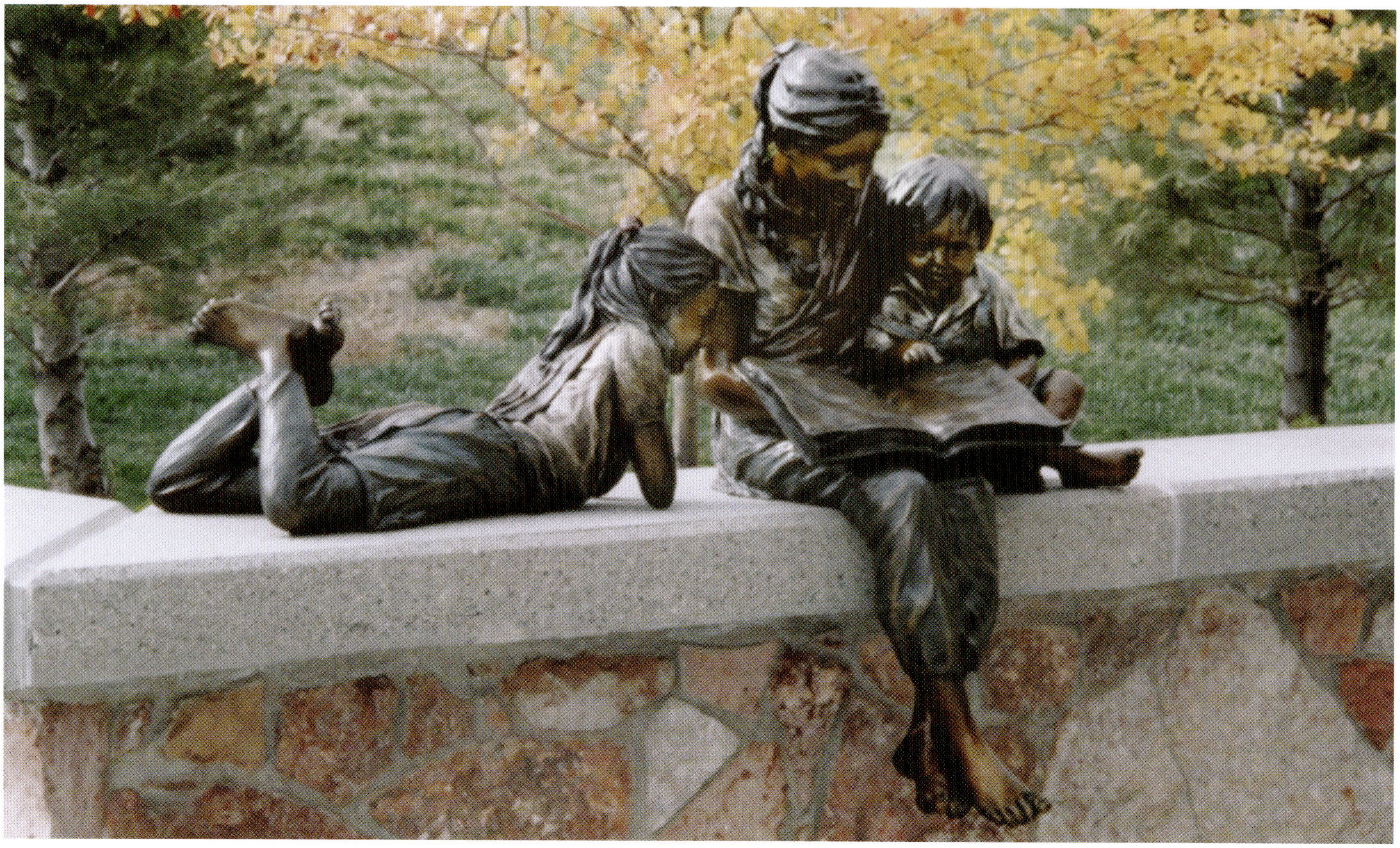

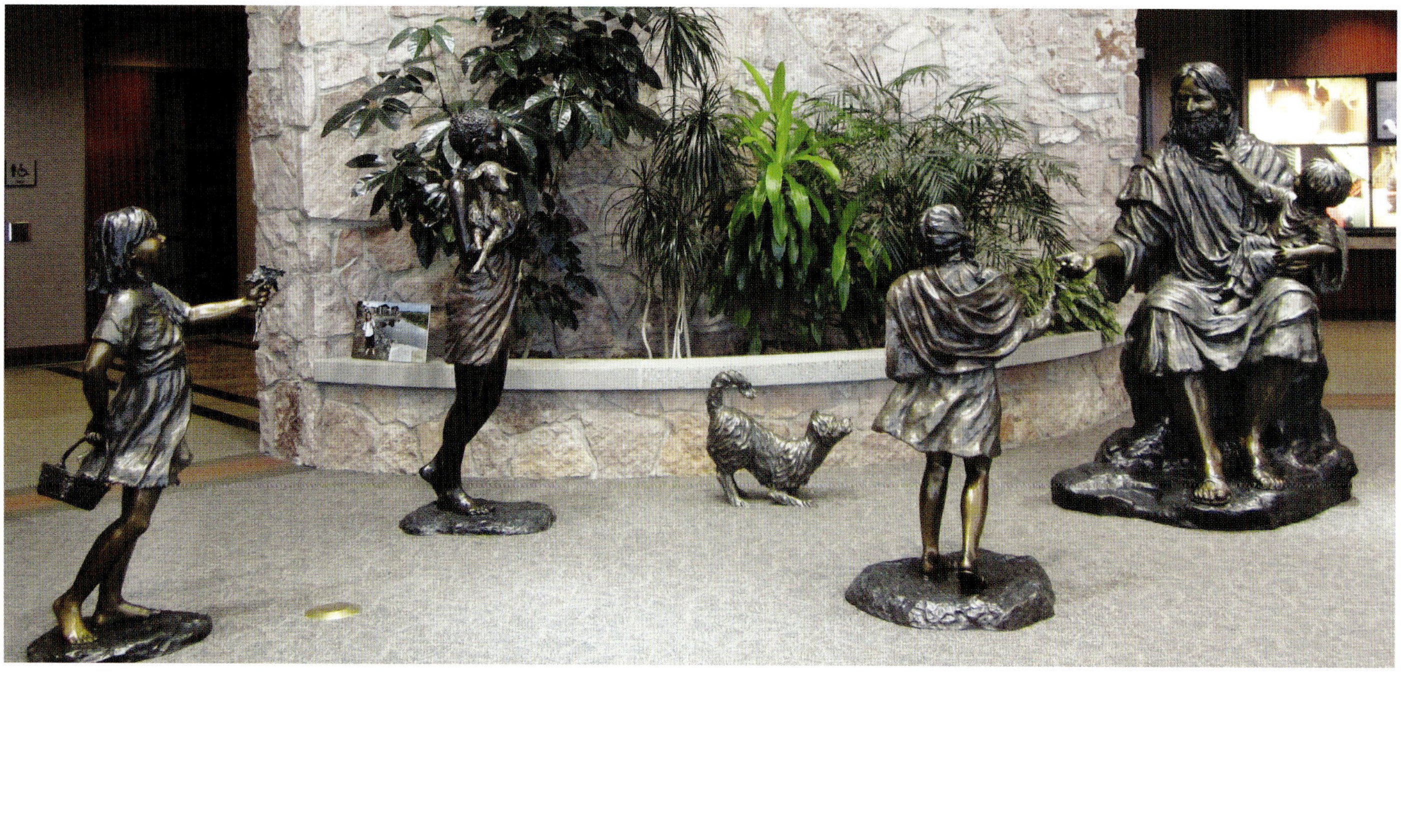

THE SCULPTURES OF COMPASSION INTERNATIONAL

12290 Voyager Parkway, Colorado Springs, Colorado

Compassion International is a Christian organization committed to helping children in poverty in 26 countries through child sponsorship, medical care, education, and other important gifts. I have sponsored two children, in Kenya and Peru, for over 15 years, and have grown to love and respect this organization. Through letters, a sponsor develops a relationship with each child and has the opportunity to make a big impact on a life by doing so little.

Compassion International was begun in South Korea in 1952 by missionary Everett Swanson, who was ministering to U.S. troops. He was deeply touched by the thousands of street children in poverty and decided to do something to help them. "Let my heart be broken by the things that break the heart of God," was his famous quote.

In 2000, Wes Stafford, the president of Compassion International, called me to discuss creating a series of bronze sculptures that would reflect their ministry to children in spiritual, economic, social and physical poverty all over the world. Between 2000 and 2007, I created 15 life-size sculptures for their headquarters in Colorado Springs. The sculpture placements begin outside the front entrance and progress into the central lobby.

On a three-foot wall beside the sidewalk leading to the entrance sit three bronze children from India. The oldest child is reading to the two younger siblings, representing the work of Compassion in India. Often, only the eldest child will receive an education, and that child will, in turn, teach the rest of the family. As you enter the main lobby, the central focus is a seated Christ figure holding an Asian child in his lap and welcoming children from Africa, Mexico, and China.

OPPOSITE
Untitled sculptures created for Compassion International
© 2000–2006 Rosalind Cook.

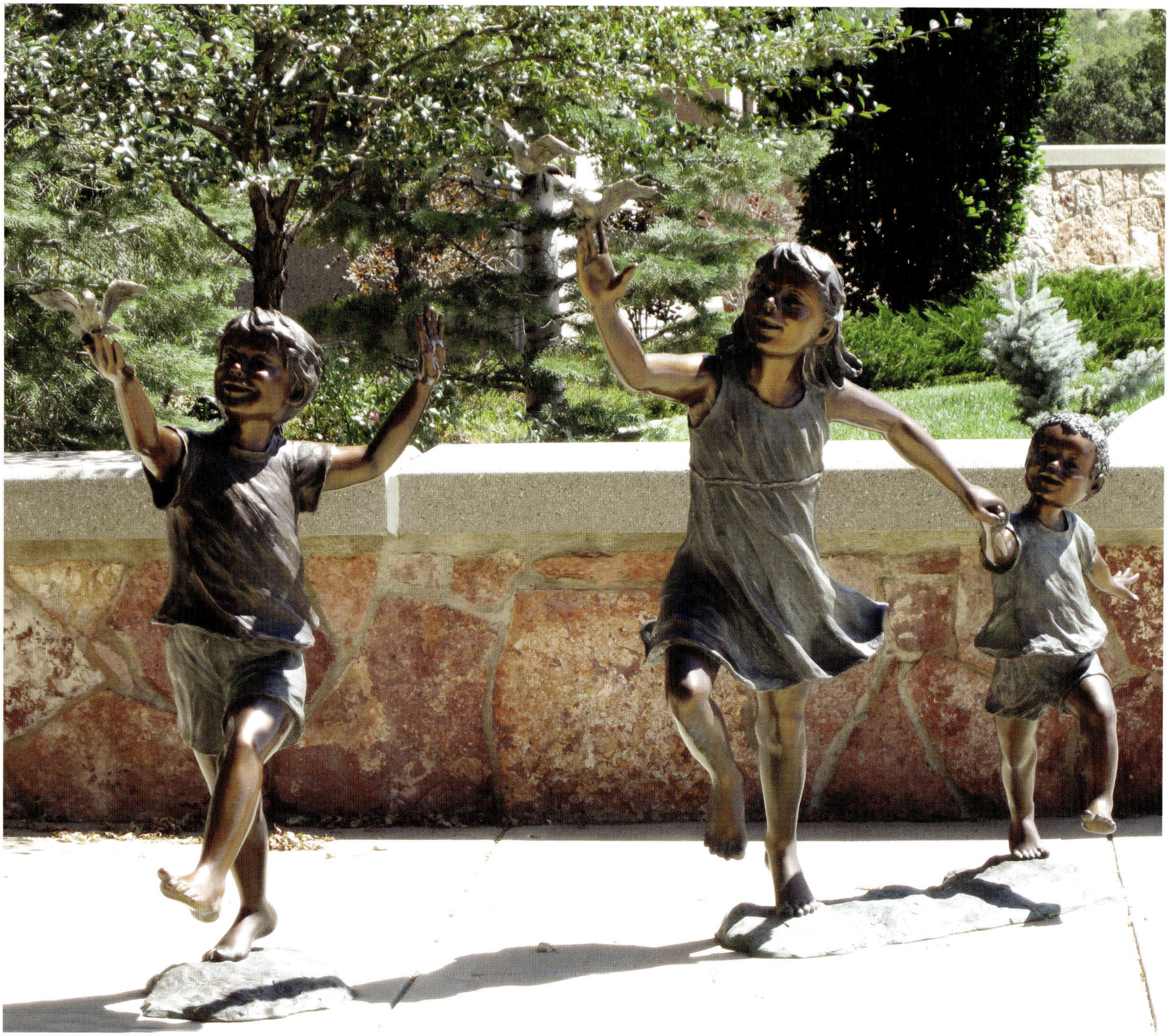

THE SCULPTURES OF COMPASSION INTERNATIONAL

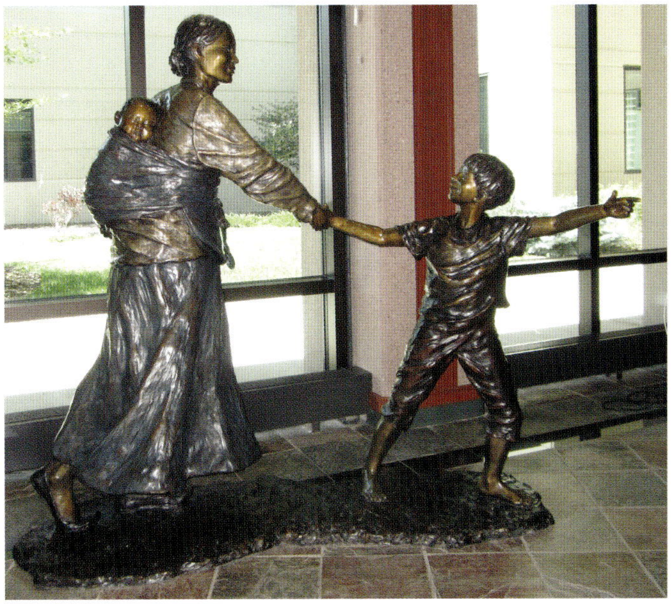

Just inside the entrance is a sculpture of a Korean mother with her baby on her back and her young son pulling her toward the sculpture of Christ. These works have become an interactive teaching tool as visitors hear the Compassion story and have their photos made with the sculptures.

The last sculpture created for Compassion, situated outside as you leave the building, was commissioned with the purpose of representing children set free from the despair of poverty, while knowing that God loves them. As I prayed, my imagination saw barefoot, happy children running and releasing doves. I love this sculpture and the impact it makes. This sculpture trio symbolizes the results of the tireless work Compassion International does in the lives of young children.

OPPOSITE
Set Free, © 2006 Rosalind Cook.

ABOVE
Korean Mother and Children,
© 2001 Rosalind Cook.

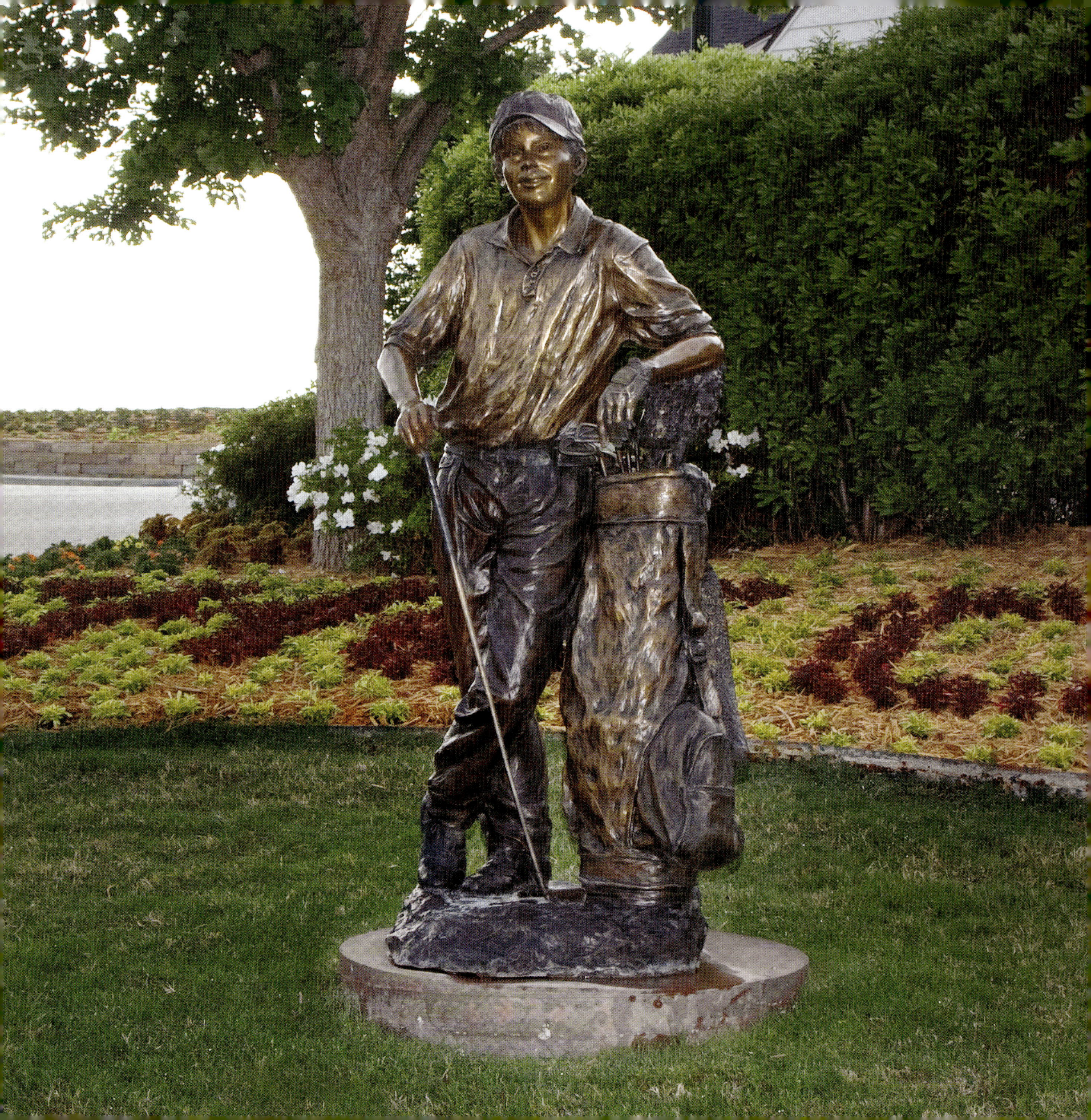

SOMEDAY

Southern Hills Country Club, 2636 East 61st Street, Tulsa, Oklahoma

In 1935, Southern Hills Country Club officially opened on land donated by oilman Waite Phillips. The club consisted of an Olympic-size pool, a stable and riding paths, a polo field, tennis courts, a skeet-shooting range, a clubhouse, and a championship golf course. The impressive clubhouse resembled a 17th-century English manor house.

One August day in 2000, I received a phone call from Dave and Clydella Hentschel, who were working with Southern Hills Country Club and the USGA on the details for hosting the U.S. Open Golf Tournament at Southern Hills the following July. Clydella told me that at most golf tournaments, the players would receive a piece of crystal or a trophy, which was often left in their lockers. "We want something special to give the golfers. Would you create a bronze sculpture that would be given to each player?"

You must realize that at this time I knew nothing about golf. I immediately called my husband, Hal, at work and told him I had been asked to do a sculpture for the U.S. Open coming up in July. Then I asked him, "What is the U.S. Open?" I had to hold the phone away from my ear because Hal was so excited he shouted, "Call them right back and tell them *'Yes!'* "

After much research, I decided that I did not want to depict another golfer swinging a club as had been done so many times. I then thought, "What do all these golfers have in common?" It is not their education, race, or culture, but the fact that as young men, they all had a dream that maybe "someday" they could make a living playing the game of golf, a game that each loved so much.

OPPOSITE
Someday,
Photo by Don Kreutzweiser.

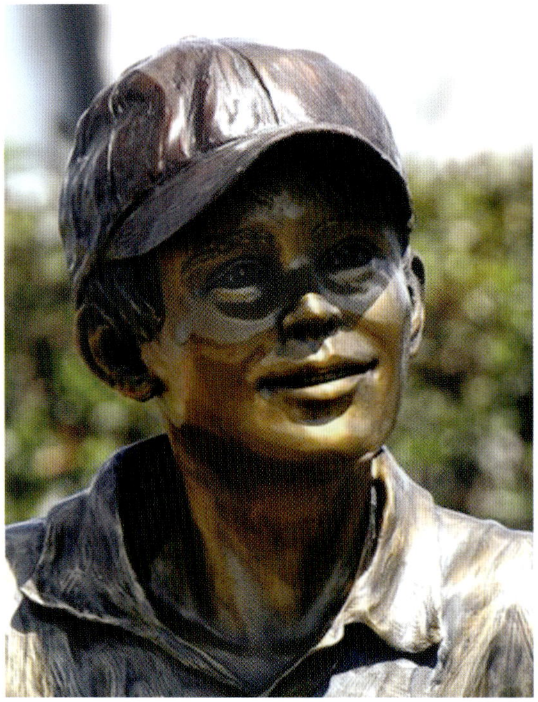

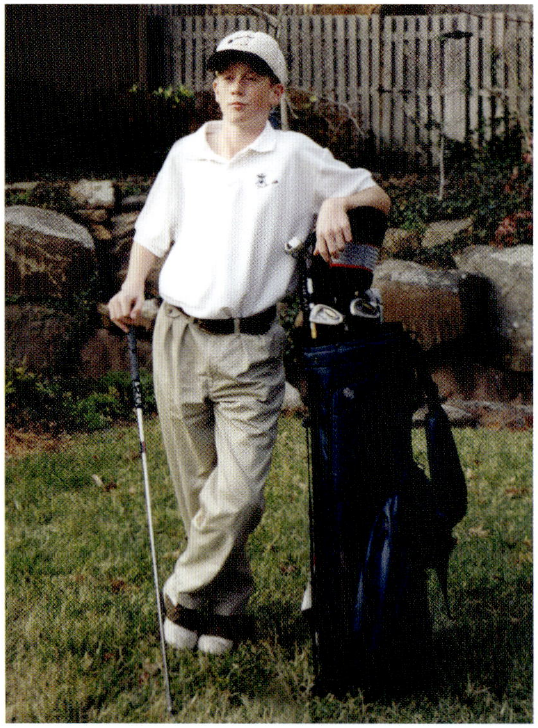

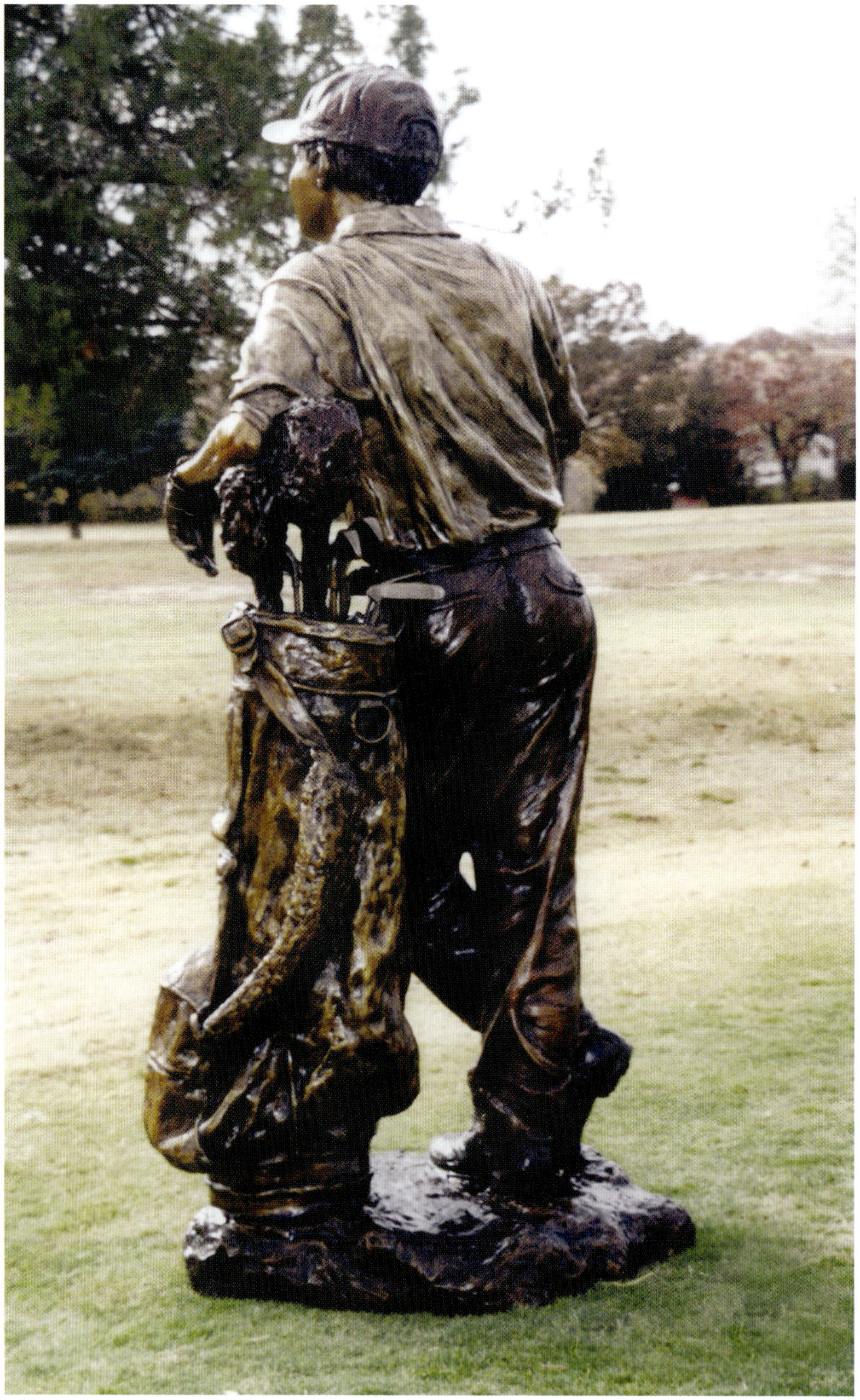

SOMEDAY

I borrowed a neighborhood teenager, Scott Allen, who played golf, and used my son's golf clubs for reference. I began working on a strong composition that would alter a lot of the "verticals" made by legs, golf bag, and a golf club. I had Scott leaning on the bag, looking out into the distance with one leg crossed in front of the other, and I juxtaposed the golf club at an angle. This created a strong triangular composition, integrating many angles, which is very masculine and interesting. It was a relaxed pose seen often on the course. My goal was to create a young man looking over the course and dreaming of what his game could be.

It was Dave Hentschel who came up with the name *Someday*, which was the perfect title for the sculpture. Each golfer received a 13-inch signed and numbered bronze. Tiger Woods received #1 of the edition because he was the winner of the previous year's U.S. Open. There was also a separate edition casting that could be purchased by members of Southern Hills Country Club, which underwrote the castings for the golfers' bronzes.

A life-size casting of *Someday* is permanently installed near the golf shop of Southern Hills Country Club. To honor Al Bush for his contribution to golf and to the club for volunteering as chairman of the 2001 U.S. Open and 2007 PGA golf championships, the club placed another life-size casting at the First Tee of Tulsa at Mohawk Park Golf Course, 5701 East 36th Street North, Tulsa, Oklahoma. This teaching program introduces golf to the youth of our city.

I must say that golf is now a big part of my life since Hal has retired, and today I love the game. My golf prayer is always, "Lord, let me not be ashamed!"

OPPOSITE, CLOCKWISE FROM UPPER LEFT
Someday (detail), © 2001 Rosalind Cook.
Photo by Don Kreutzweiser. / Young Scott Allen, my model for *Someday*. / Rear view of *Someday*.
Photo by Don Kreutzweiser.

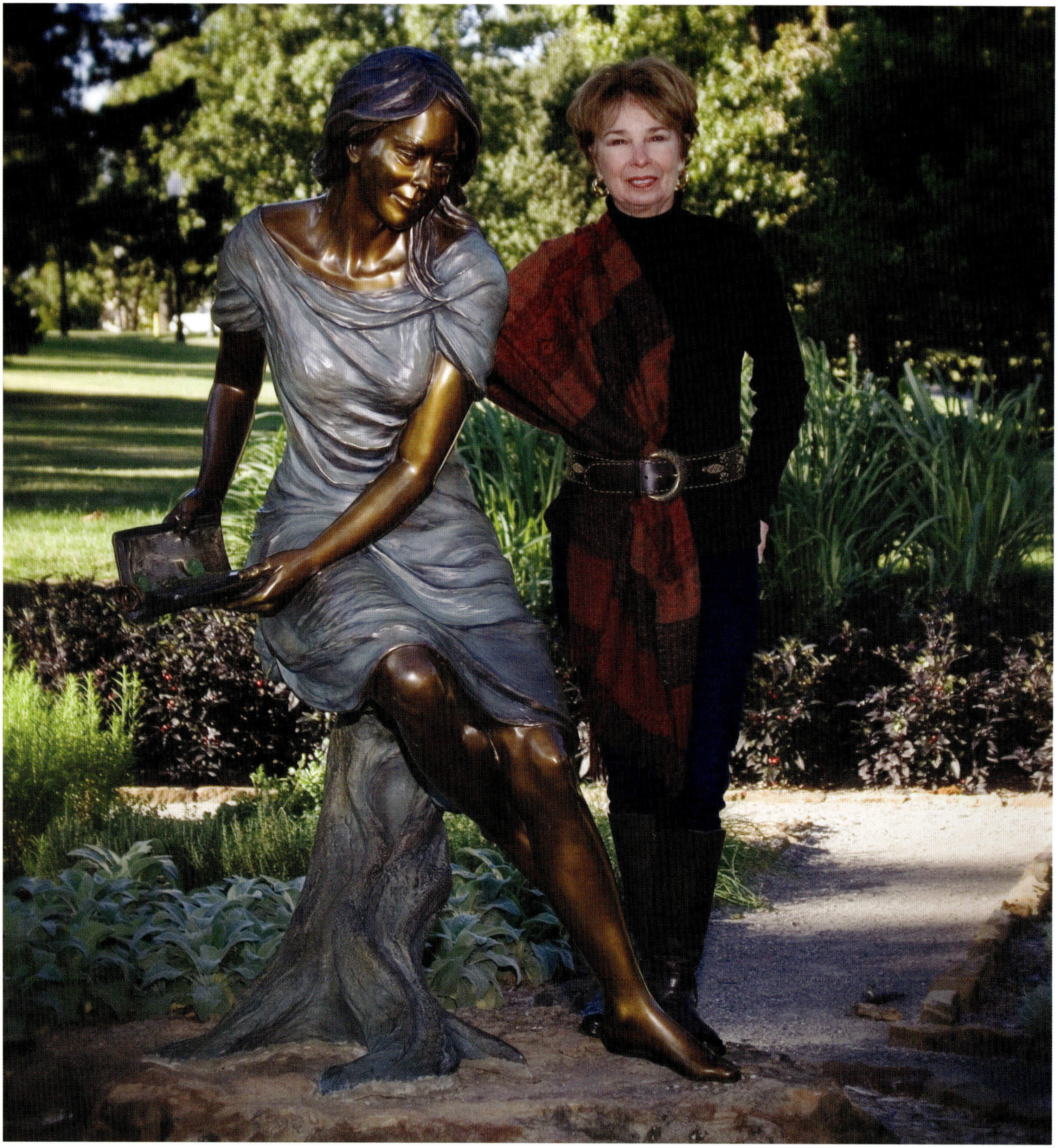

POEMS AND PROMISES

Anne Hathaway Herb Garden, Tulsa Garden Center in Woodward Park
21st Street and Rockford Avenue, Tulsa, Oklahoma

In 1909, the 45-acre tract of land located at the corner of 21st Street and Peoria Avenue, which would become Woodward Park, was purchased by the City of Tulsa for $100 an acre from the father of Helen Woodward, who had received it from a land allotment. Helen was a 14-year-old minor at the time, and this sale was done without her consent. After she grew up and married, Helen battled the City for the land for years, ultimately losing her case before the Oklahoma Supreme Court.

In 1935, the Tulsa Rose Garden was created adjoining Woodward Park, using hand labor and work horses. The project was funded by a federal grant as part of the Great Depression Recovery Program. Today Woodward Park is one of Tulsa's beauty spots, and through the years many of the trees and plantings have been given to the park by caring citizens.

In 1996, having recently returned from Italy, where I studied the sculptures of the Renaissance masters, I was challenged to create a sculpture using my new knowledge. I wanted to incorporate the principles of design I had learned in order to create movement and unity within a stationary figure. The result was this young lady reading a book of poems, seated on a twisted tree stump.

I juxtaposed the planes of the head, shoulders, pelvis, and legs at angles to one another, which created a spiraling effect and strong lines. I duplicated forms such as the round "S" curves of her hair, the tree, and her clothing. I purposefully projected her foot over the base, so as to invite the viewer "in," as opposed to the sculpture appearing "untouchable."

OPPOSITE
Rosalind with *Poems and Promises*, © 2003 Rosalind Cook.
Photo by Don Kreutzweiser.

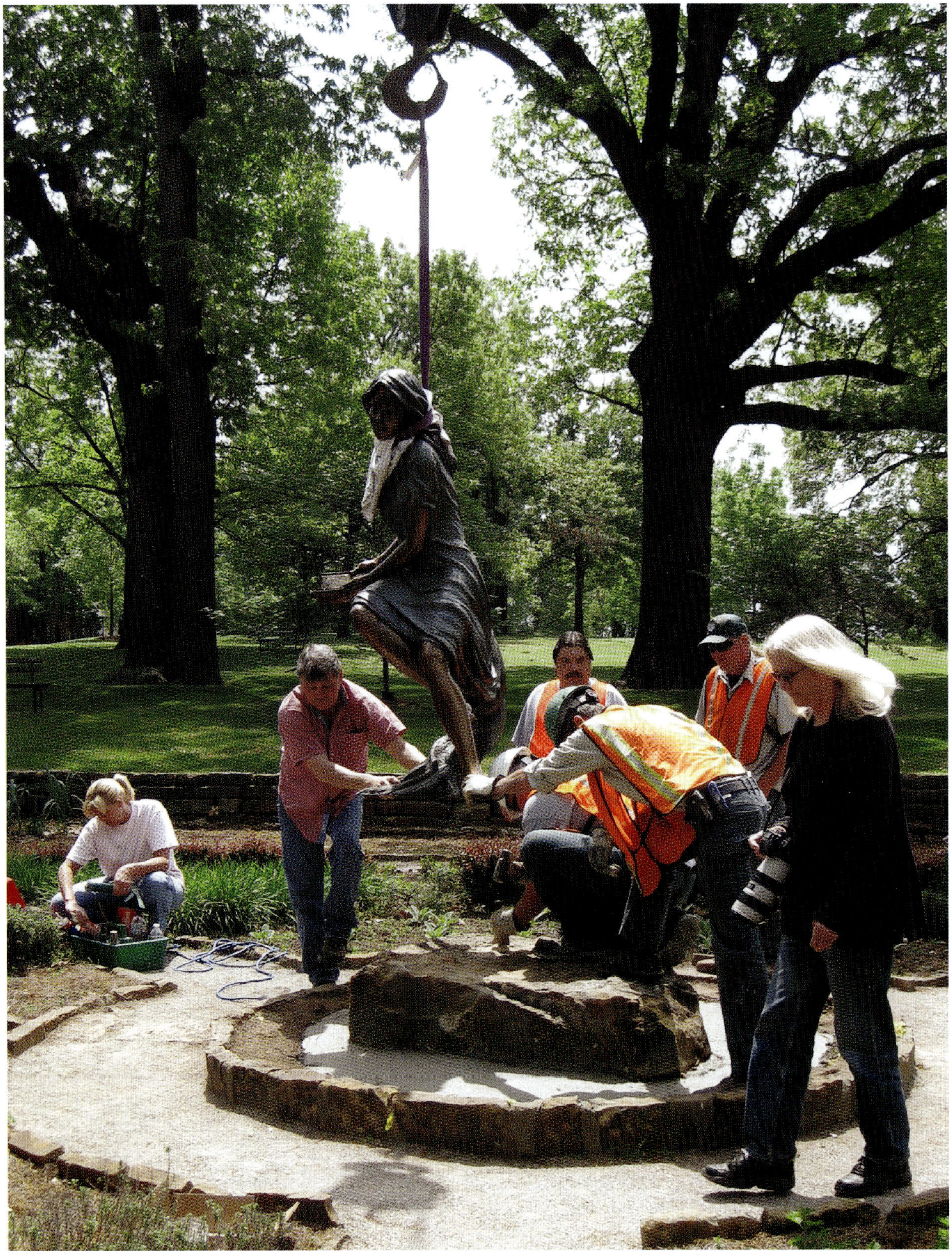

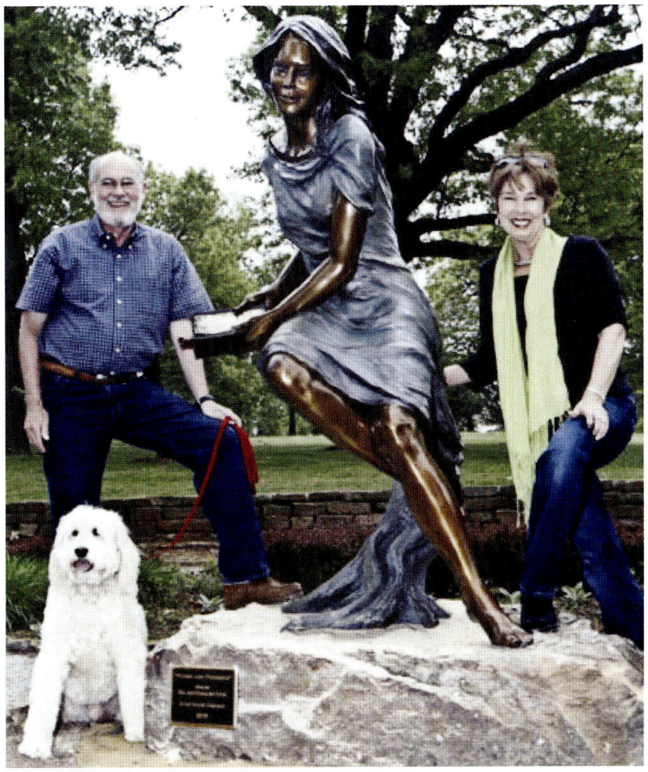

An 18-inch edition of 35 sold out quickly, so I created an enlargement of life-size plus 15 percent. In 2010, Hal and I gave a casting of *Poems and Promises* to the city of Tulsa in appreciation for the city's support of my career. After a meeting with Peggy Helmerich and Maureen Turner, who is a horticulturist for the City of Tulsa, it was decided to situate *Poems and Promises* as the focal point of The Anne Hathaway Herb Garden in Woodward Park, the park where our young children had played.

The Tulsa Garden Center held a contest to choose a line of poetry to be written on the pages of the book in the sculpture. Since Anne Hathaway was married to William Shakespeare, his famous line, "A rose by any other name would smell as sweet," was chosen. I welded a bronze rose in the crease of her poetry book for the finishing touch.

OPPOSITE
Workers install *Poems and Promises* in the Anne Hathaway Herb Garden.

ABOVE
Hal, Aspen, and Rosalind with *Poems and Promises*. Photo courtesy of *Tulsa World*.

STORY TIME FOR THREE

Bristow Public Library, 111 West 7th Street, Bristow, Oklahoma

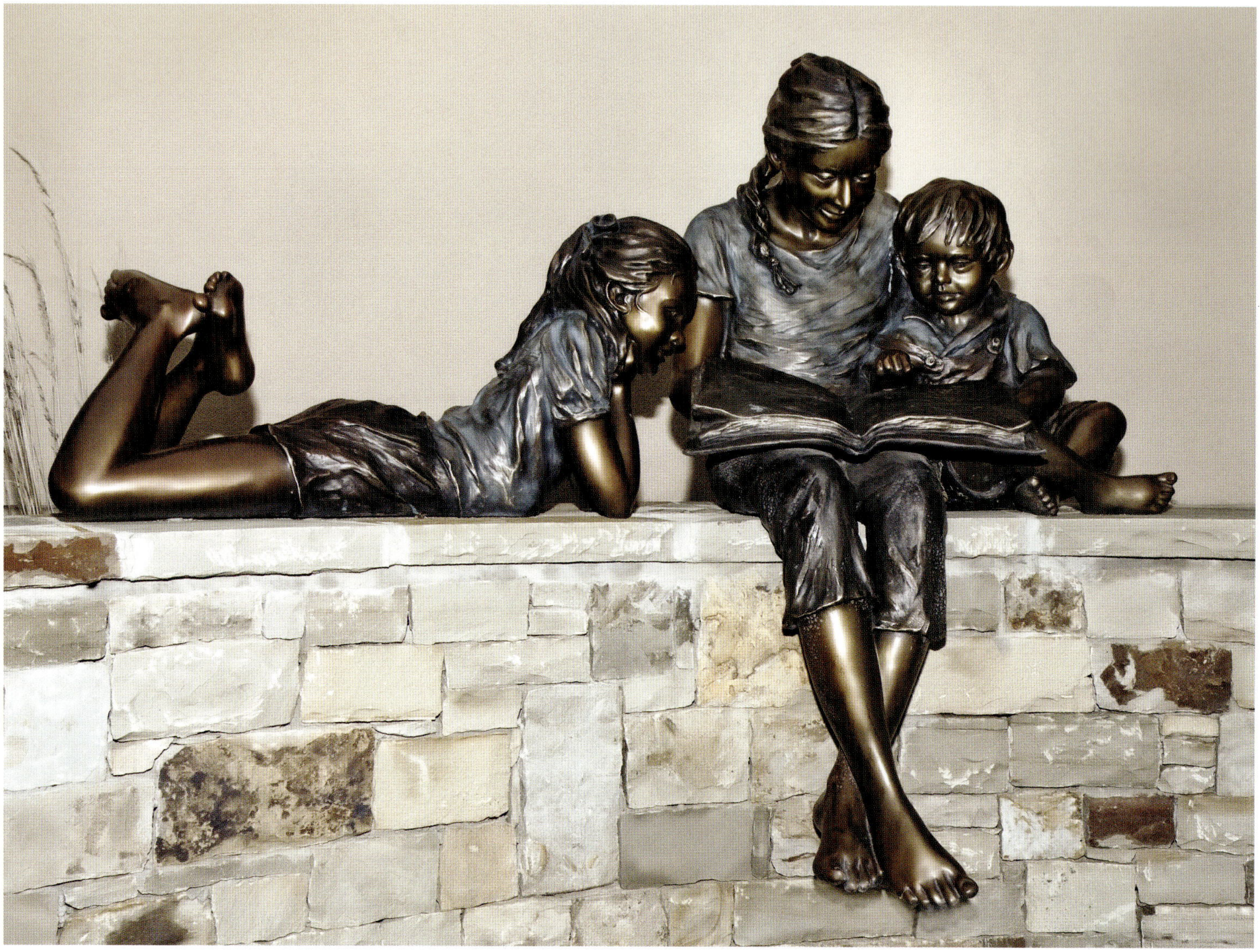

In 2013, I was contacted by Roger Collins representing The Bristow Library Board Inc. The board purchased *Story Time for Three* for the entrance to the newly renovated Bristow Public Library. This sculpture in one of its variations incorporates three children.

STORY TIMES

In 2004, I designed a sculpture for libraries and schools that not only would be an interactive sculpture for children but also one that would allow flexibility in numeric combinations and variety in marketing. My three little models were neighbors: Isabelle and Grant Marshall, children of Cary and Cindy Marshall, and Katlyn O'Sullivan, daughter of Kevin and Karen O'Sullivan. *Story Time* may be purchased as a single, double, or triple figurative sculpture.

STORY TIME FOR TWO

Henry Zarrow Regional Library, 2224 W. 51st Street, Tulsa, Oklahoma

Mr. Henry Zarrow was one of Tulsa's most beloved philanthropists and businessmen. He was affectionately known as "Mr. Henry." In 2005, Mr. Henry came to my studio to order a sculpture for the regional library named in his honor, The Henry Zarrow Regional Library. He decided on *Story Time for Two*. In January 2014, Tulsa lost one of its dearest philanthropists, "Mr. Henry" Zarrow, at age 97.

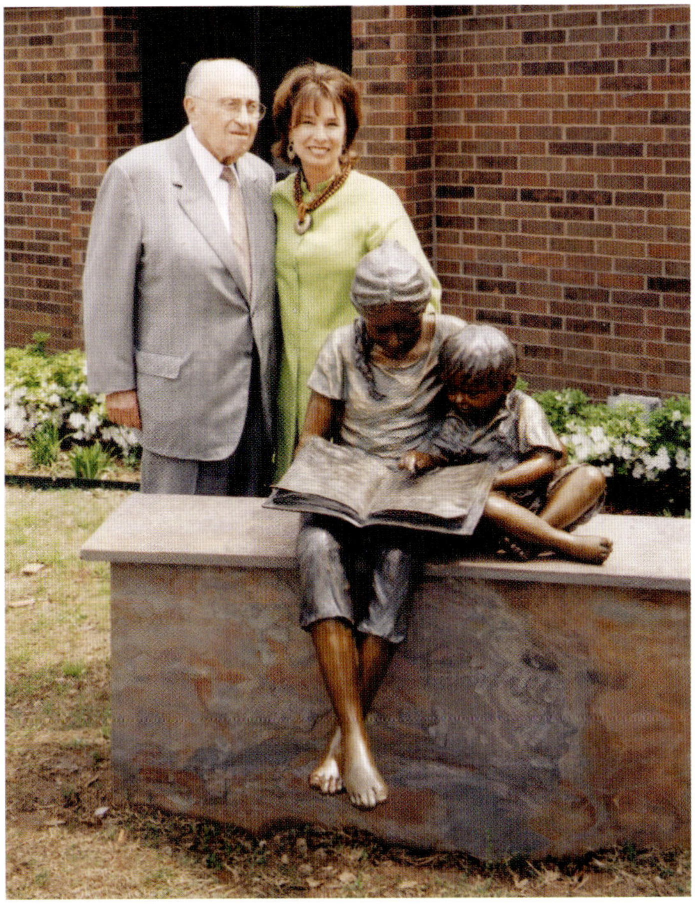

OPPOSITE
Story Time for Three, © 2005 Rosalind Cook. Photo by Don Kreutzweiser.

RIGHT
"Mr. Henry" and Rosalind with *Story Time for Two*, © 2005 Rosalind Cook.

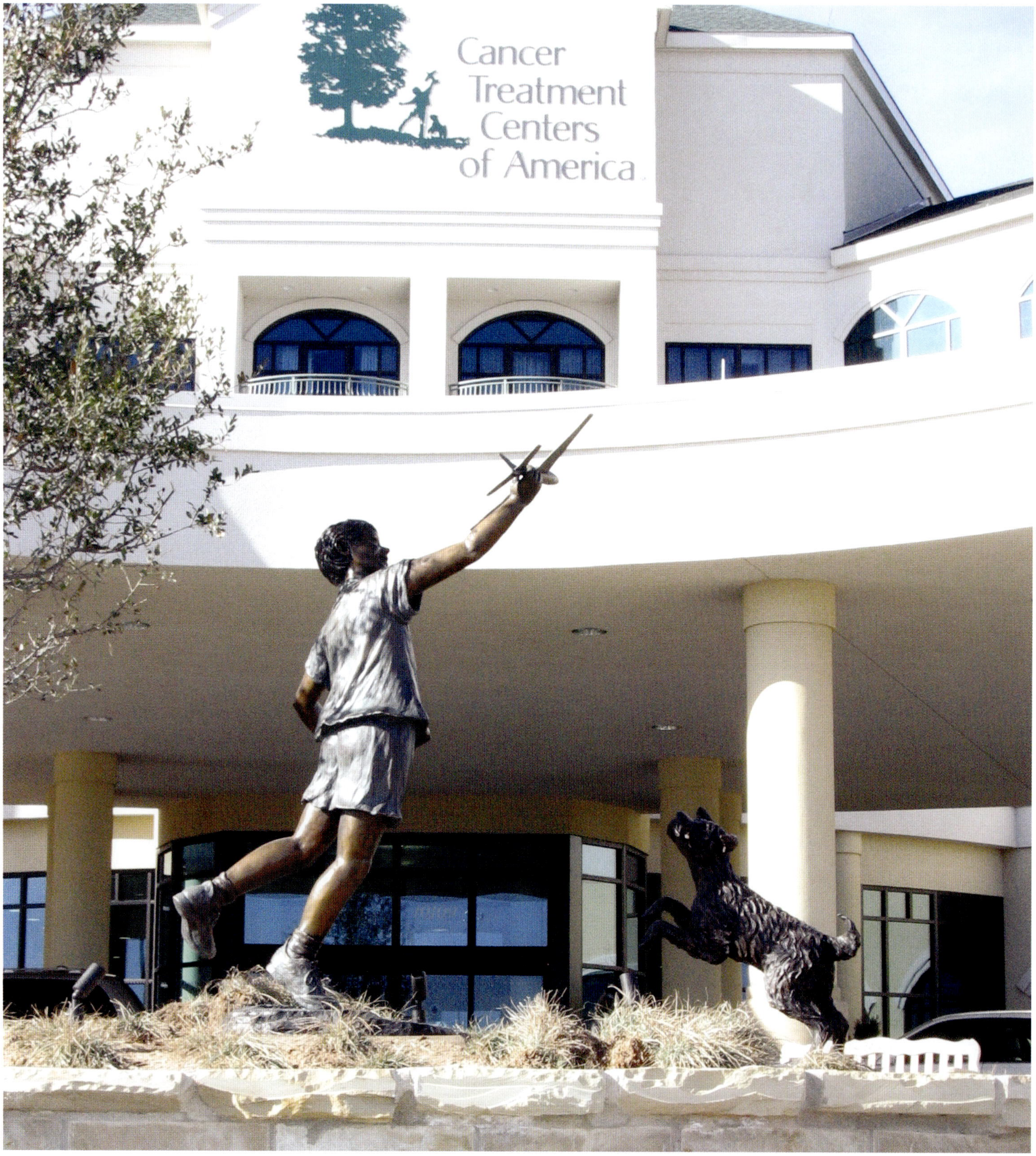
Cancer
Treatment
Centers
of America

CELEBRATE LIFE

Cancer Treatment Centers of America, 10109 East 79th Street, Tulsa, Oklahoma

The Cancer Treatment Centers of America was started by Richard Stephenson, whose mother had died of cancer. He was not happy with the treatment and care she had received and vowed to build a hospital system that would be devoted totally to the treatment and care of cancer patients.

I only knew Kristen Shriks as someone who sang in our church choir and had the voice of an angel. Kristin called me one day in 2005, inviting me to meet her employer, who happened to be Mr. Stephenson. He asked me to duplicate in bronze the Cancer Treatment Centers of America logo of a young boy flying a toy airplane with a big dog leaping beside him. The third element in the composition was to be a tree. This image was taken from his family's life experience and he named this logo *Celebrate Life*, which is an uplifting creed of CTCA hospitals.

I agreed to give him an exclusive on this sculpture as it would be placed at every Cancer Treatment Centers of America that would be built. To date, these hospitals are across the country and my sculpture, *Celebrate Life,* is at the entrance to each. The hospitals are located in Tulsa, Oklahoma; Philadelphia, Pennsylvania; Zion, Illinois; Goodyear, Arizona; and Newman, Georgia.

My husband, Hal, has flown his plane for Angel Flights, bringing cancer patients to CTCA for treatment and returning them home. So in several ways, this was a significant project for both Hal and me.

OPPOSITE
Celebrate Life, © 2005 Rosalind Cook.

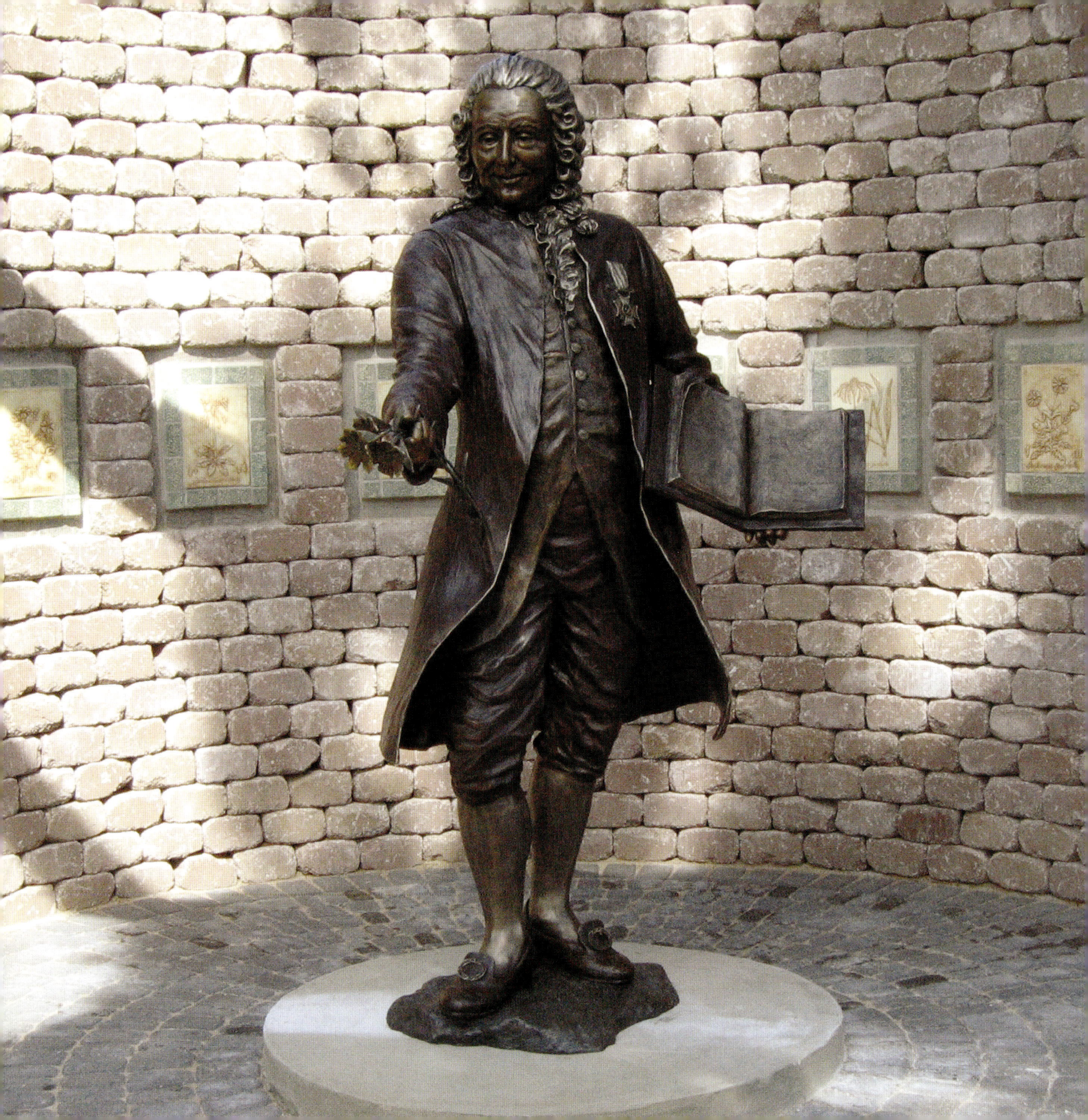

CAROLUS LINNAEUS

Linnaeus Teaching Garden of Tulsa, 2435 South Peoria Avenue, Tulsa, Oklahoma

The original mansion that is now The Tulsa Garden Center was completed in 1920, at a cost of $100,000. The architect was Noble Fleming, and the original owner was David R. Travis, who lived in his mansion for only three years. The next owner was merchant Arthur Hull. From 1932 to 1950, the property was owned by George Snedden. The mansion was then acquired by W.G. Skelly, who never resided in the home. The City of Tulsa purchased this mansion in 1954 to become the Tulsa Garden Center. The Linnaeus Teaching Garden, located on the grounds behind the mansion, is an ongoing project of the Tulsa Garden Center as a viewing and teaching garden.

In 2005, I was commissioned by the Tulsa Garden Center to create a sculpture of Carolus Linnaeus, known as the Father of Botany. Linnaeus was a Swedish botanist, physician, and zoologist, who laid the foundation of binomial nomenclature (the classification of living things into the categories of genus and species).

This sculpture was to be the focal point of the Linnaeus Teaching Garden, which has become a primary site for viewing by locals and visitors to Tulsa. Barry Fugatt, director of horticulture for the Tulsa Garden Center, had the vision for this garden. With a great deal of work and help, he saw this vision through into a reality and also developed an extensive docent teaching program, which serves the public on site and brings noted horticulturists from all over the United States to the garden for lectures and teaching.

OPPOSITE
Carolus Linnaeus, © 2005 Rosalind Cook.

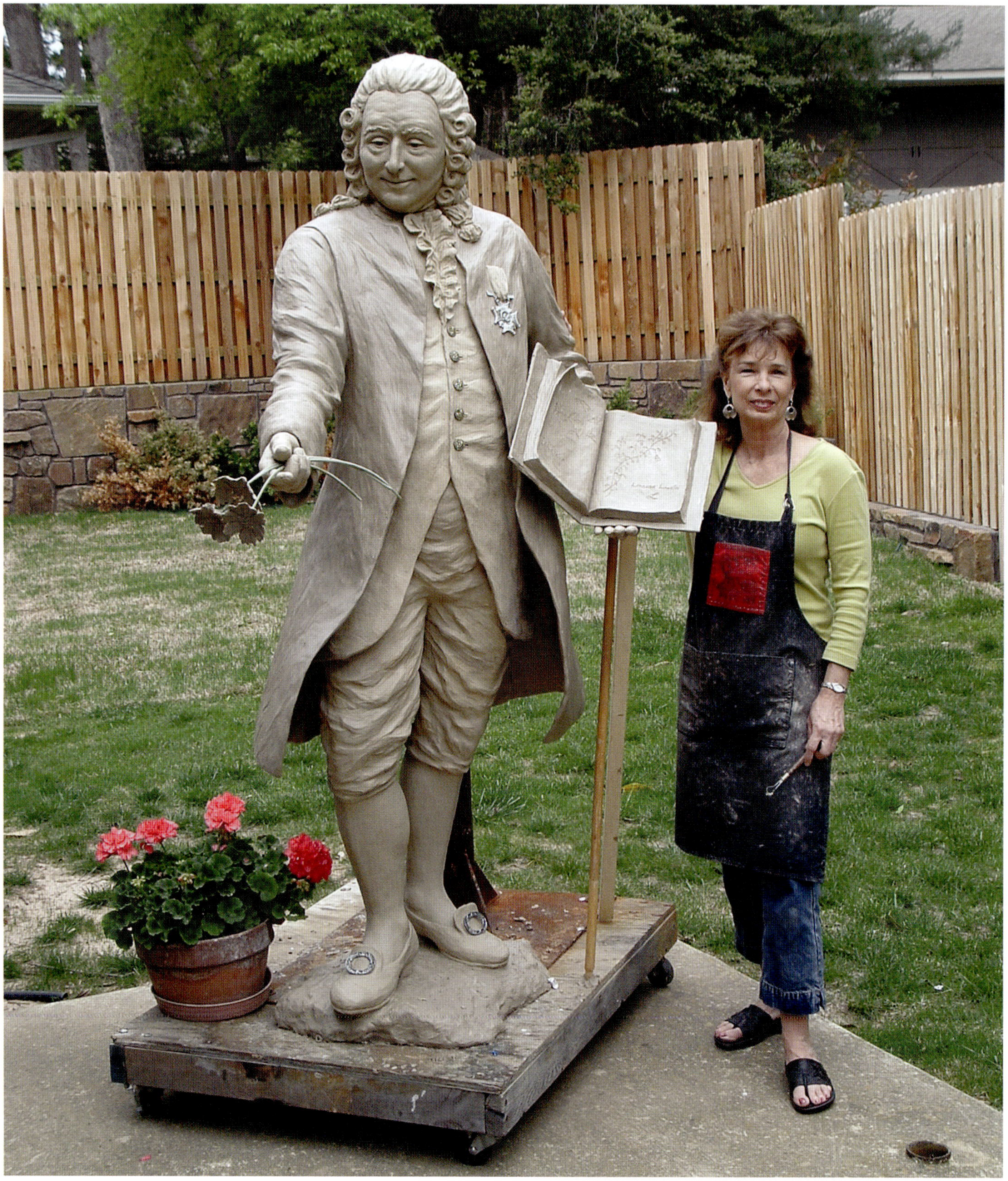

CAROLUS LINNAEUS

I have always loved the challenge of researching a historical character. This seven-foot sculpture is a very good likeness of Linnaeus, taken from his wedding portrait. He is in dress clothes of the 1700s and is assuming the pose taken by men of that day. I created him doing what he loved best—teaching—as he did 300 years ago. In his left hand is his book of botanical drawings showing the Linnaeus Borealis, a plant named for him and signed with his signature, a flourishing "L." His right hand is holding out a Gaillardia, the Oklahoma State wildflower, in which a few ladybugs are hiding for children to find.

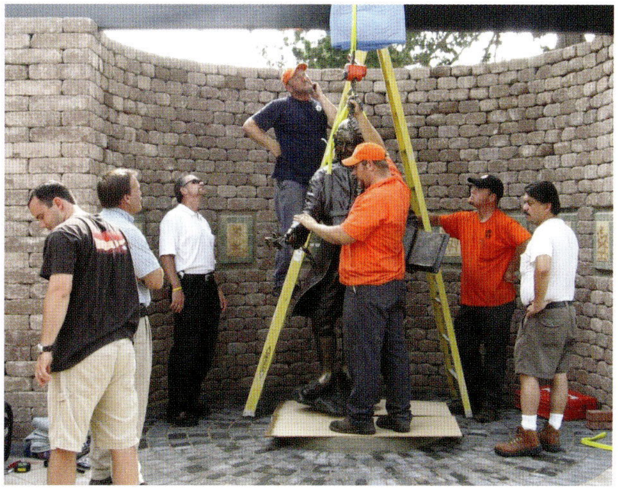

The sculpture and gardens were dedicated on June 8, 2006. The sculpture was generously underwritten by Bryan Close, a great philanthropist and owner of many of my sculptures. An 18-inch version of this sculpture, fondly called "Mini Linni," is available for sale to benefit the Tulsa Garden Center.

OPPOSITE
In my backyard with the clay sculpture of *Carolus Linnaeus*.

ABOVE RIGHT
The installation of *Carolus Linnaeus* in the Tulsa Garden Center.

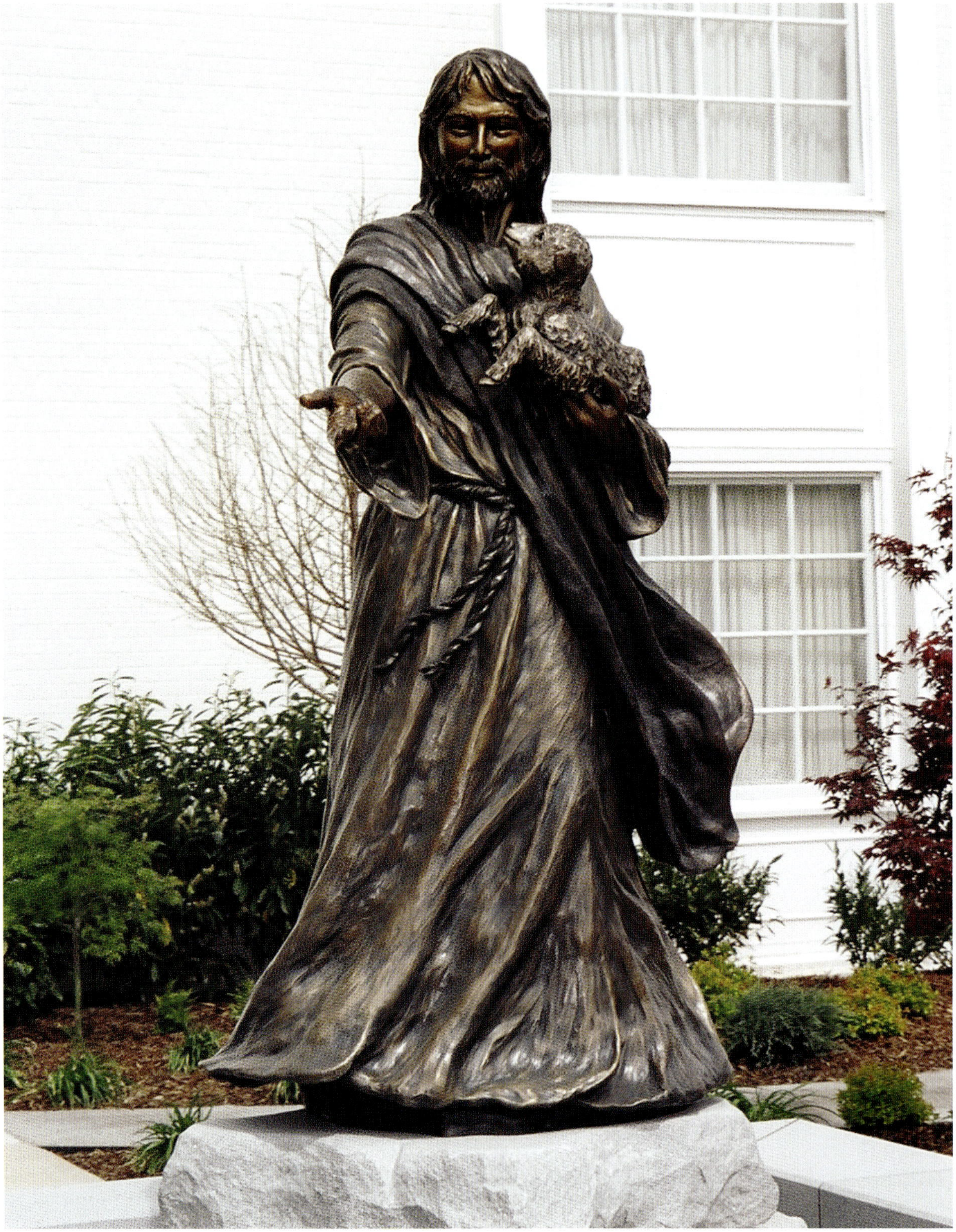

CHRIST, OUR GOOD SHEPHERD

Kirk of the Hills Presbyterian Church, 4102 East 61st Street, Tulsa, Oklahoma

The Kirk of the Hills Presbyterian Church was established by 100 members in 1961. The membership quickly grew, and in 1965 the construction of today's edifice began. Designed in the Colonial style of architecture, with its beautiful tall white steeple, "The Kirk" is one of Tulsa's most recognizable churches.

I had always hoped for the opportunity to create a sculpture of Christ as our Shepherd. Years ago I read a book by Phillip Keller entitled *A Shepherd Takes a Look at The 23rd Psalm*. It gave me many new insights into this Biblical metaphor.

Kirk of the Hills was designing a prayer garden and wanted a sculpture as its focal point. I was given free reign to create it, and what could be more appropriate for a prayer garden than a reminder of the love, care, and power of Jesus as the Good Shepherd? So, this long-ago wish became a reality. In my research of depictions of Christ as a Shepherd, I could not find one portrayal in which the lamb in His arms was looking at Christ; the lamb was always looking out. I chose to emphasize our dependency upon the Lord's guidance in our life by depicting the lamb in this sculpture looking into the face of Jesus.

A wonderful "mistake" occurred in the foundry process of this sculpture. When I was sculpting His outstretched hand, I used wires as armatures for the fingers. Those wires were all connected in the palm of the hand, creating a small knot of wiring that protruded through the clay surface. I had instructed the wax workers at the foundry to be certain to remove the knot when the sculpture was in wax and to smooth out the palm of the hand. When the bronze sculpture arrived at Kirk of the Hills, I saw a very rough scar on the palm of Christ's hand where the impression of the wire knot remained. One of the installers said to me how wonderful it was that I had left a scar on the palm of His hand to remind us of Christ's sacrifice for us. I could only smile and say, "Thank you."

OPPOSITE
Christ, Our Good Shepherd, © 2008 Rosalind Cook

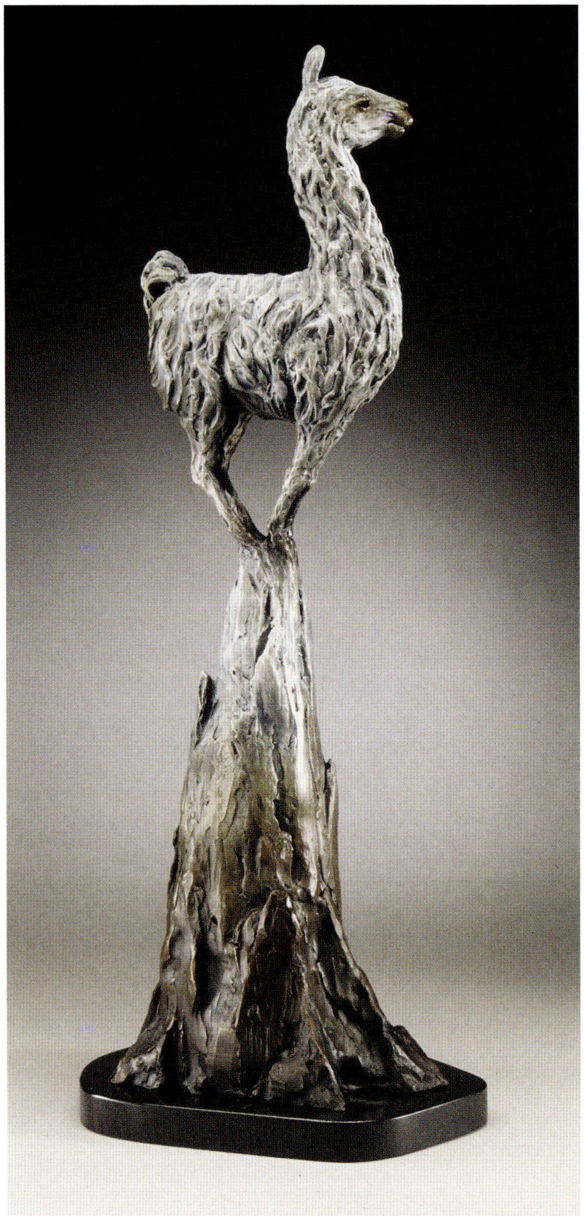

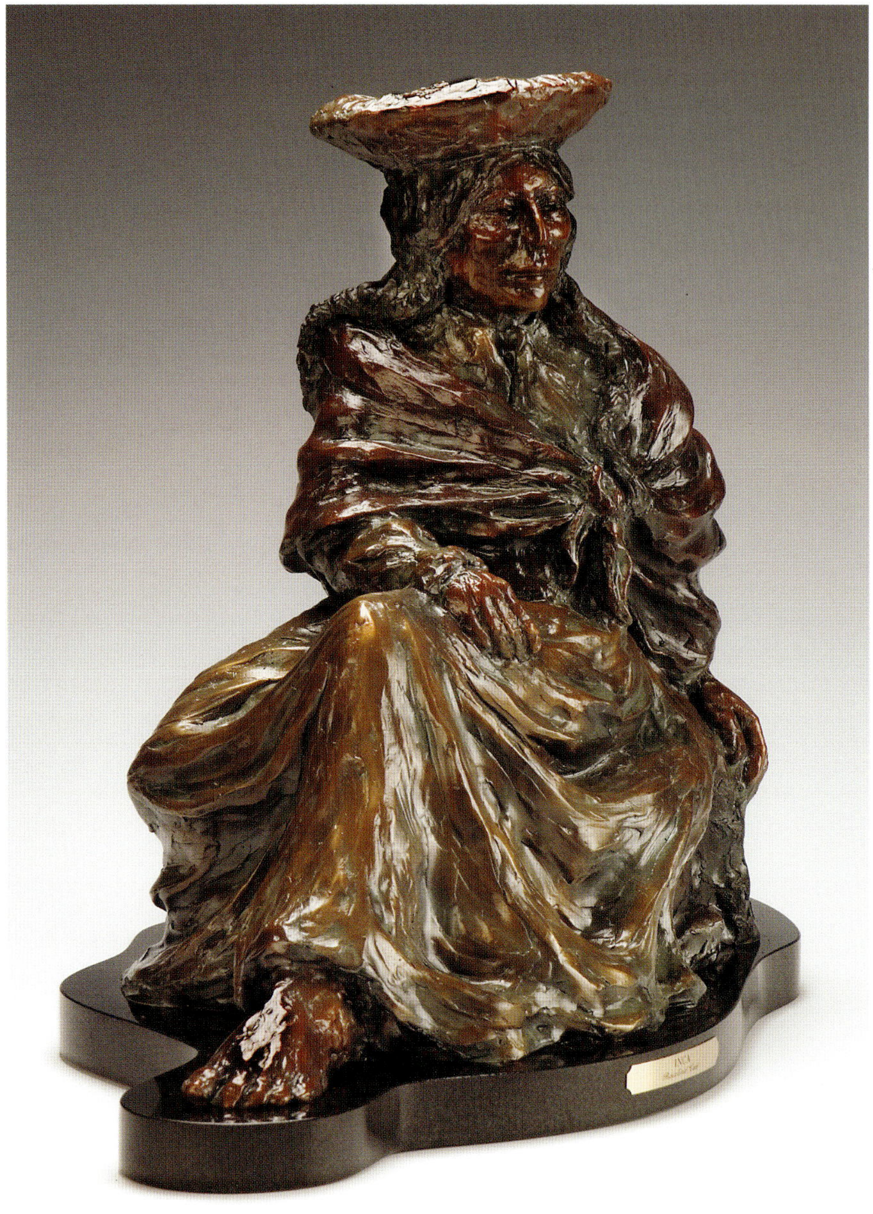

TWO PERUVIAN SCULPTURES

My Peruvian childhood forever will be a part of my view of the world. We lived among the native people and animals who had an influence on my life and for whom I hold great affection. Their traditional customs and way of life continue to provide an endless source of subject matter.

ATTITUDE IN ALTITUDE

This sculpture is a bit on the humorous side. While living in Peru, I grew to understand the nature of the llama. Used as beasts of burden, they will lie down if carrying more than 70 pounds of load. Llamas are very proud and often temperamental. My llama displays her pride as she is perched on the peak of a mountain. She illustrates a life lesson: "our attitude determines our altitude." As I was explaining this sculpture's significance to my six-year-old grandson, Noah, he asked me, "Mimi, where am I on that mountain?" I replied, "Noah, you will always be at the top!"

INCA

This sculpture is of a typical older woman of the Incas, and purposefully depicts pride and strength. In reality, the Inca women are oppressed, though they are the backbone of a family. The triangular composition, the upward tilt of the chin, the abnormally large hands, and large, bare feet communicate strength and fortitude.

OPPOSITE LEFT
Attitude in Altitude, © 2002 Rosalind Cook.
Photo by Mel Schockner.

OPPOSITE RIGHT
Inca, © 2007 Rosalind Cook.
Photo by Mel Schockner.

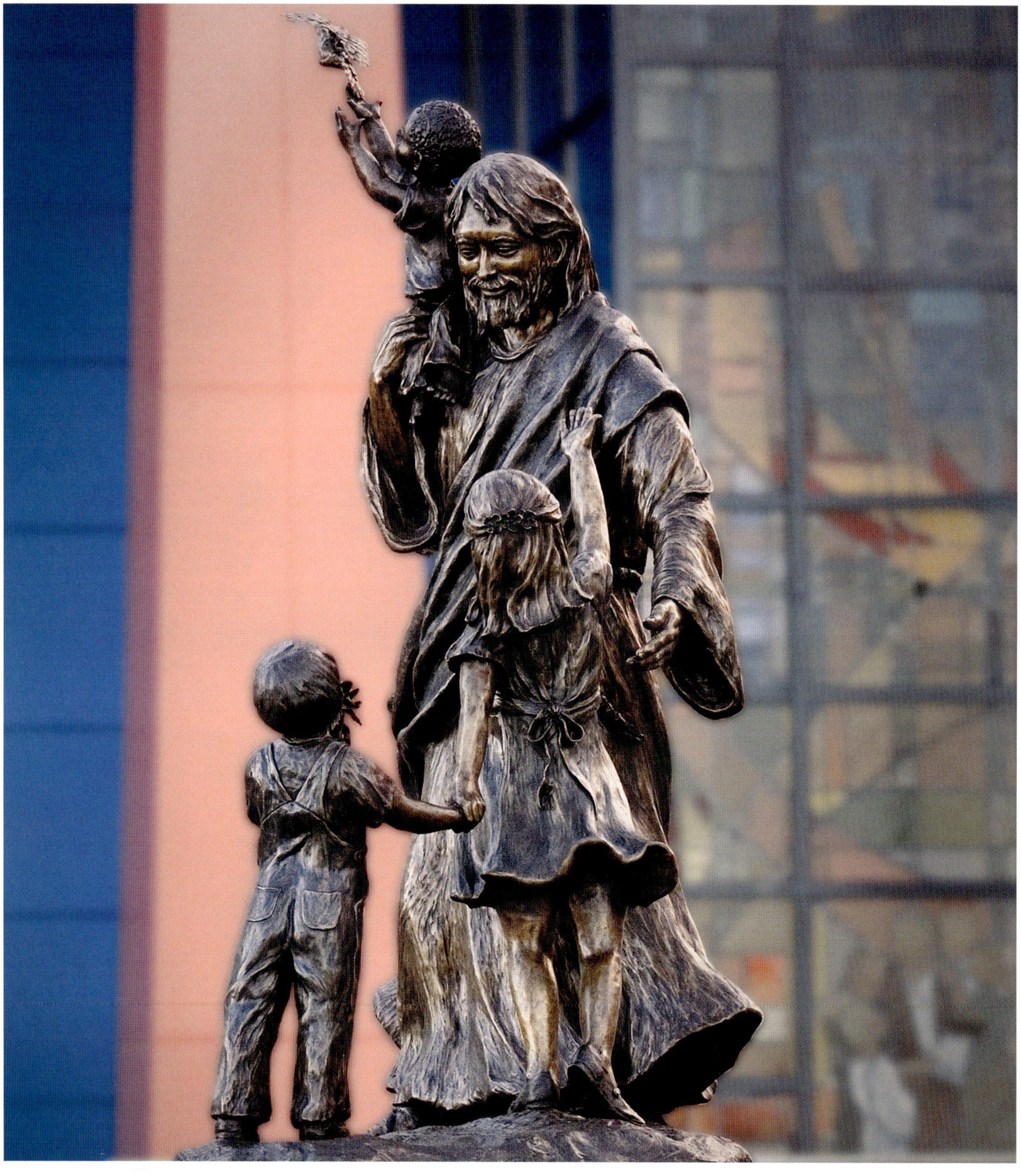

CHRIST'S LOVE FOR THE CHILDREN

Saint Francis Children's Hospital, 6161 South Yale Avenue, Tulsa, Oklahoma

Saint Francis Hospital, founded by Mr. and Mrs. William K. Warren Sr., opened its doors in 1960 with a six-story building. Today, there are five additional hospitals in the Saint Francis campus, located at the intersection of South Yale and East 61st Street.

In 2007, Jake Henry, CEO of Saint Francis Hospital; Robert Butler, CFO; and Sister Barbara Anne Gooding came to my studio to discuss a representational sculpture for the entrance to The Children's Hospital that was under construction. Since it is a Catholic hospital for children, the subject matter was clear. After seeing the future placement, I realized that the sculpture needed to be monumental in size and must also be deciphered from every angle, as it was to be placed inside a circular drive between two of the hospitals.

As I thought about the composition, I imagined the smallest child sitting on the shoulder of a strong, loving Christ and reaching up for a flying dove. Two other children of varied races are coming to Christ, creating a strong oblique, triangular composition. The child on Christ's shoulder reaching up to the dove adds an inspirational and heavenly dimension.

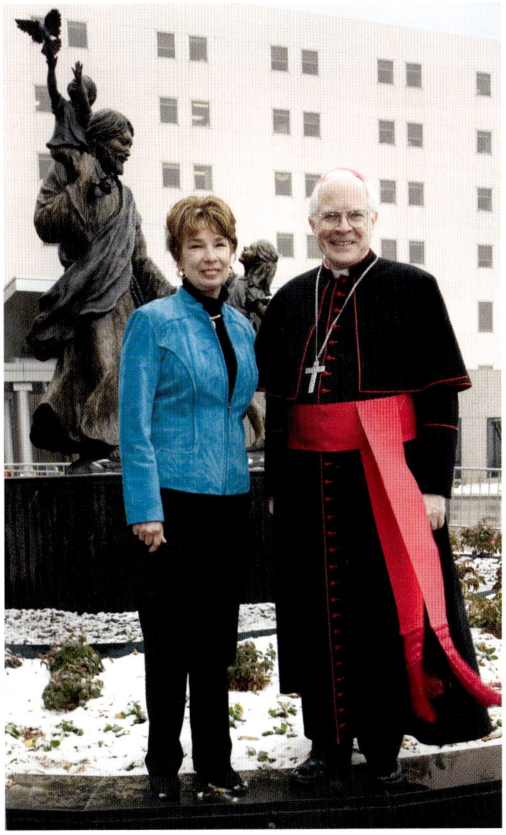

OPPOSITE
Christ's Love for the Children, © 2008 Rosalind Cook.
Photo by Don Kreutzweiser.

RIGHT
Bishop Edward J. Slattery blessed the newly opened Children's Hospital at Saint Francis Hospital.

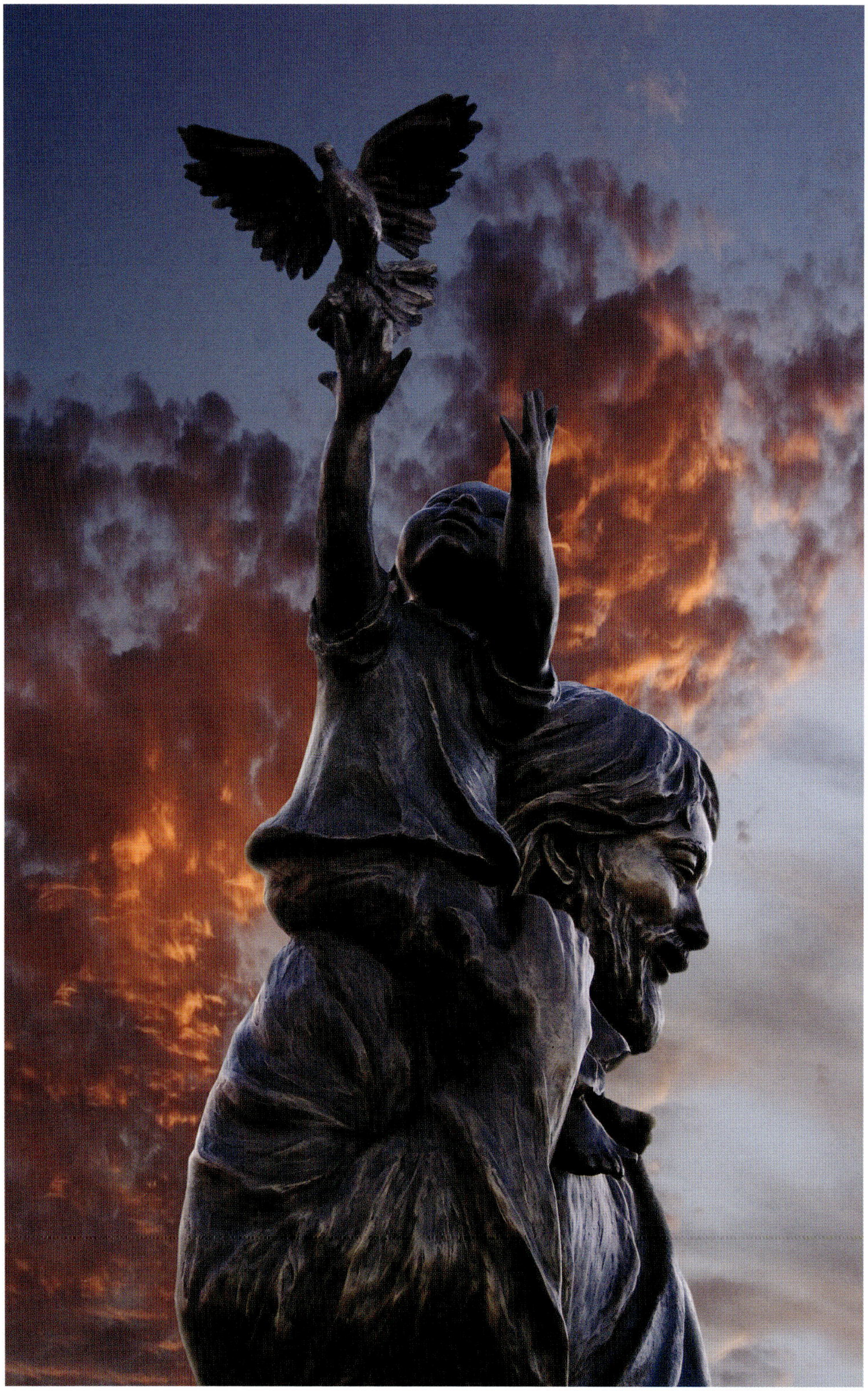

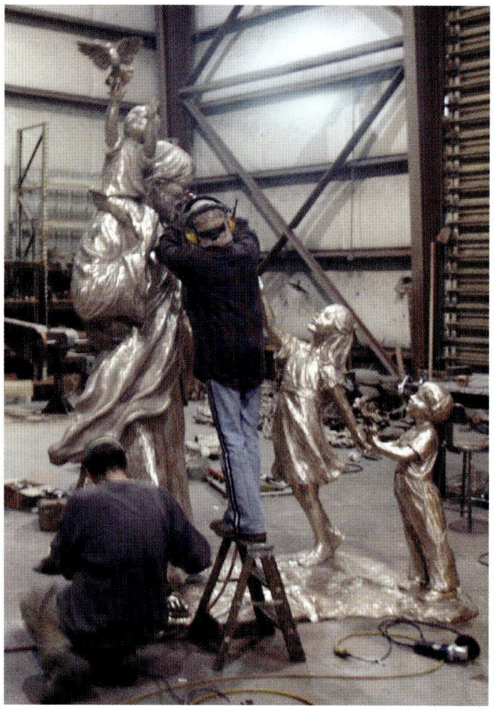

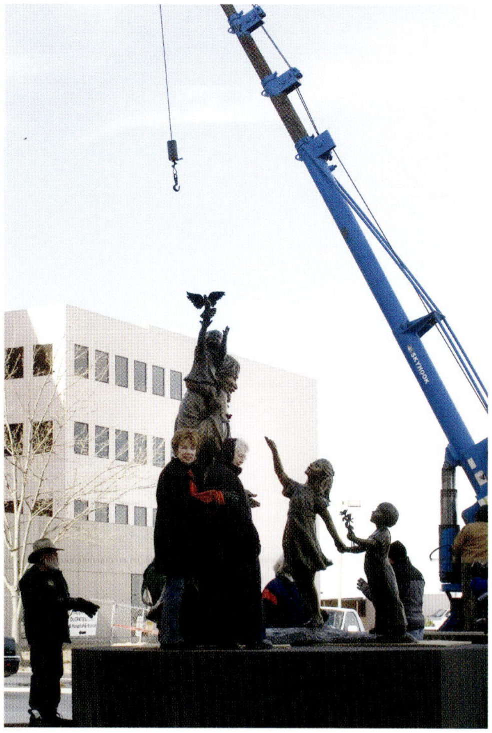

Working on this sculpture was such a pleasure, for often the nuns from Saint Francis would come to the studio and pray for me, which was certainly an added blessing. Mold makers came to my studio, and after the molds were completed they were taken to the foundry in Colorado. After the sculpture was cast and finished, it was loaded onto a flatbed trailer for its journey to Tulsa. At its delivery, the driver of the truck remarked, "This sculpture almost caused a few wrecks on the way. Can you imagine seeing a ten-foot Jesus coming down the interstate?"

The dedication of the hospital and the unveiling of the sculpture took place on a snowy January day. The Marine band played, officials spoke before dignitaries and guests in the bleachers, who were all holding umbrellas, and I unveiled the sculpture. Many of our friends from Crested Butte, Colorado, flew into Tulsa for this celebration. What a joyful day!

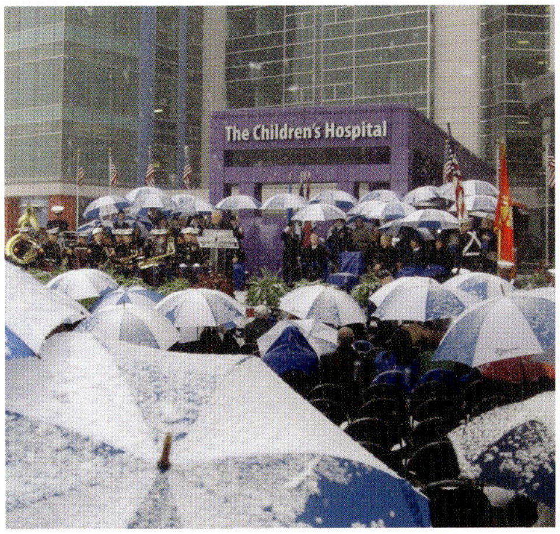

I continue to receive notes and emails from family members whose children are hospitalized at Saint Francis Hospital telling me what hope and comfort my sculpture gives them.

OPPOSITE, CLOCKWISE FROM LEFT
Christ's Love for the Children (detail), © 2008 Rosalind Cook. Photo by Don Kreutzweiser. / *Christ's Love for the Children* at the foundry. / Installation of *Christ's Love for the Children*

ABOVE RIGHT
It was a snowy day for the opening of The Children's Hospital at Saint Francis Hospital.

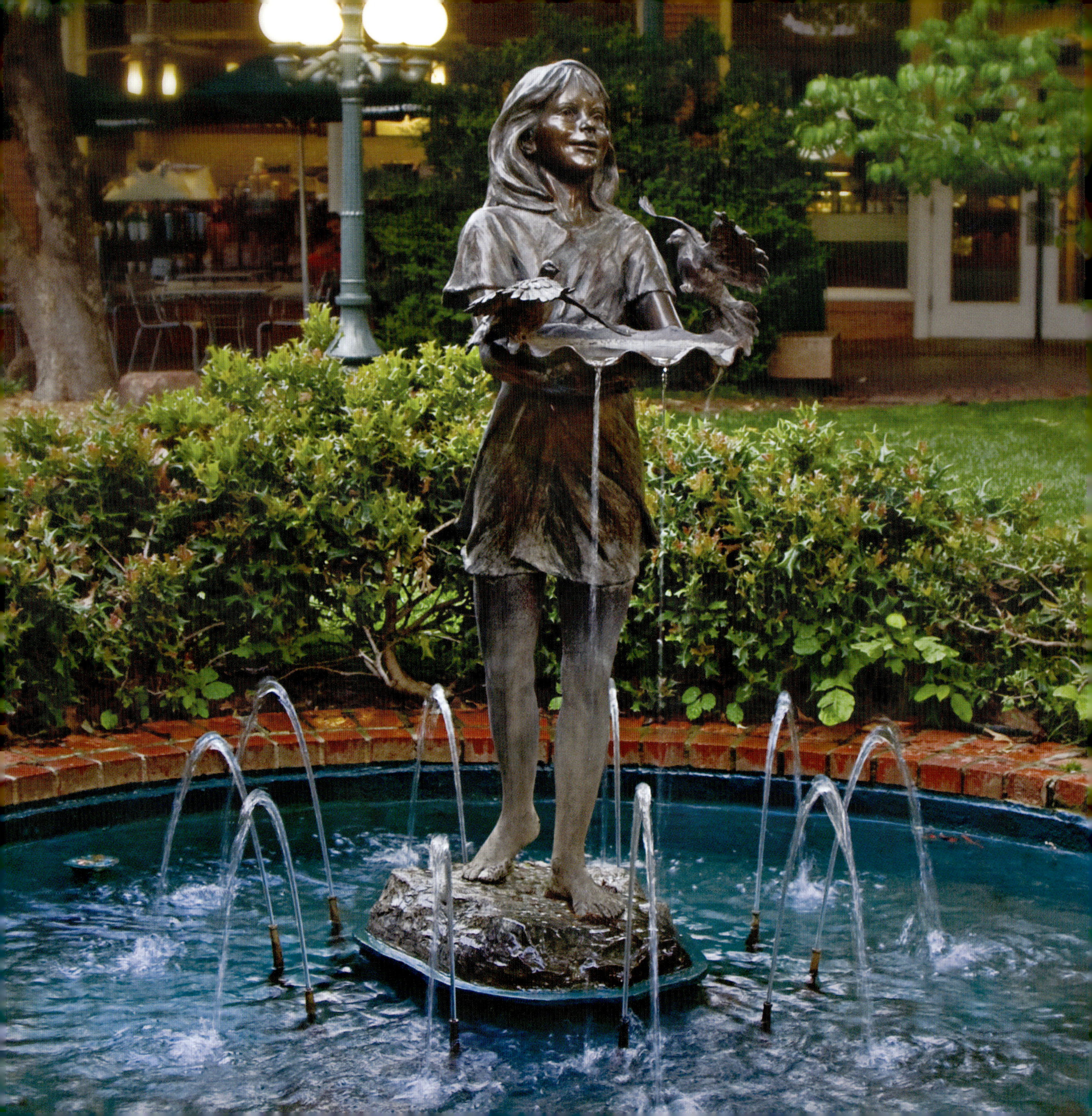

THE SCULPTURES OF UTICA SQUARE SHOPPING CENTER

South Utica and 21st Street, Tulsa, Oklahoma

WELCOME, FRIENDS

My Goddaughter, McKenna Brady, was the model for *Welcome, Friends*, created in 1995. She signed her name under the skirt when it was in clay, and now she is forever cast in bronze.

Having no knowledge of dove anatomy, I purchased a live and a "deceased" dove at a farmer's market. The deceased dove was kept in a sealed bag in the freezer so that I could study its anatomy and manipulate the wings. The other dove lived freely in my studio so that I could observe her fly, land on her water bowl, and move about. Named after Amelia Earhart, Amelia lived with me for three months until the sculpture was completed in clay. I then took her out into the countryside and released her. Three days later, while working in my studio, I heard pecking on my window—it was Amelia! She flew in and out of my studio until she left me, most likely for a mate.

In 1997, the well-known Tulsa painter Leonard Wren and I were having a two-man show at Saks Fifth Avenue in Utica Square. *Welcome, Friends* was prominently exhibited. Walt Helmerich, chairman of Helmerich & Payne, Inc., and his wife, Peggy, attended the show. The Helmerichs also own Utica Square, an upscale shopping center in Tulsa. They told me they had searched Europe for the perfect sculpture for the fountain at Utica Square and had now found it in *Welcome, Friends*.

Mrs. Helmerich later told me that one day she and her friends were observed at Utica Square looking under the skirt of the sculpture for the signature of McKenna. I wish I could have seen that!

OPPOSITE
Welcome, Friends, © 1995 Rosalind Cook.
Photo by Don Kreutzweiser.

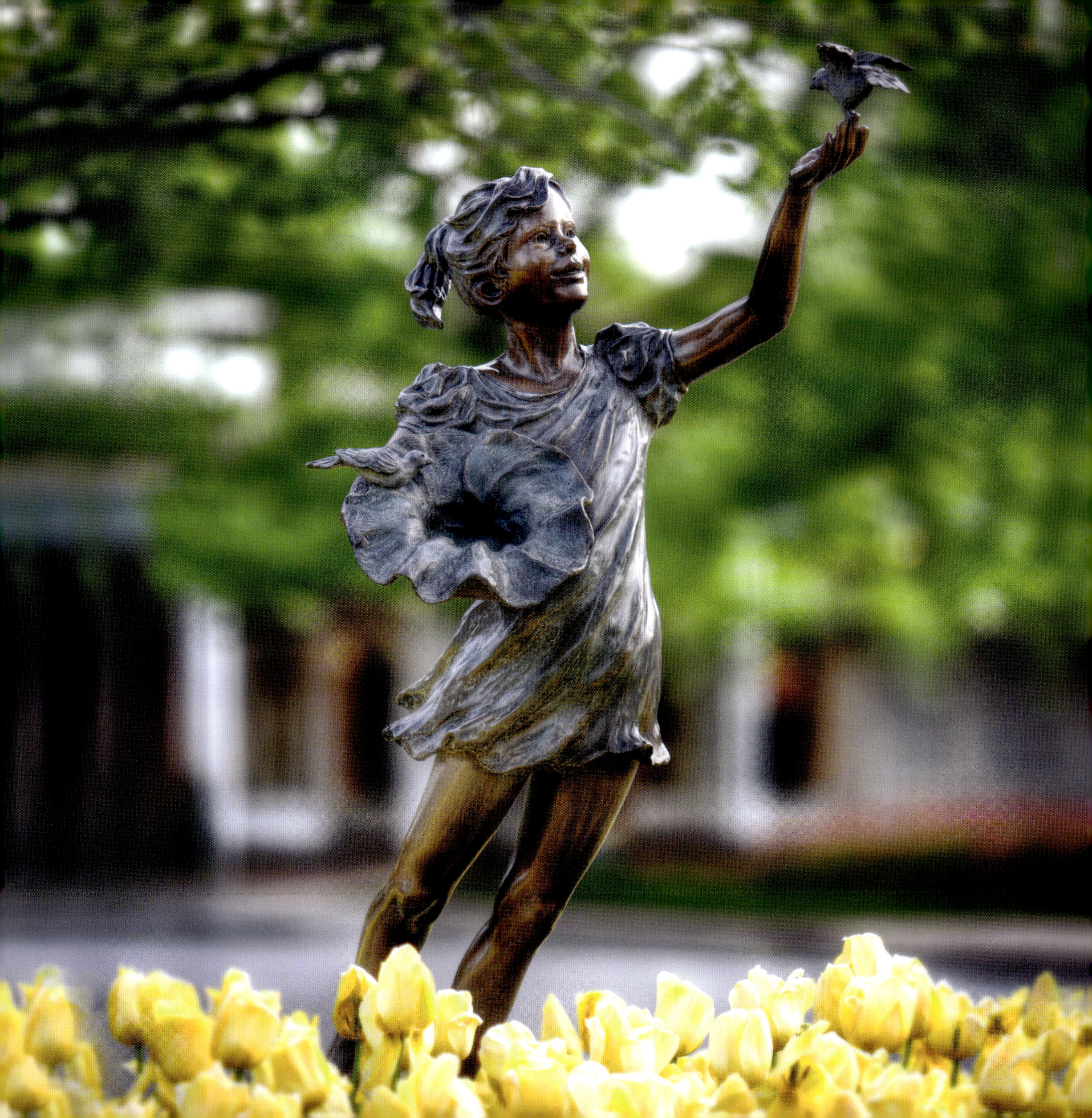

THE BIRD FEEDER, WINDY

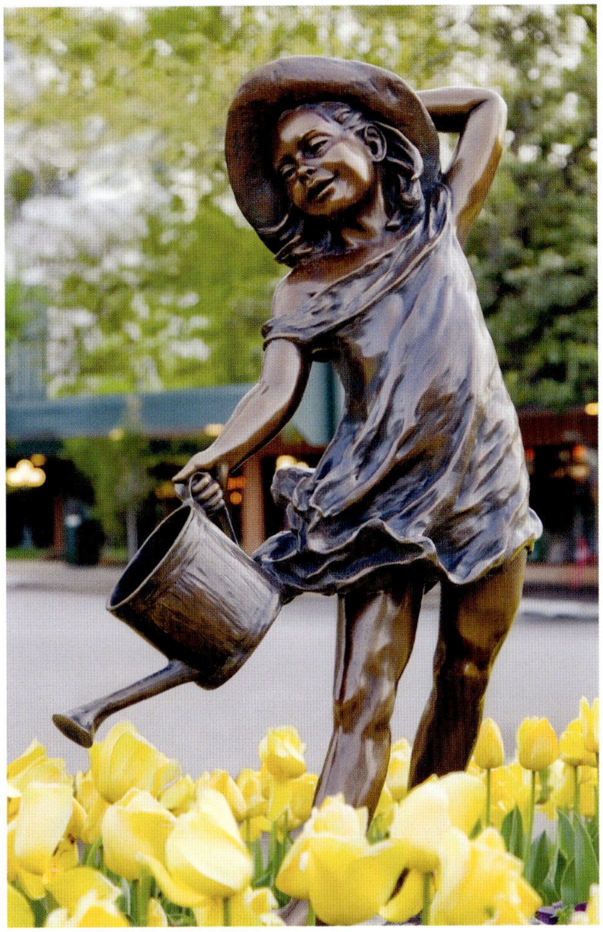

This pair of complementary sculptures can be seen in the two flower beds at the center of Utica Square. Though created in separate years, these two young girls, both the same size, are representative of aspects that have brought me success as a sculptor. After a basic idea is conceived, I create a maquette (a small model), building in strong elements of design and composition. In each of these sculptures one can see a strong major diagonal line, and an "S" curve, which is very feminine. Also, one can see repetitions of circular forms and triangular shapes that create unity within the sculpture and draw the eye back into the piece. Capturing movement within a static form, as if the wind is blowing, is accomplished by the treatment of hair and flowing clothing. Both pieces can be used as optional fountains.

OPPOSITE
The Bird Feeder, © 2000 Rosalind Cook.
Photo by Don Kreutzweiser.

ABOVE
Windy, © 1996 Rosalind Cook.
Photo by Don Kreutzweiser.

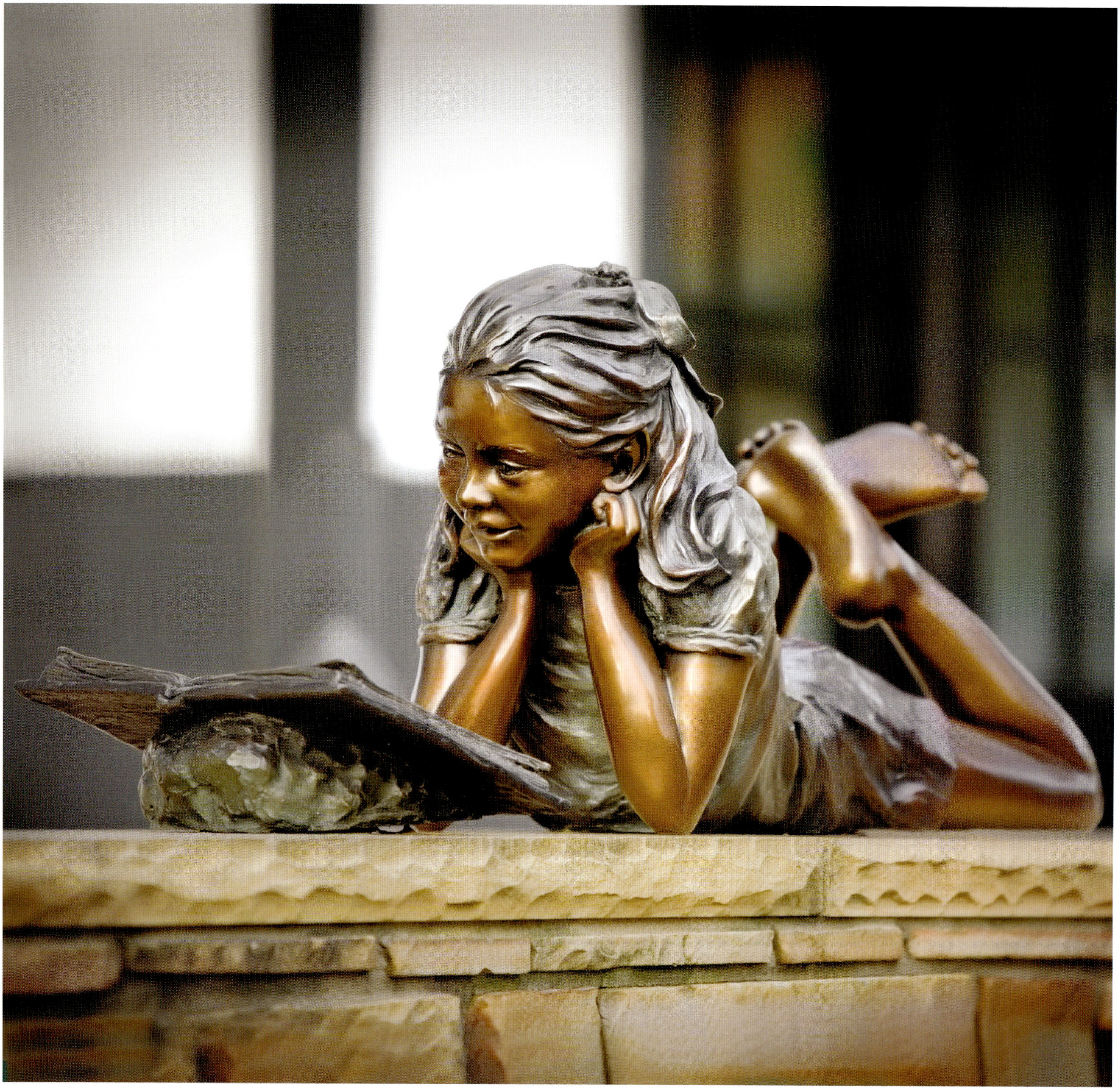

STORY TIME FOR ONE

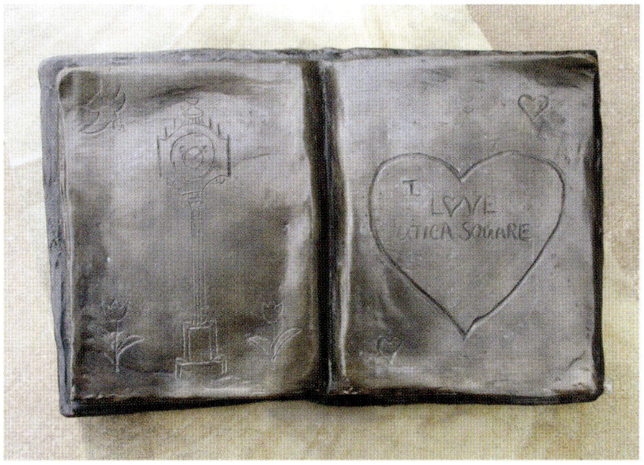

One day as I was walking into Pottery Barn Kids at Utica Square, there was a boy about three years old tickling the feet of *Story Time for One,* which depicts a little barefoot girl lying on her belly, reading a book, with her legs crossed in the air. This little boy was trying to get a response out of her. Several years ago, Walt Helmerich called me to order this sculpture, which he had seen on my website. However, he wanted something special on the pages of the book she was reading. I decided to do a line drawing of the iconic Utica Square clock. On the opposite page I drew a big heart that simply says, "I love Utica Square," in handwriting as if a child had written it. Mr. Helmerich loved it!

OPPOSITE
Story Time for One, © 2004 Rosalind Cook.
Photo by Don Kreutzweiser.

ABOVE
The book in *Story Time for One.*

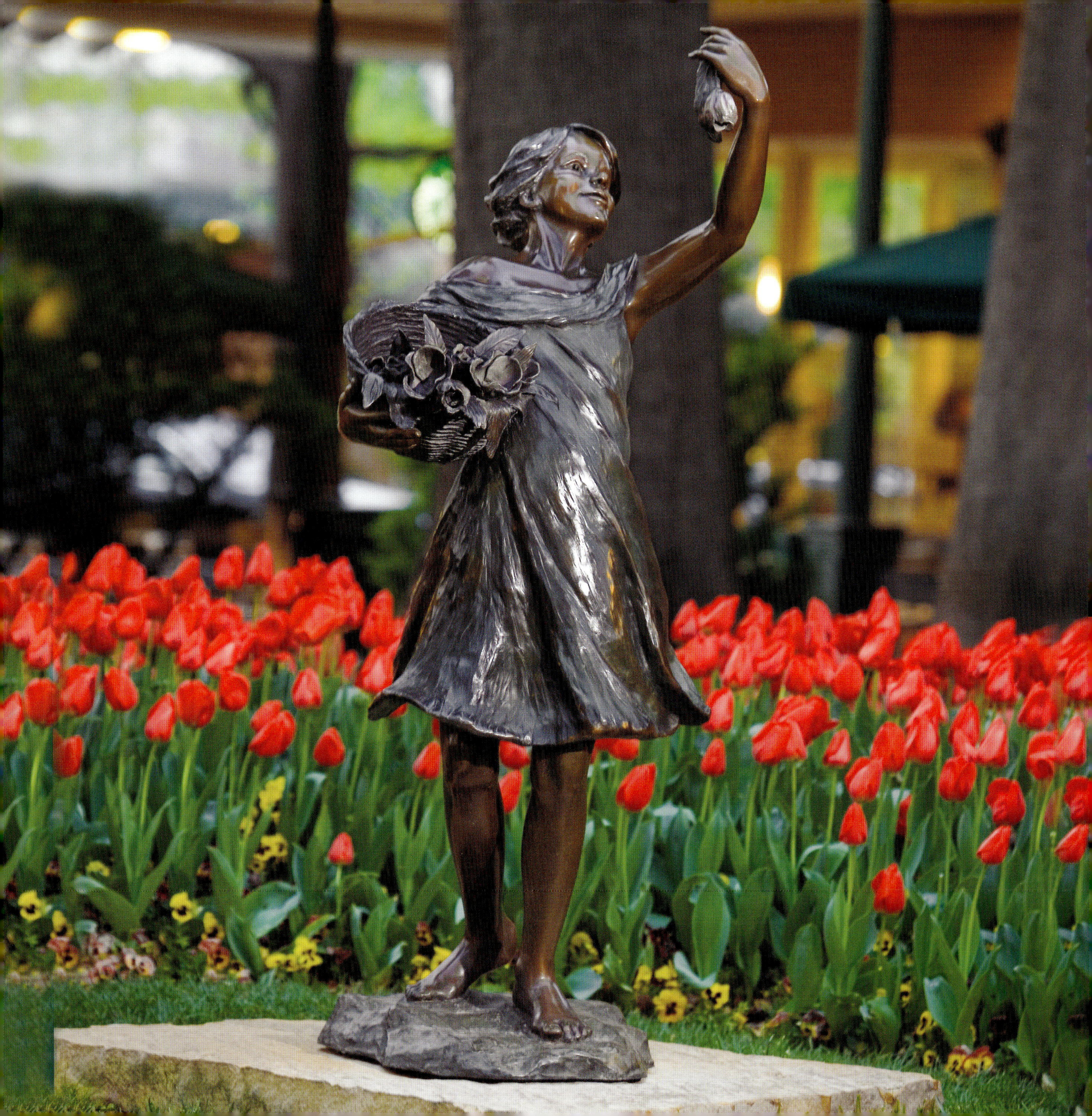

BEAUTIFUL BOUNTY

Early in 2010, Walt Helmerich called and said that he and his wife, Peggy, would like to visit my studio to discuss another sculpture for Utica Square. At the time, I happened to be working on a speculative piece to market to the wine industry and wine enthusiasts. It depicted a romantic young lady harvesting grapes. The basket in her arm was overflowing with grapes, and she was holding up a cluster in the other hand, viewing them with awe and admiration.

After discussing this piece as a possibility for Utica Square, Mr. Helmerich asked if I could change the grapes into flowers on the sculpture in progress, and he asked what the price would be. I explained that the harvest needed to be grapes as it was for the wine industry. Nothing more was said and we parted congenially.

Within three days I received a check with full payment for this piece, and on the bottom of his check he wrote, "Flowers, NO grapes." In visiting *Beautiful Bounty* in Utica Square, you will see her basket overflowing with tulips, and she is admiring a tulip in her uplifted hand.

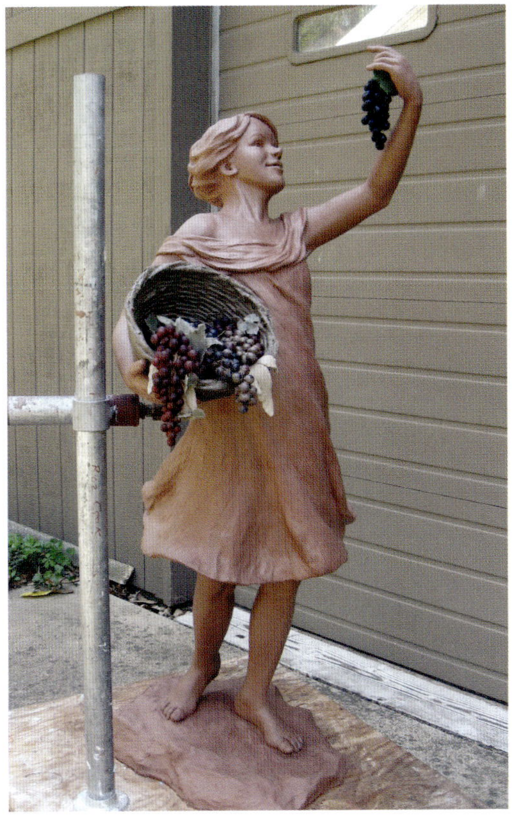

Beautiful Bounty is the last piece of sculpture Walt Helmerich purchased from me before his death in 2012. He was a wise and great philanthropist who left his indelible mark on Tulsa.

OPPOSITE
Beautiful Bounty, © 2011 Rosalind Cook.
Photo by Don Kreutzweiser.

ABOVE RIGHT
The original clay version of *Beautiful Bounty*, with grapes!

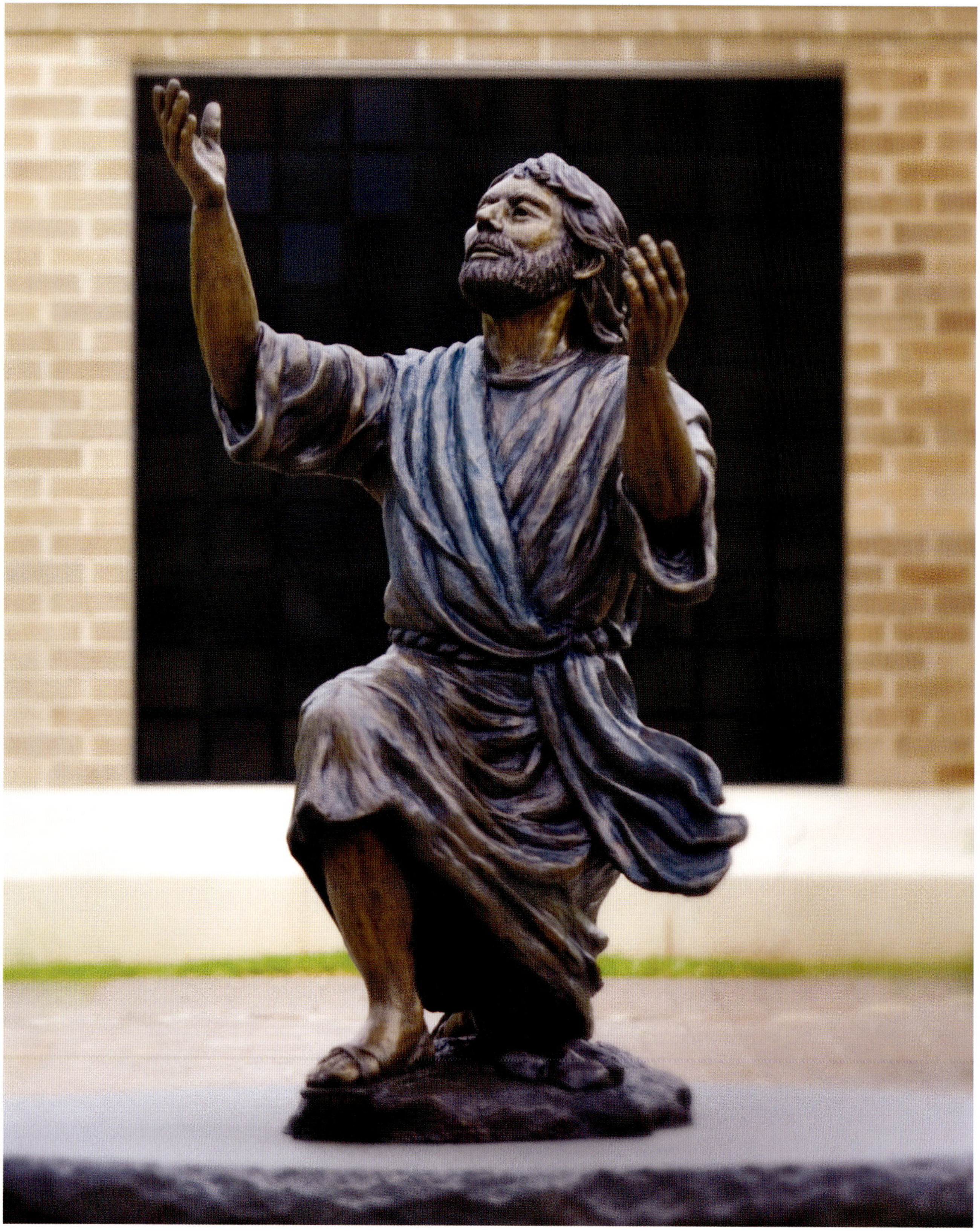

THE SCULPTURES OF ASBURY UNITED METHODIST CHURCH

6767 South Mingo Road, Tulsa, Oklahoma

INTERCESSION

In 2008, I was asked to create a sculpture of Christ for the new Columbarium Garden at Asbury United Methodist Church. I chose to depict Christ kneeling on one knee as He prays for the intercession of all believers. This prayer, found in John 17, even describes his body position during the prayer, which I used for this sculpture.

REVEREND BILL MASON

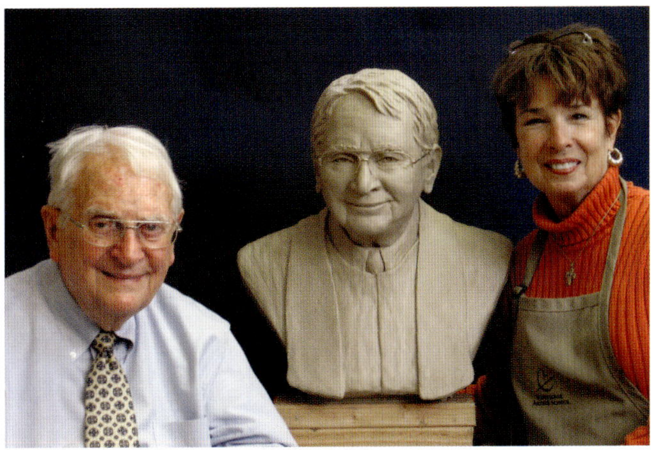

I feel privileged to have been asked to capture in bronze the spirit of Reverend Bill Mason, retired senior pastor of Asbury. For 29 years, Reverend Mason led the church's growth from a start-up church to a congregation of over 8,000 members. As the portrait evolved, Reverend Mason would sit in my studio and tell me stories of his life and ministry. He is one of the kindest, most Christ-like people I have ever known. He was very happy with the results of this sculpture, which today is located in the Mason Chapel at Asbury United Methodist Church.

OPPOSITE
Intercession, © 2008 Rosalind Cook.
Photograph by Don Kreutzweiser.

ABOVE
Reverend Bill Mason, © 2011 Rosalind Cook.
Photograph by Bill Kohl.

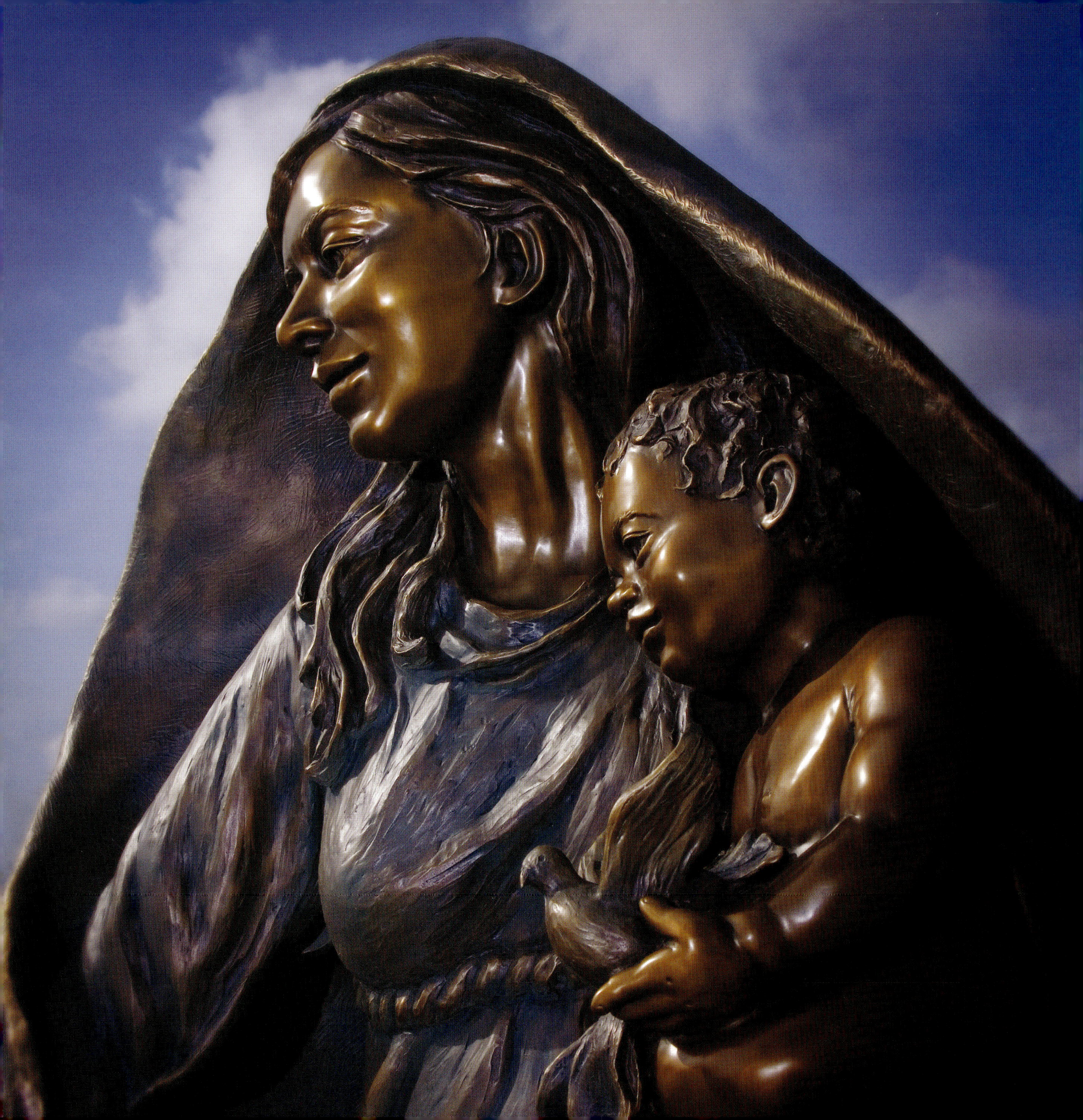

THE POOR VIRGIN OF NAZARETH
WHO HOLDS IN HER HANDS THE WEALTH OF THE WORLD

Catholic Charities, 2450 North Harvard Avenue, Tulsa, Oklahoma

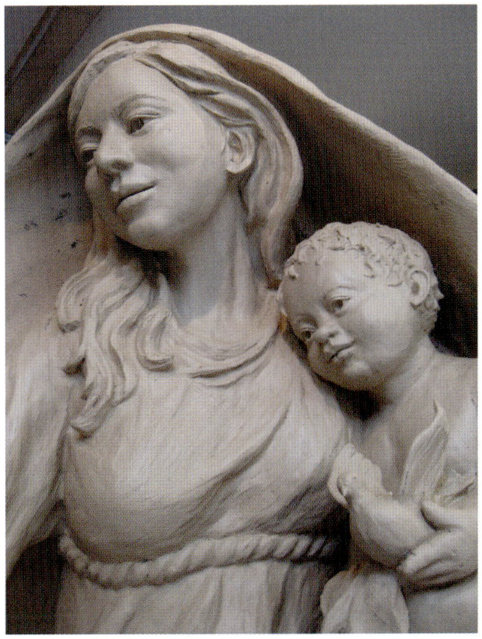

The Catholic Charities serves over 50,000 clients a year through ministries such as feeding and clothing programs, adoption, counseling, dental and medical care, and education. Its mission is "to be Christ's merciful love to those who suffer." In 2008, Catholic Charities was building a new campus at Pine and North Harvard in order to house all of their ministries in one location. My dear friends Rich and Sally Minshall, co-chairmen for the capital campaign, asked me to meet with them and Bishop Edward Slattery, bishop of the Catholic Diocese of Tulsa. They came to my studio to discuss the commission of a large sculpture for the facility's entrance. Bishop Slattery is an amazing man with vision and a passion for helping the poor and oppressed. I immediately warmed to his kindness and his delightful sense of humor.

They wanted a sculpture depicting the Mother Mary holding the Christ Child. Bishop Slattery gave me three criteria to follow: Mary had to be historically accurate, she had to be feminine without being sensual, and she had to be inviting and welcoming to the viewer. As a sculptor, I readily accept guidelines for a commission, but I must have freedom to create the design and composition. I began to pore over photos from my studies in Italy, and the maquette took form following the criteria.

OPPOSITE
The Poor Virgin of Nazareth (detail), © 2009 Rosalind Cook. Photo by Don Kreutzweiser.

ABOVE
The clay version of *The Poor Virgin of Nazareth*.

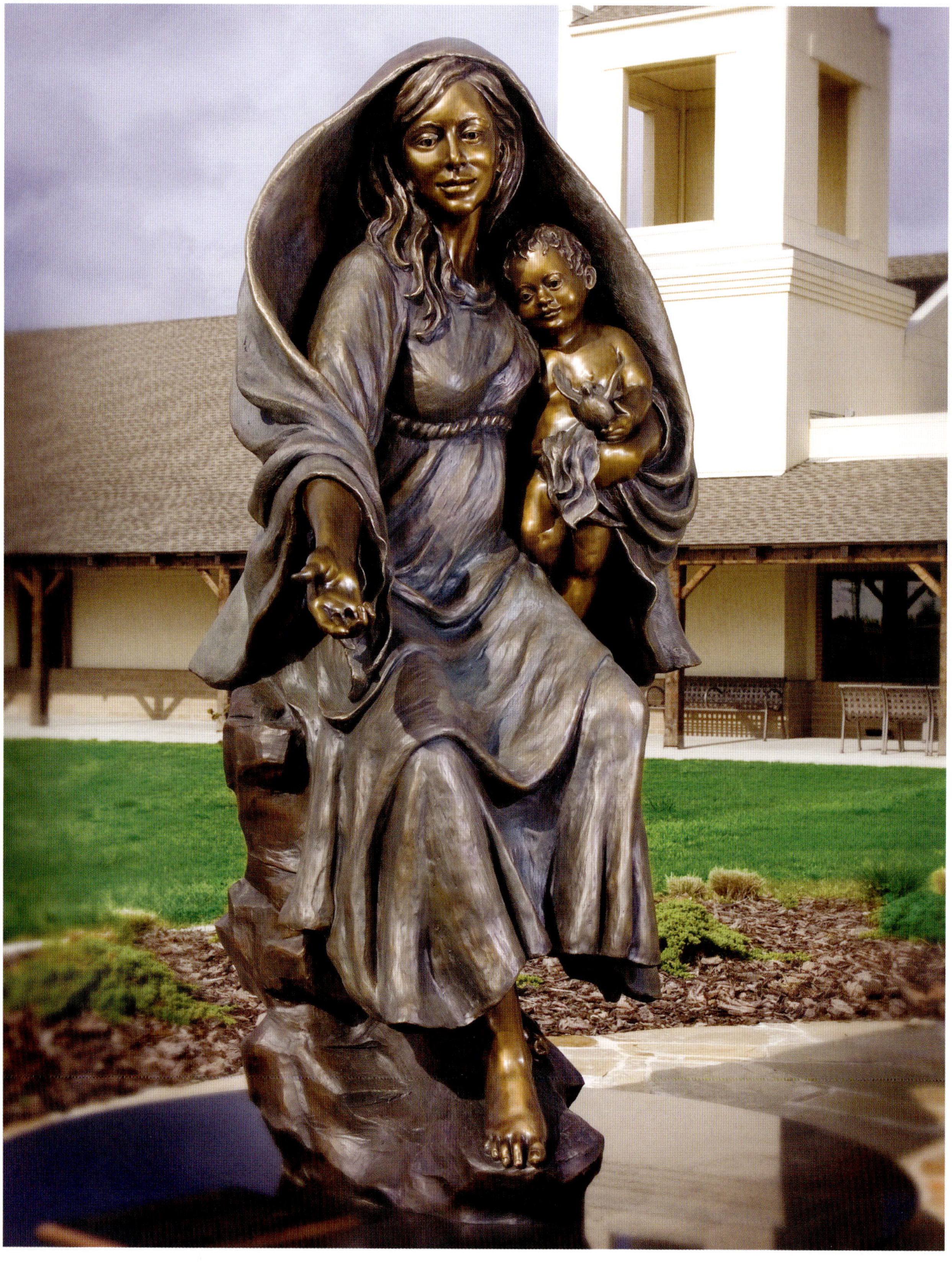

THE POOR VIRGIN OF NAZARETH
WHO HOLDS IN HER HANDS THE WEALTH OF THE WORLD

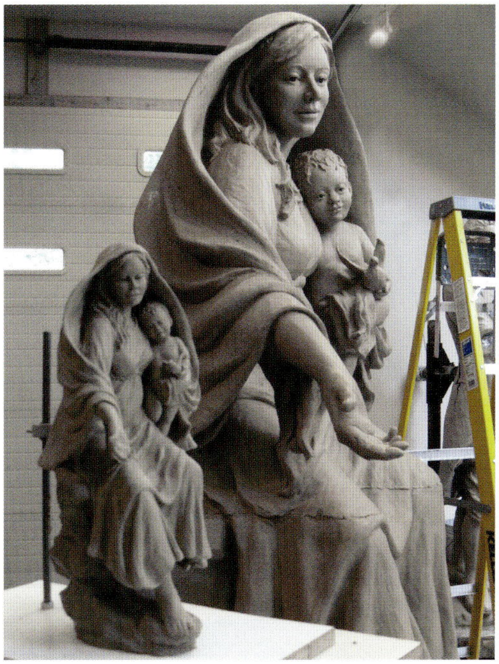

Historically, Mary would have been around 15 or 16 years old, and was from a working-class family. So, I sculpted her barefooted and simply clothed. On this eight-foot-tall sculpture, the drapery defining her form is feminine and flowing. Reality is only a point of departure, so I really had fun with the head cloak, creating a "grotto of protection" over the figures of Mary and the Christ Child.

As in the Renaissance masters' works, her foot projects over the base so that there is no barrier between Mary and the viewer. Her free arm is reaching to the viewer. The Christ Child is standing slightly on His own, yet leaning into His mother. He holds a dove, symbolic of the Holy Spirit.

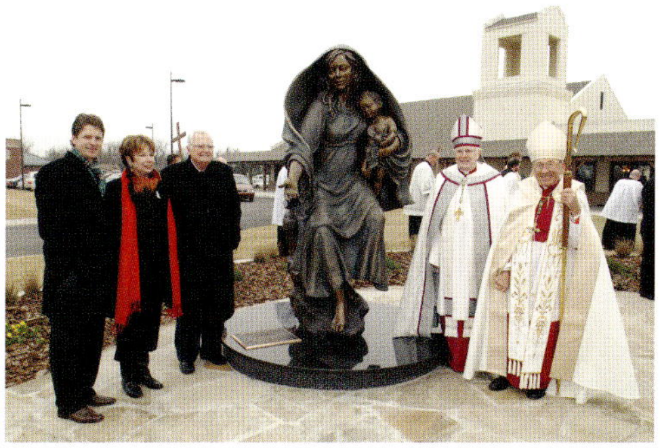

Mr. William K. Warren Jr. generously underwrote this sculpture and dedicated it to the Warren family. Sales of the 18-inch bronze of the large sculpture continue to benefit Catholic Charities.

OPPOSITE
The Poor Virgin of Nazareth, © 2009 Rosalind Cook. Photo by Don Kreutzweiser.

ABOVE LEFT
The maquette and the full-size clay sculpture in my studio.

ABOVE RIGHT
The dedication ceremony of *The Poor Virgin of Nazareth*.

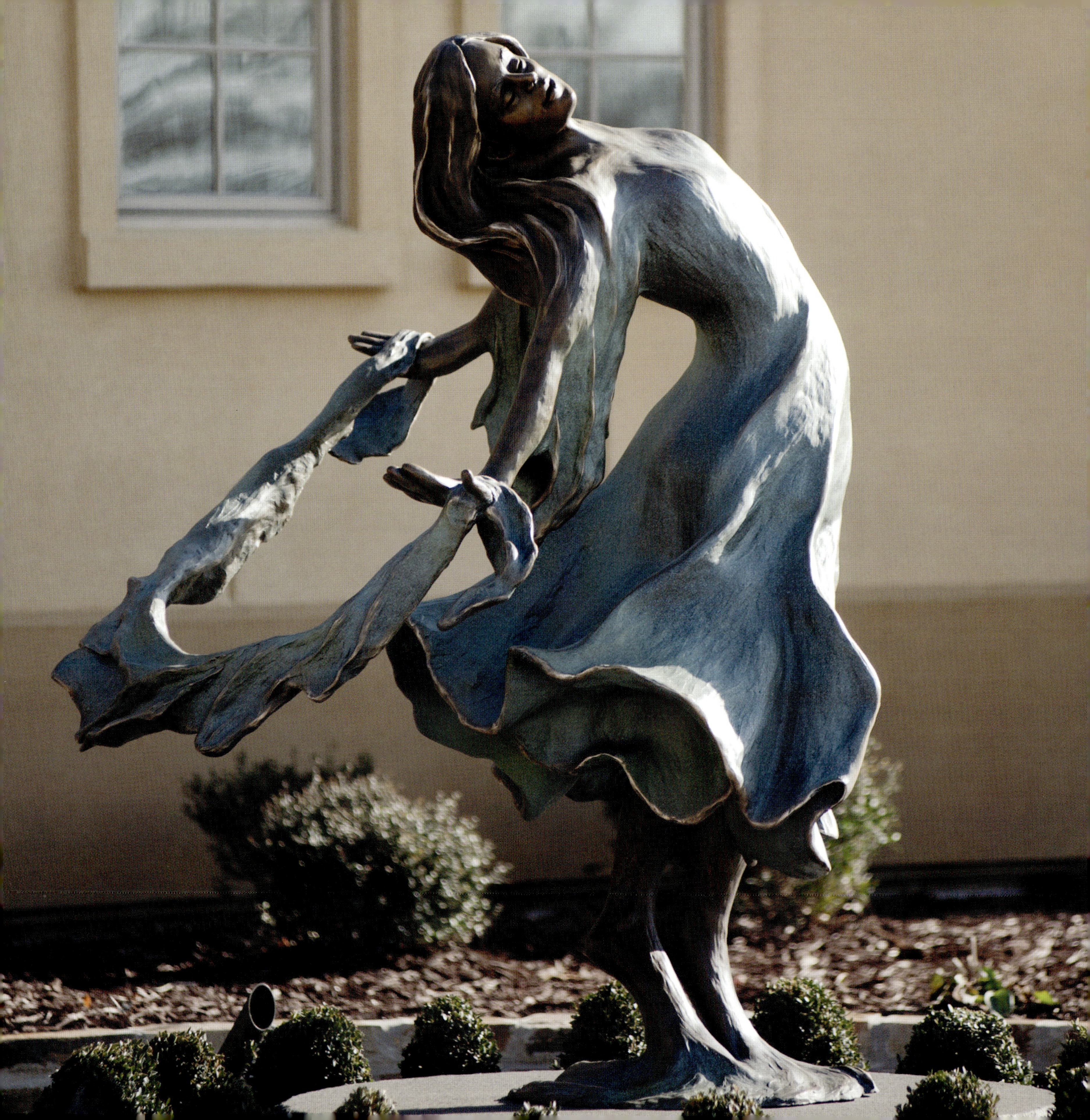

YOUNG IN SPIRIT, BREAKING FREE

Montereau in Warren Woods, 6800 South Granite Avenue, Tulsa, Oklahoma

Young in Spirit is a six-foot version of a sculpture named *Breaking Free* that is 28 inches high. *Breaking Free* was a piece that came deep from my heart, as she is the epitome of what it feels like to be set free from anything that has oppressed us or kept us from being all we can be. She is lost in abandon and joy.

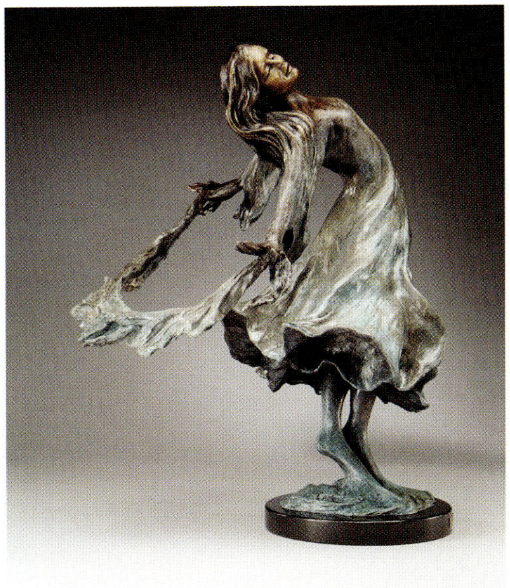

The edition of 37 sold out quickly, and I was told amazing stories from several buyers of their personal stories of "breaking free." Her picture was even used on the cover of a book by a life coach in Colorado.

Representatives of Montereau in Warren Woods, a retirement center in South Tulsa, came to my studio to discuss a sculpture for their campus. They saw *Breaking Free* and felt that the spirit of this young woman would be perfect in a six-foot size for the entrance to the campus of Montereau. She was named *Young in Spirit* and will forever lift the spirits of the residents and visitors of Montereau.

OPPOSITE
Young in Spirit, © 2011 Rosalind Cook.
Photograph by Nathan Harmon.

ABOVE
Breaking Free, © 2011 Rosalind Cook.
Photograph by Mel Schockner.

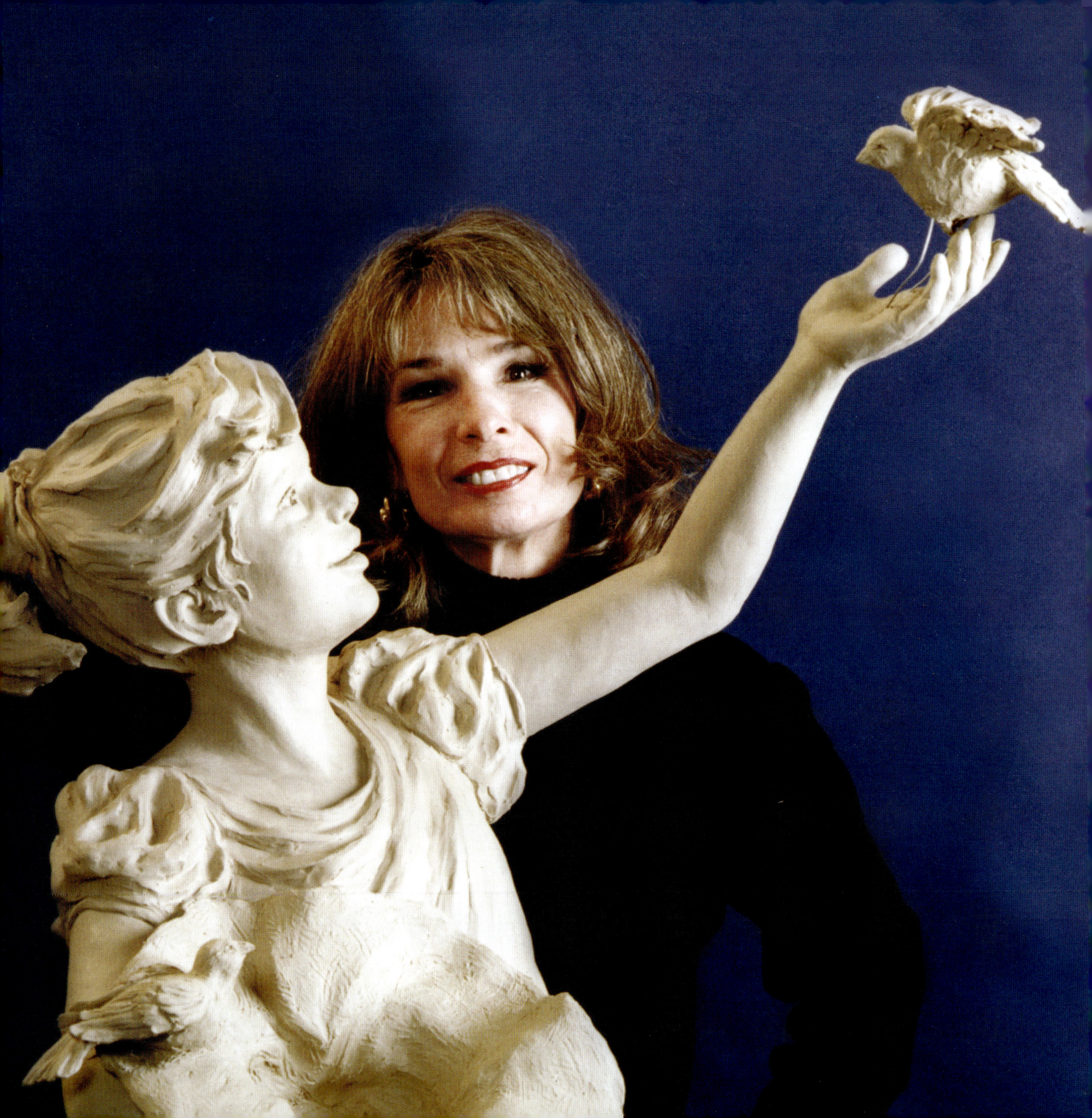

GIVING FROM THE GIFT

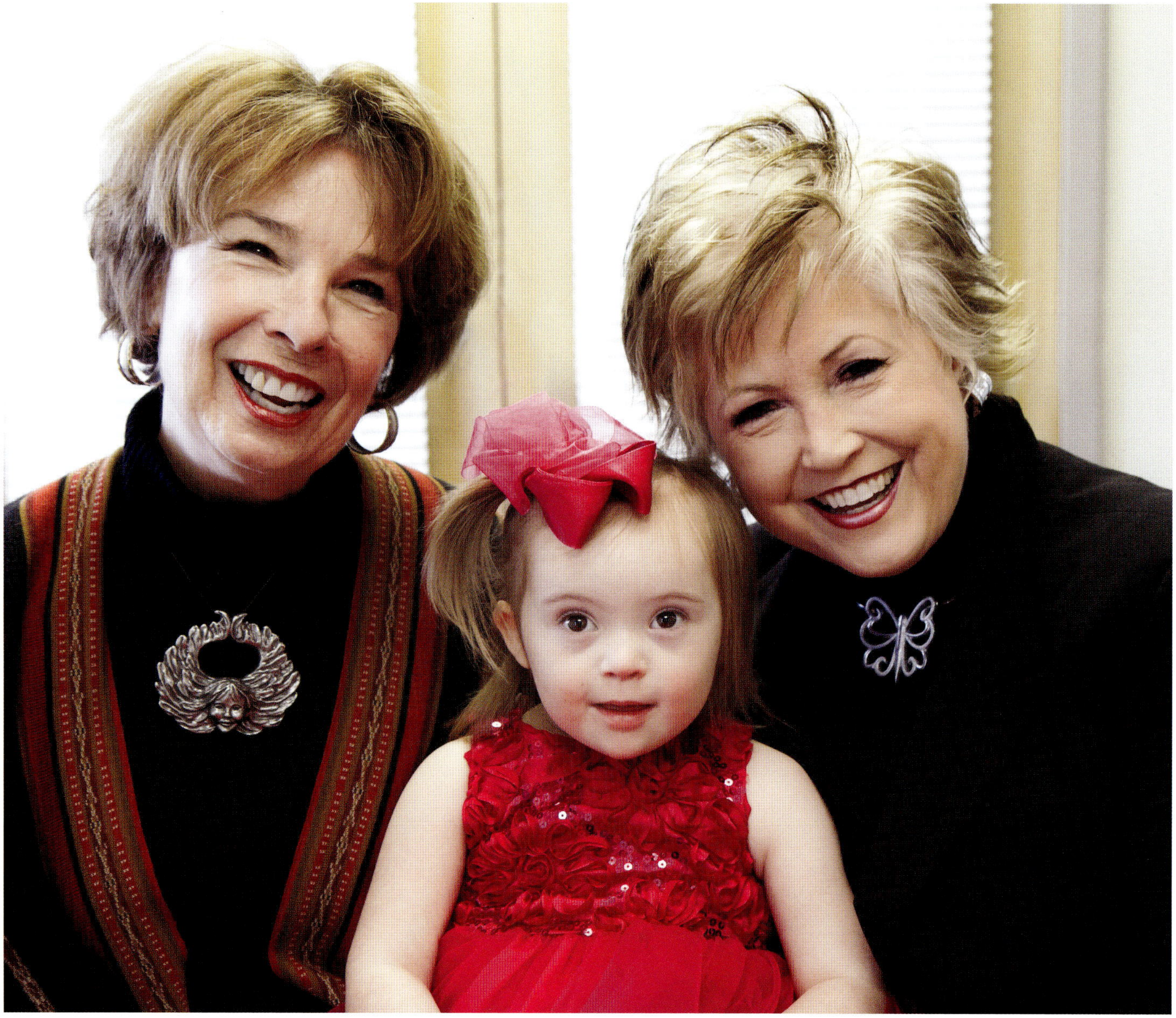

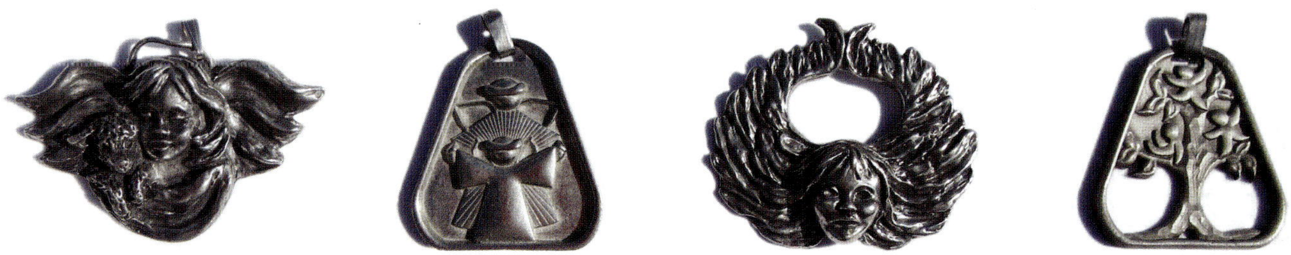

HELPING ONE ANOTHER

Winston Churchill put forth the concept that we make a living by what we get, but we make a life by what we give. I have enjoyed the benefits of being a successful sculptor, but never so much as when I am able to use my talents to encourage or benefit others. In a way, giving and sharing take my sculpture from a career level to an even higher plane that makes it truly significant and of lasting value. Through the years, the giving and sharing has come to me in many ways: invitational speaking engagements, teaching sculpture classes, studio tours, and creating sculptures to represent or benefit nonprofit organizations. I would like to share a few of these opportunities that have made my work significant for others. I also share these to encourage others to use their gifts and talents to benefit this world in some way.

THE LITTLE LIGHT HOUSE

Soon after moving to Tulsa in 1974, and having been a special-education teacher, I began my volunteer work at The Little Light House, a Christian developmental center for children with special needs. Hal and I have been involved with this center ever since.

PAGE 118
Rosalind with the clay version of *The Bird Feeder.*
Photo by Bill Welch.

OPPOSITE ABOVE
Rosalind with Marcia Mitchell, founder and former executive director of The Little Light House, and Vivianna Smith, student at The Little Light House.

OPPOSITE BELOW
Pewter ornaments created for The Little Light House.

The Little Light House operates tuition-free and is fully supported by donations. I had the idea to create an ornament/pendant, have it cast in pewter, and make it available to sell on behalf of this wonderful organization. From 1997 to 2000, these small works of art raised more than $35,000 each year.

Hal and I continue to donate one sculpture each year to be auctioned at the annual Little Light House Garden Party. At this auction my sculpture always sells for more than its actual value, reflecting the goodness of the people of Tulsa.

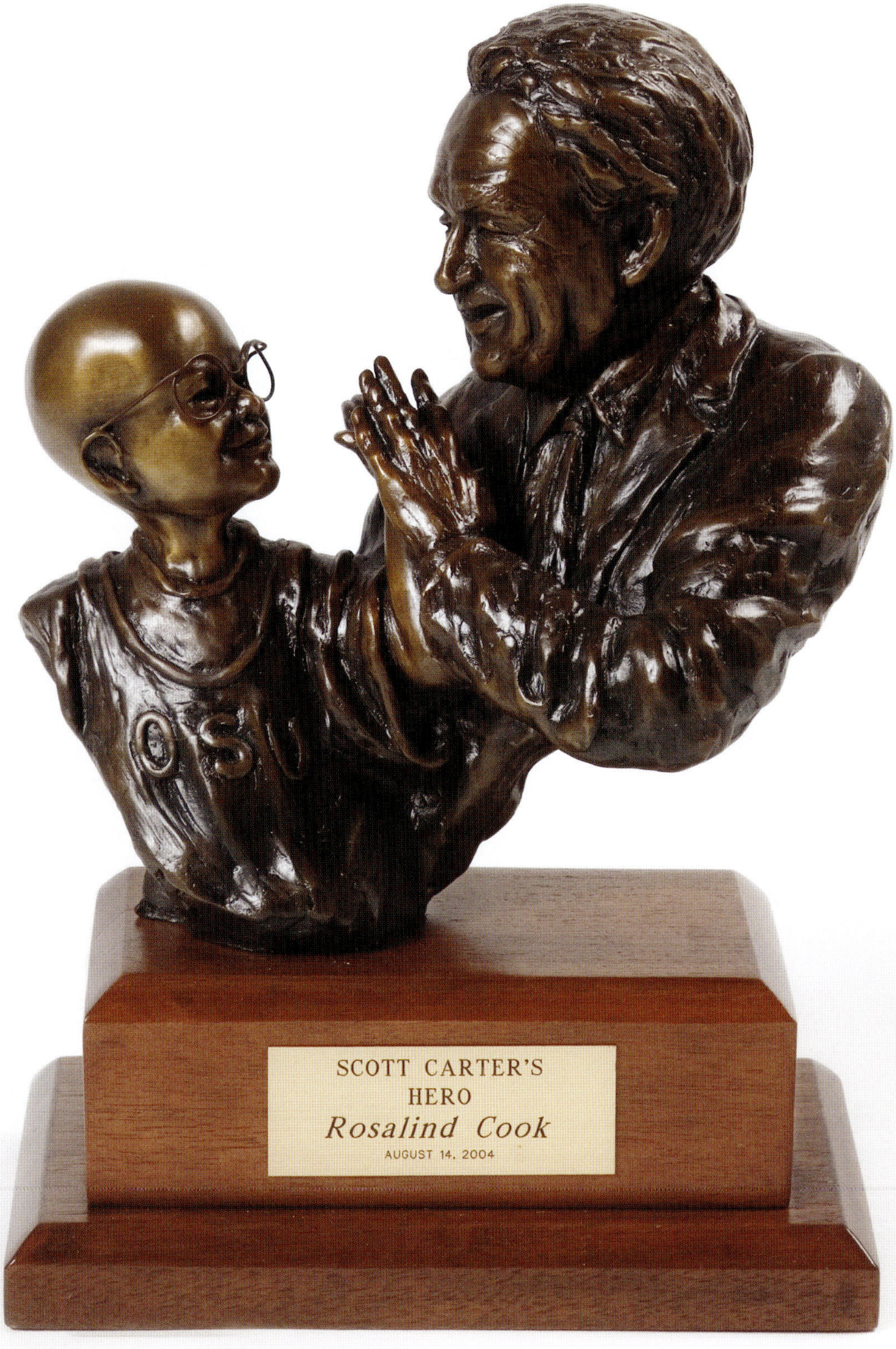
OSU
SCOTT CARTER'S
HERO
Rosalind Cook
AUGUST 14, 2004

THE SCOTT CARTER FOUNDATION

Mike Carter, Athletic Director of Oral Roberts University, and his wife, Paula, lost their 13-year-old son, Scott, to bone cancer in 1993. Scott had been an unabashed and loyal fan of Oklahoma State University basketball.

Coach Eddie Sutton invited Scott to sit on the bench with the players during the games, which became the thrill of Scott's short life. In an effort to fulfill their son's dream of finding a cure for childhood cancer, Mike and Paula began The Scott Carter Foundation, and asked me to create an award to be given annually. The sculpture I created depicts Scott and Eddie Sutton giving each other a "high five."

In creating this award, which was to be a surprise to Eddie, I worked from the coach's own photos. Both his sons and his wife, Patsy, would stop by and tell me to add more wrinkles or jowls. I normally lessen the effects of aging when I am doing a portrait sculpture, but I was told that the jowls created a true image of Eddie. They were right: everyone who sees this award immediately recognizes the distinctive face of Eddie Sutton.

OPPOSITE
The Scott Carter Foundation award, *Scott Carter's Hero*,
 Photo by Don Kreutzweiser.

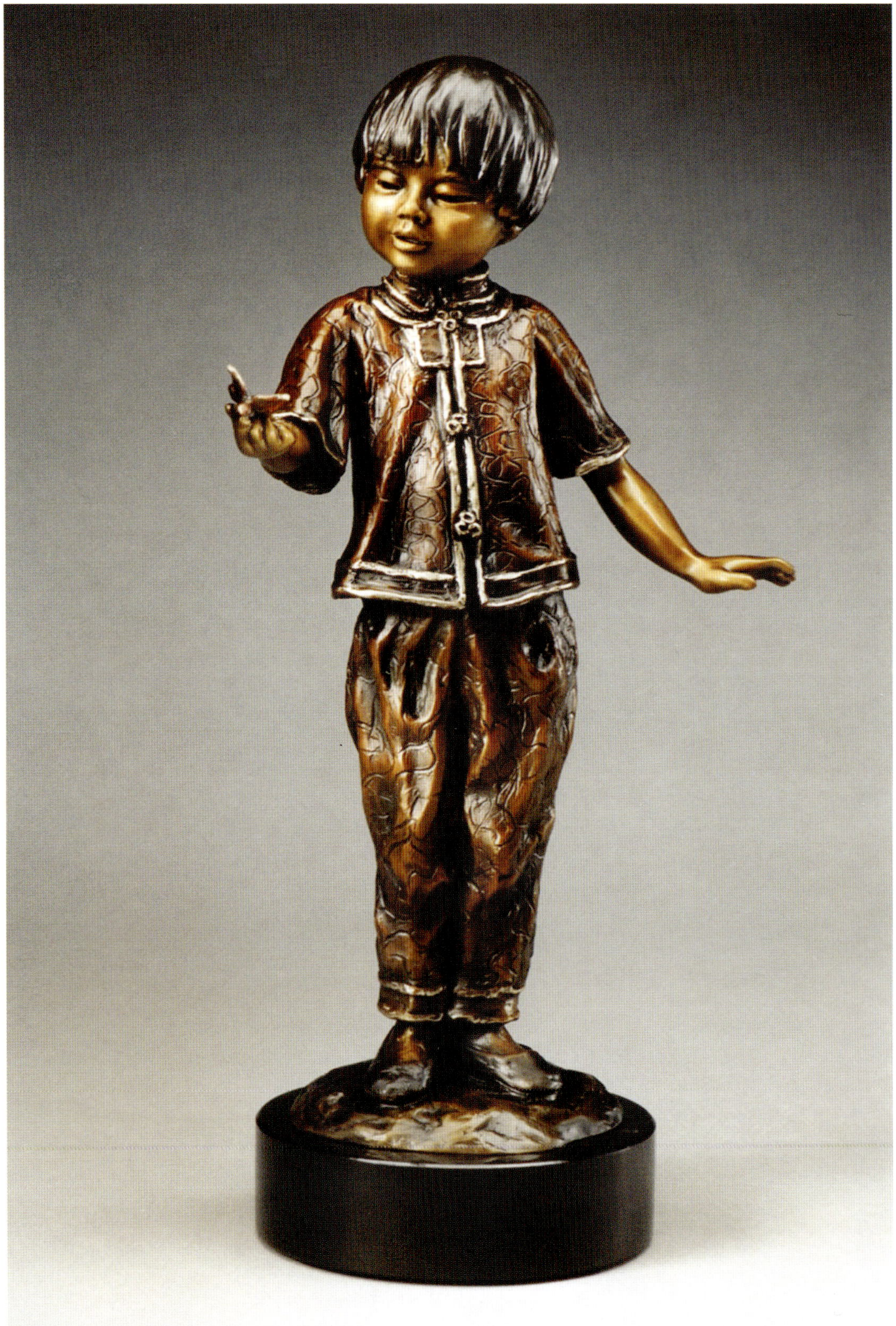

DILLON INTERNATIONAL

The Dillon International was created in 1972 by Jerry and Denise Dillon as Oklahoma's first licensed international adoption agency. Through their efforts Dillon International has provided loving families for abandoned or orphaned children from Korea, China, and ten other foreign countries. The Dillons' story of how this agency came into being is yet another example of what can happen when one person has a vision and acts on that vision.

In 2002, a young mother and her newly adopted Chinese child came over to play in my yard so that I could take photos of the little girl for a sculpture I would create to benefit Dillon International. Dressed in her little Chinese silks and with her straight, black hair, I marveled at the way Maddie, daughter of Sam and Nancy Smith, moved around the yard in such delicate ways that were so in keeping with her Asian heritage. From this experience came a sculpture, *Butterfly*. The butterfly represents the new life for both the child and the adoptive family.

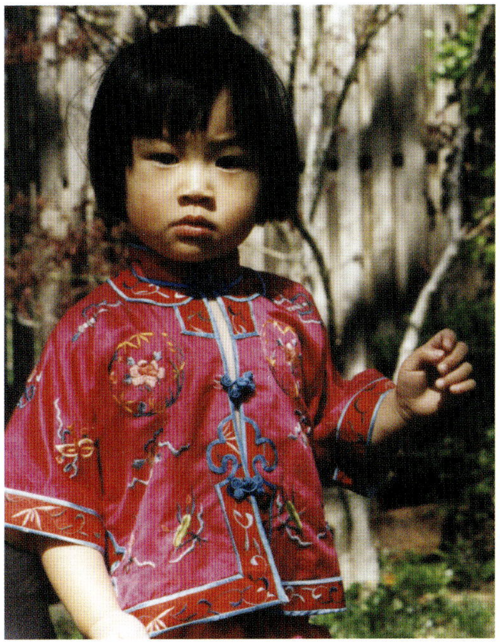

OPPOSITE
Butterfly, © 2002 Rosalind Cook.
Photo by Mel Schockner.

RIGHT
Little Maddie Smith, my model for *Butterfly*.

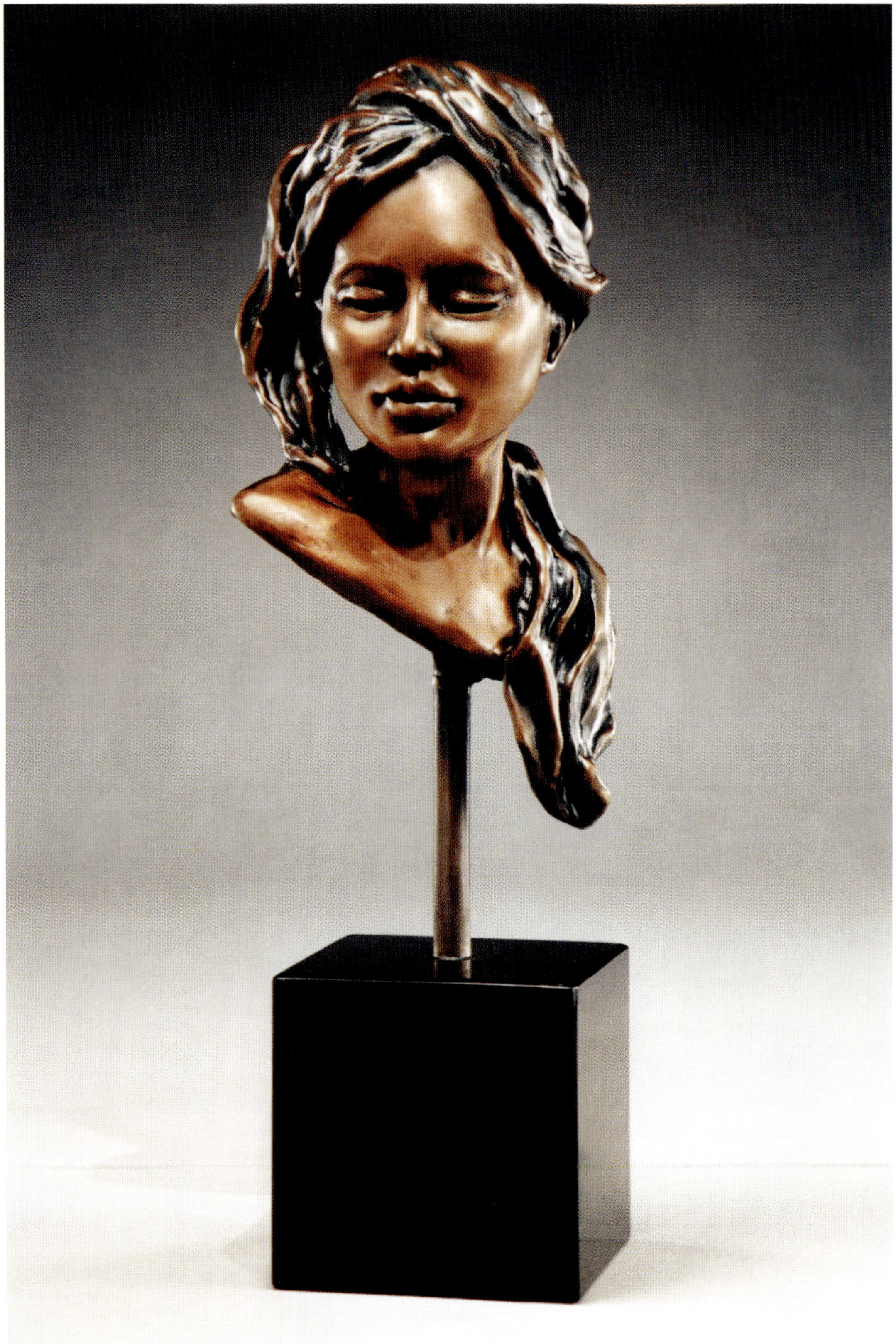

TULSA PROJECT WOMAN

TPW As a part of the Susan B. Komen Pink Ribbon network, Tulsa Project Woman provides mammograms, diagnostic procedures, and surgical services for women who have no health insurance or have limited financial resources. In any given year, they will assist about 1,800 women.

Sally and Rich Minshall were having dinner with Hal and me one evening. Afterward, Sally was in my studio when she shared with me that she and Rich were chairmen for the Pink Ribbon event that would benefit Tulsa Project Woman. She wondered if I had a sculpture they could use as part of the fundraiser.

Only weeks before, I had been working on a study of a small head of a woman wearing a turban. As Sally and I were talking, my eyes rested on this small study. I immediately thought, "This is it!" for she had neither hair nor breasts to define her, and yet she was feminine, strong, and full of hope. This sculpture could be used to raise money for Tulsa Project Woman through many castings, rather than just a one-time sale. That very night we named her: *Her Name is Hope.*

But there is more to this story. That week, I took the clay study to the Bronze Horse foundry in Pawhuska, Oklahoma, and explained to Sue, who works my waxes, that this piece was going to be used as a fundraiser for Tulsa Project Woman. Sue gasped and her eyes filled with tears. She told me that she had just been diagnosed with breast cancer and had no insurance. Her doctor was working to have her expenses covered by Tulsa Project Woman. I was so moved that I asked Sue to share her story at the benefit dinner where we would present the sculpture as a fundraiser for Tulsa Project Woman.

After careful thought and consideration, Sue felt that it might be a part of her healing process and agreed to speak. She bravely and beautifully shared her heartfelt story, and I saw tears in many eyes as she spoke. *Her Name is Hope* raised a great deal of money that night, and continues to do so.

OPPOSITE
Her Name is Hope, © 2002 Rosalind Cook.
Photo by Mel Schockner.

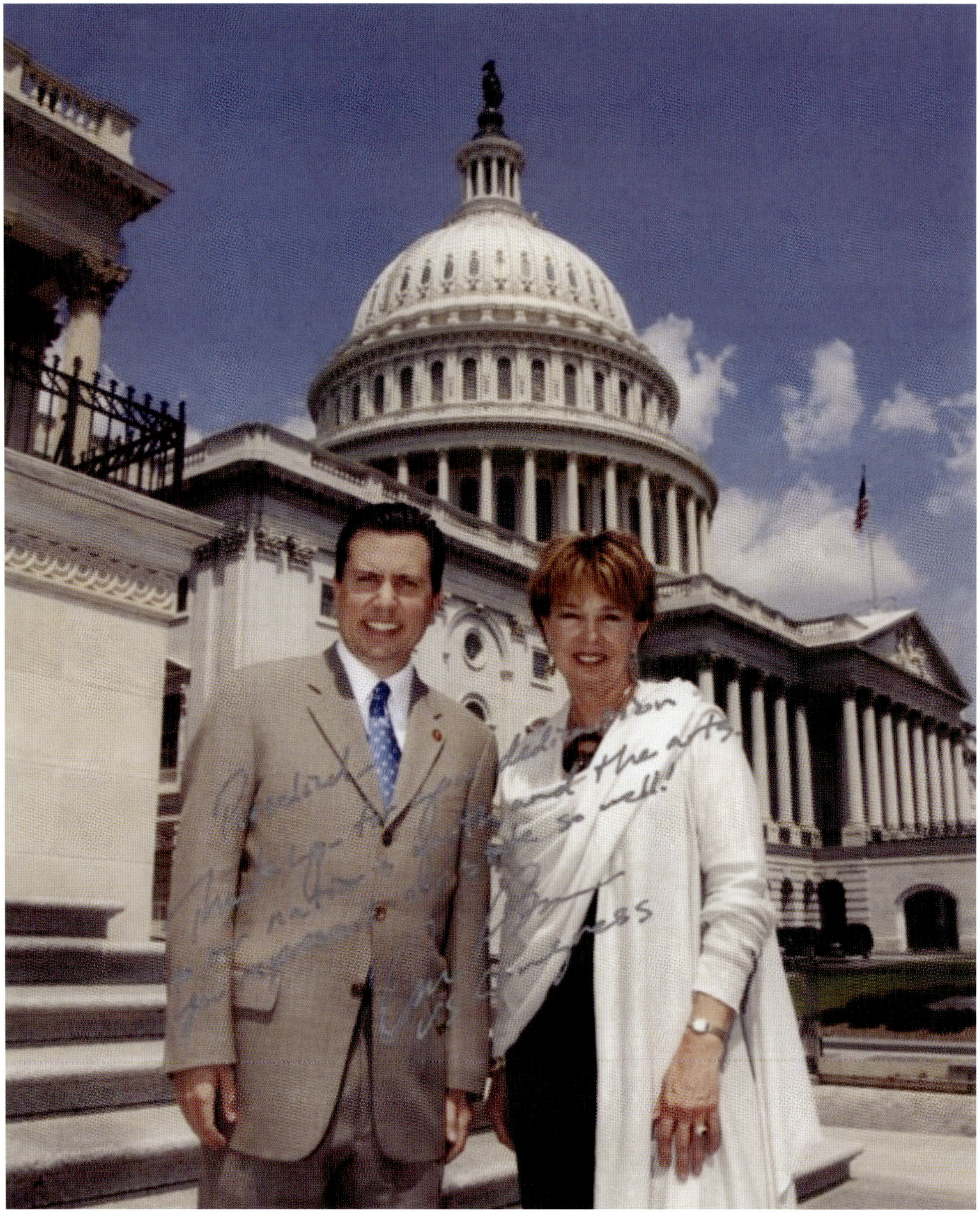

THE NATIONAL CONGRESSIONAL ART COMPETITION

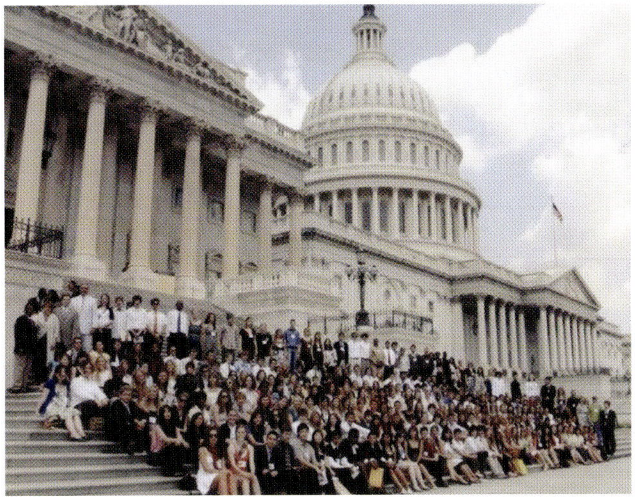

In 2008, I received a call from Oklahoma Congressman Dan Boren asking me to be the speaker for the National Congressional Art Competition in Washington, D.C. This program recognizes one high school art student from each of the 437 congressional districts in the United States. The students are invited to come to Washington, exhibit their work, meet with congressional officials, and attend a lecture and program in the Library of Congress by an accomplished professional artist. That speaker was *me!*

Through the years, I had done many speaking engagements, but this one had a new purpose. I had the opportunity to encourage, challenge, and advise budding artists from all over the country. What a responsibility, for it has been my experience that there are so many talented artists who have no idea how to move ahead with their art.

I was so excited to tell these young people that their gift of art should be developed and shared. I encouraged them to set goals, both short range and long range, to "bloom wherever they were planted" by entering local shows, and to think creatively about opportunities to show their work. Finally, I shared that a part of becoming a significant artist was to use their gifts to benefit others. It was thrilling to see these young artists light up and grab on to all the possibilities that lay ahead them.

OPPOSITE
Dan Boren and Rosalind at the United States Capitol.

ABOVE
Winners of the National Congressional Art Competition.

NONPROFIT ORGANIZATIONS

Tulsa has always been a giving city. These many givers have been an inspiration and a model for me in my giving. Using my work to benefit others makes my sculpture more significant and lasting in its purpose. Additional organizations I have supported through my sculpture are: The Salvation Army, Alzheimer's Association, Muscular Dystrophy, Cystic Fibrosis, Resonance, Tulsa Girls' Art School, other area schools, and many more nonprofit organizations.

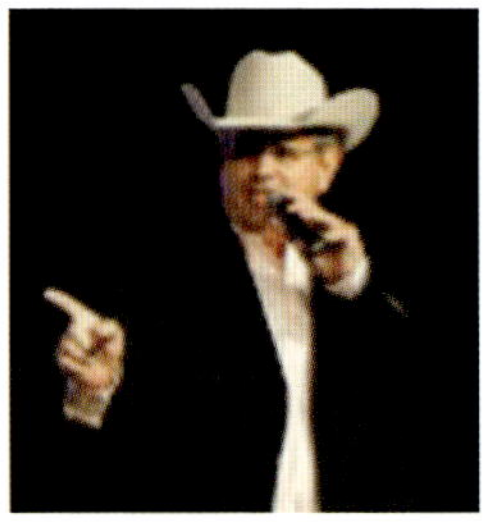

And now I want to recognize a gentleman who is truly a giver and has been a very successful auctioneer at many of the charity auctions where my work has been sold. The man in the big white Stetson is Mr. Jay Litchfield, who gives his talents and time to help the many organizations in the great city of Tulsa. Hats off to you, Mr. Jay!

THE ROSALIND COOK ARTISTIC ENCOURAGEMENT FOUNDATION

I have often been asked to be a judge for school art exhibits and competitions. I quickly became aware of how very hard the art teachers of our city work and how very small their budgets are. In 2008, I established a foundation through the Tulsa Community Foundation, where senior high school art teachers could apply for funds for specific art projects in their classes.

These funds are awarded to outstanding art teachers chosen through the Tulsa Arts and Humanities Council to receive the Rosalind Cook Artistic Encouragement Award, presented at the council's annual awards presentation each spring. Through the years these awards have benefited the following high schools: Nathan Hale, Will Rogers, McClain, Booker T. Washington, Edison, Memorial, East Central, Traice Academy, Owasso, and Project 12.

MADONNA HOUSE OF CATHOLIC CHARITIES

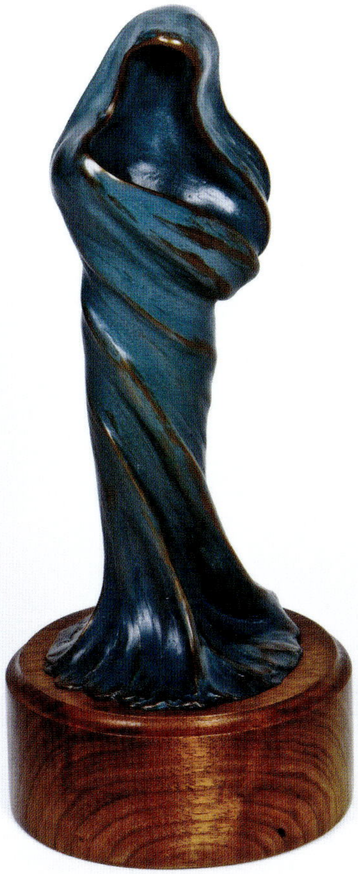

The Madonna House is a part of the many-faceted Catholic Charities and provides housing, counseling, and training for pregnant women choosing life and wanting a fresh start. Ronnie Donnelly called me in 1995 and explained that Madonna House wanted to present an annual award in the form of a bronze sculpture to those who had greatly benefited the mission of Madonna House.

The fact that this sculpture would be used as an award dictated some parameters within which to work. It had to look like an award. I wanted to convey the mission of the organization but without limitations as to personhood. I came up with a very organic, impressionistic form in which one can see a mother and child within the negative spaces. This sculpture has served its purpose well by honoring many outstanding volunteers and philanthropists through the years.

OPPOSITE
Jay Litchfield, auctioneer

ABOVE
The Madonna House award, © 1995 Rosalind Cook. Photo by Don Kreutzweiser.

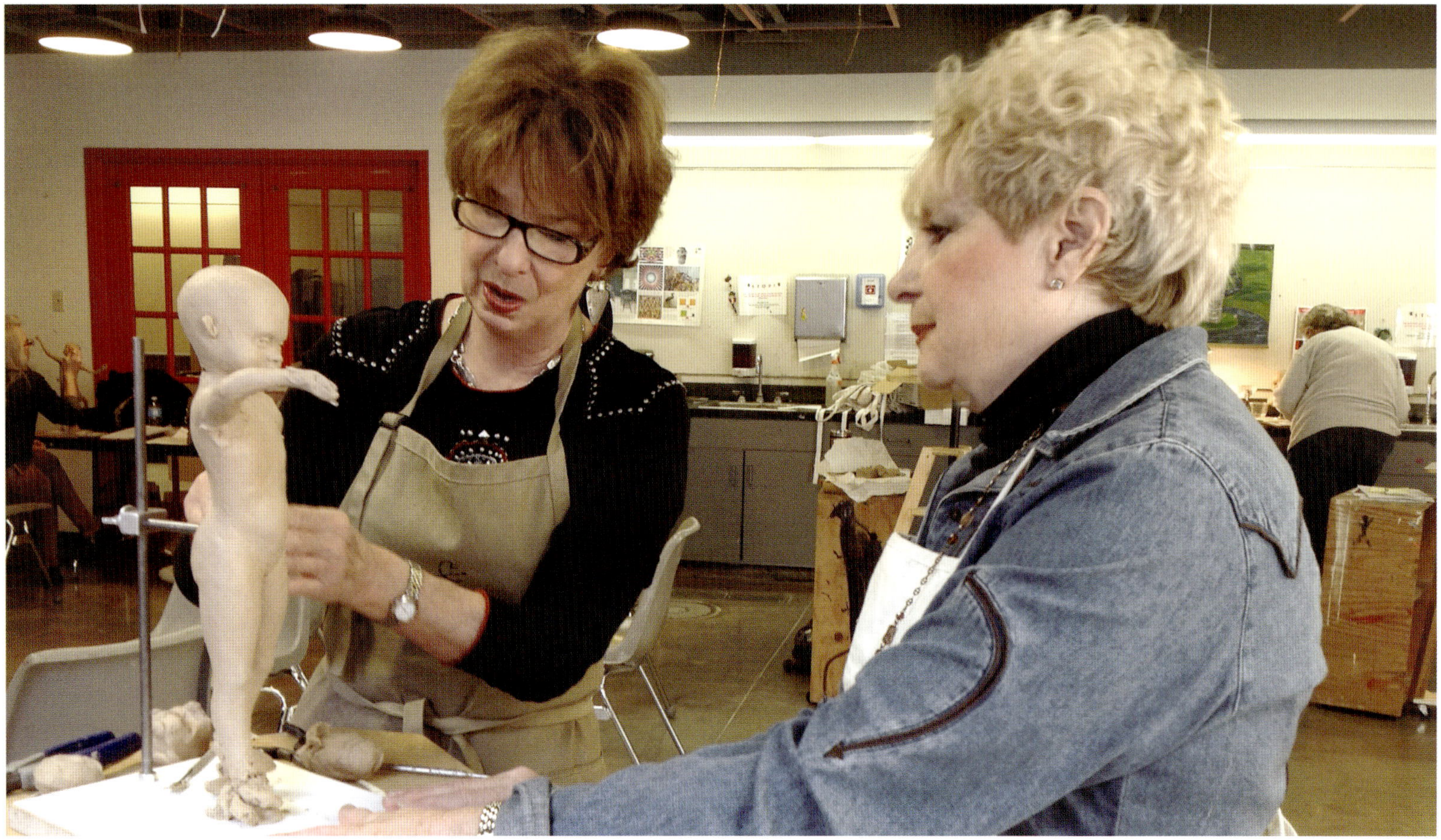

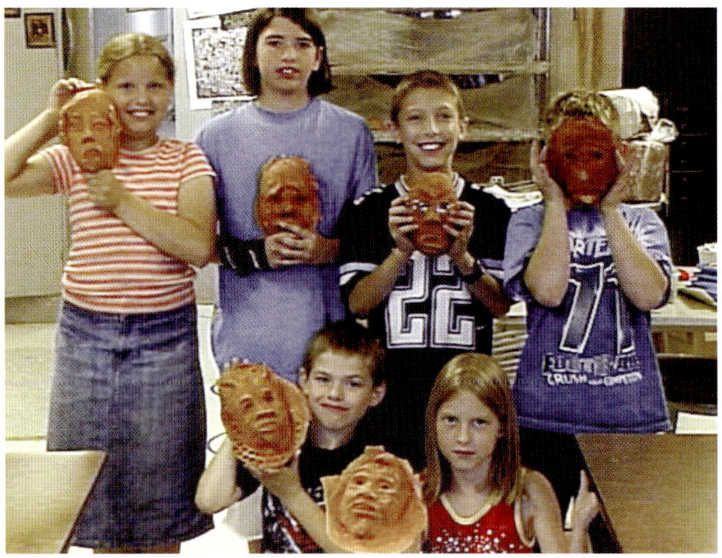
22
71

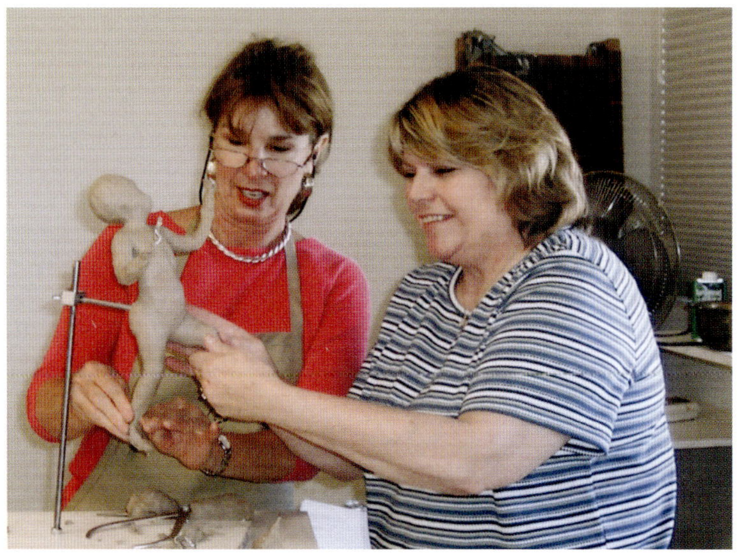

TEACHING VENUES

My sculpting success has allowed me to pursue another passion, that of teaching sculpture classes. Rather than be a distraction to my personal sculpting career, teaching has added dimenstion to my growth as an artist. I have taught adult classes at the Loveland Academy of Art in Colorado; the acclaimed Scottsdale Artists School in Arizona; Fechin Institute in Taos, New Mexico; Philbrook Museum in Tulsa; and many private venues across the country.

I first began teaching because I wanted to inspire others and give them the tools they would need to progress. Little did I know the many benefits teaching would have in store for me. First of all, I have to be organized and devise a progressive plan for a five-day workshop, or whatever the time dictates. Within the overall plan are goals to accomplish for each half-day session. People skills are very important as well. Being sensitive to each student's needs and personality is crucial. Students need to have their confidence built, as they may be exposing their inner self through their work for the first time. This is a precious gift to a teacher, and it must be treated with respect. There is a fine line between pushing too hard and yet pulling out a student's very best effort. Also, I find that as I am teaching principles and skills, those same words are carving deeper into my own mind and soul, and making me a better sculptor. I can always hear my own "teaching words" as I approach a challenging aspect of a project. Teaching truly feeds my soul, giving the gift I have been given by God to others.

OPPOSITE, ABOVE AND LOWER RIGHT
Masters Class at Philbrook Museum of Art in Tulsa, Oklahoma.

OPPOSITE, LOWER LEFT
Teaching children at Jenks East Elementary School in Jenks, Oklahoma.

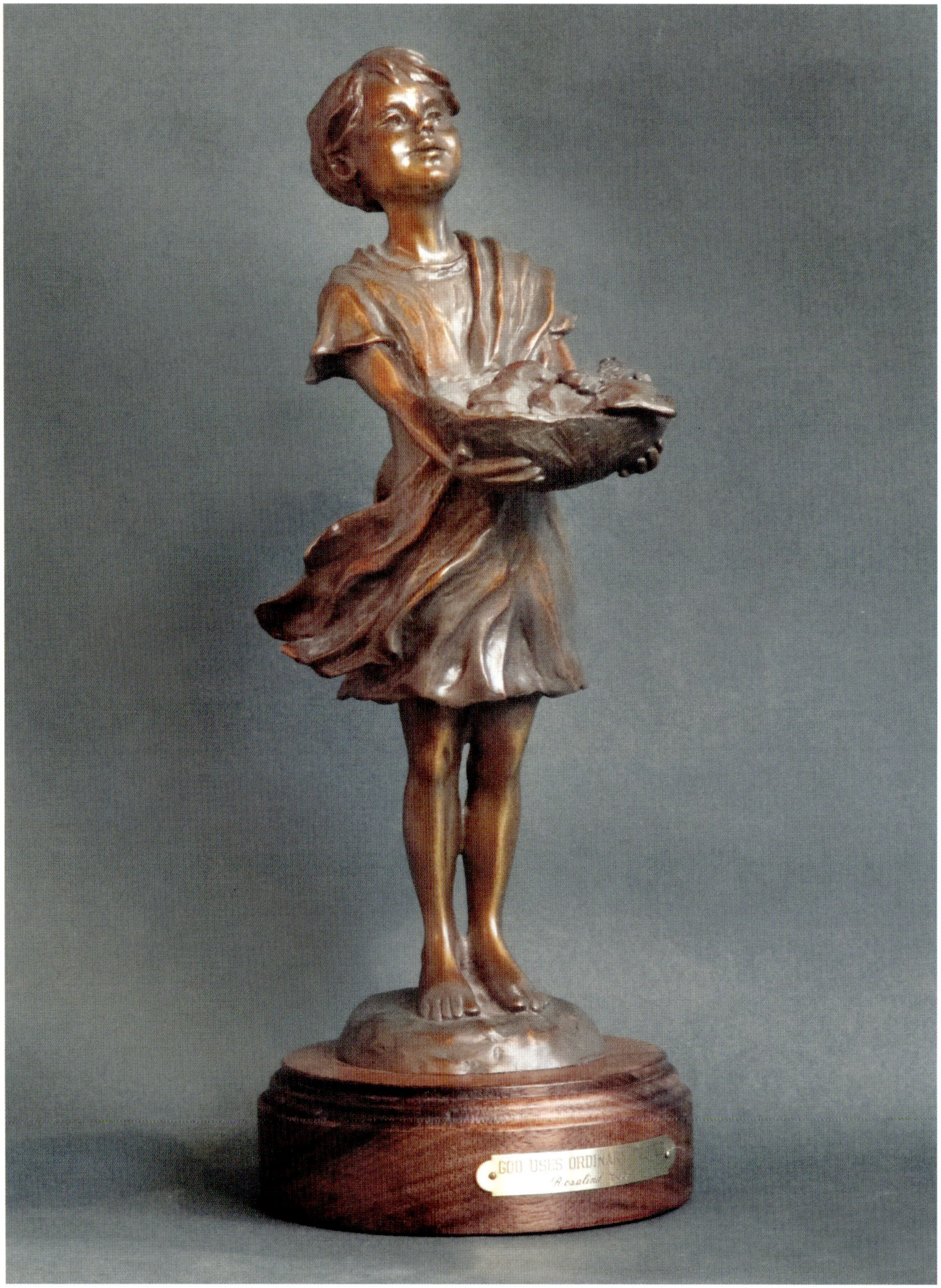
GOD USES
Rosalind

MISSION GIVING

My church, First United Methodist of Tulsa, has always held missions as a priority. We have frequent short-term trips allowing members of the congregation to serve in missions. Our family has participated in a few of these, and the experience changed our lives. One Sunday, a soloist sang a song called "God Uses Ordinary People" to accompany a sermon along the same lines. The idea came to me of creating a sculpture of the little boy in the Bible who generously gave his lunch of loaves and fishes, and with God's blessing, fed 5,000 people. This story metaphorically shows the principle of what can happen when one gives in faith. The total profits of the entire edition of 25 went toward our mission program. What took me a few days to create in the studio touched many lives: those of the missionaries and the people they served.

PHILBROOK MUSEUM FESTIVAL OF TREES

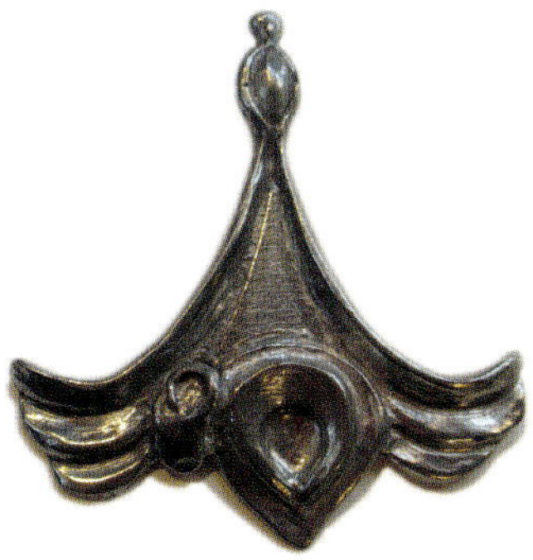

Among the many Christmas celebrations in Tulsa, Oklahoma, one of my favorites is the Festival of Trees at Philbrook Art Museum. The festival features Christmas trees created by local artists, gingerbread houses produced by local schoolchildren, and festive galas, all to benefit the museum. Each year an artist is chosen to design and create a special Christmas tree pin that is sold to patrons of the museum. I was asked to create the pin in 2007, Oklahoma's centennial year, celebrating 100 years of statehood. I chose to incorporate two iconic symbols of Oklahoma into an Art Deco design: the scissortail flycatcher and the American bison. Each pin was signed, numbered, dated, and cast in pewter at Inola Castings in Inola, Oklahoma.

OPPOSITE
God Uses Ordinary People, © 2004 Rosalind Cook.

ABOVE
Festival of Trees pin, © 2007 Rosalind Cook.

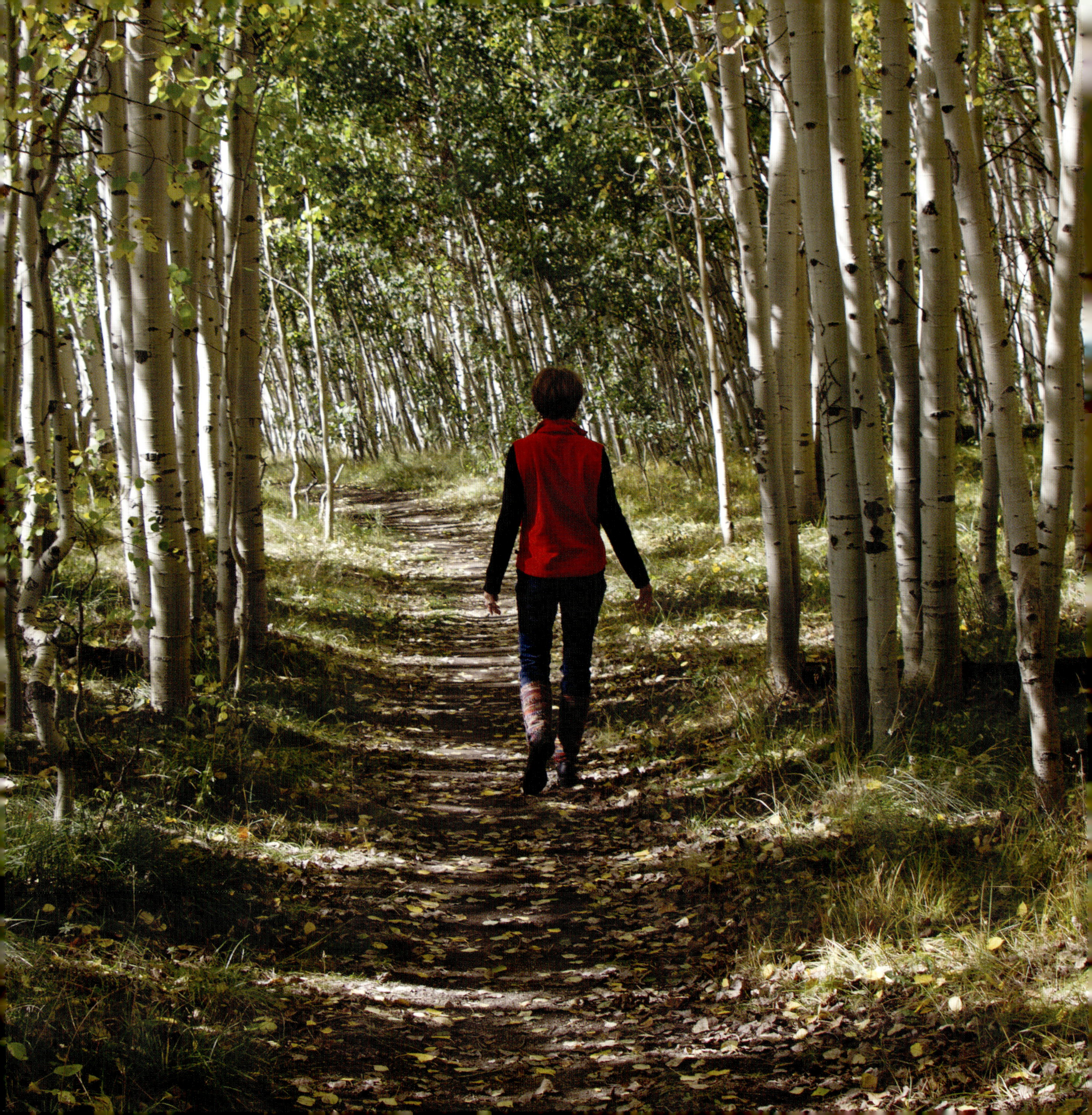

AND IN CONCLUSION

It is the desire within each of us to, in some way, "be significant." If you look up the word significant, it simply means making a difference. God has guided me through the journey of my life, showing me the paths to take. My life has been surrounded by people who have made a difference: my parents, my life partner, Hal, my children, my dearest friends, and my teachers. The city of Tulsa is filled with people who have made a difference and, in many ways, affected my life as well. My soul is fed with the love of the Holy Father, Son, and Holy Spirit, and my heart is filled with gratitude.

Here is a quote by George Bernard Shaw that deeply resonates with me and I shall leave you with this gift. The words in parentheses are my personal additions.

> *"This is the true joy in life, being used for a purpose recognized by you as a mighty one. I am of the opinion that my life belongs to the whole community (and to God) and as long as I live it is my privilege to do for it whatever I can. I want to be thoroughly 'used up' when I die, for the harder I work (and the more I give), the more I live. I rejoice in life for its own sake. Life is no brief candle to me. It is a sort of splendid torch which I have got hold of for the moment, and I want to make it burn as brightly as possible before handing it on to future generations."*

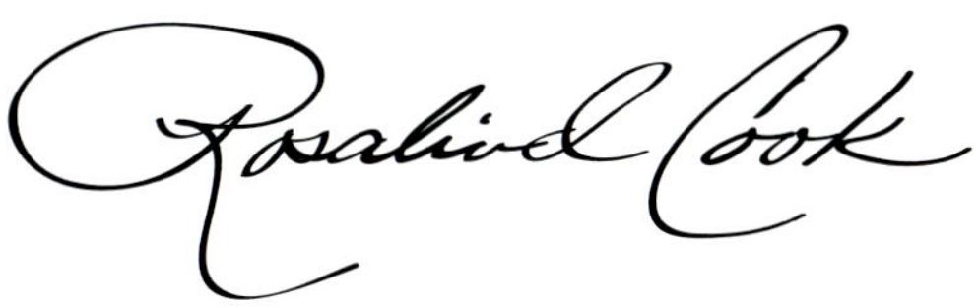

OPPOSITE
Walking a new path in Colorado.
Photo by John Miller.

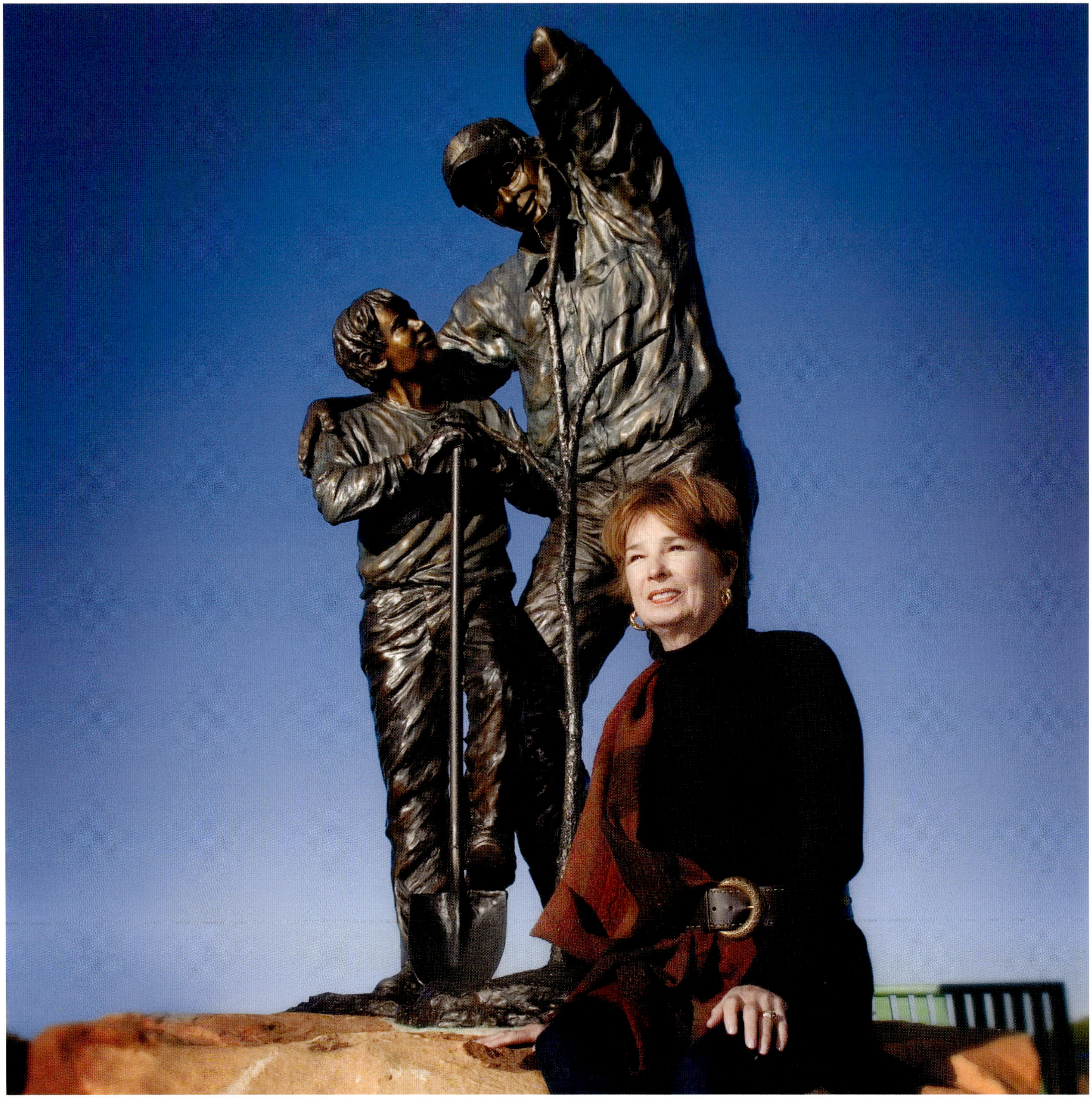

SCULPTURES IN TULSA'S PUBLIC PLACES

Harwelden, Arts and Humanities Council of Tulsa: *Celebrating the Arts**
Utica Square: *Welcome, Friends; The Bird Feeder; Story Time for One; Windy; Beautiful Bounty*
Tulsa Garden Center, The Linnaeus Teaching Garden: *Carolus Linnaeus, Father of Botany**
Holland Hall Preparatory School: *Belonging and Becoming**
Peggy V. Helmerich Library: *Legacy of Literature**
Saint Francis Children's Hospital: *Christ's Love for the Children**
Henry Zarrow Regional Library: *Story Time for Two*
Cancer Treatment Centers of America: *Celebrating Life**
Ronald McDonald House: *Finders Keepers**
First United Methodist Church: *Come Unto Me; Turning Point**
Kirk of the Hills Church: *Christ, Our Good Shepherd**
Michael Case Tennis Center, University of Tulsa: bust of *Natalie Overall Warren**
First United Methodist Church of Broken Arrow: *Come Unto Me*
Parent Child Center: *Locks and Lops and A Hare-y Carry*
River Parks: *Planting for the Future,** a tribute to Sid Patterson, founder of Up With Trees
Southern Hills Country Club, U.S. Open 2001: *Someday**
Mohawk Park First Tee: *Someday*
The Little Light House: *Abba, Father;* Locks and Lops and A Hare-y Carry; Come Unto Me*
Saint Simeon's Retirement Village: *The Bird Feeder*
Herman and Kate Kaiser Library: busts of *Herman Kaiser, Kate Kaiser**
Asbury United Methodist Church: *Intercession,** bust of *Reverend Bill Mason**
Catholic Charities campus: *The Poor Virgin of Nazareth Who Holds In Her Hands the Wealth of the World**
Catholic Charities, Madonna House annual award,*
Woodward Park, Anne Hathaway Garden: *Poems and Promises*
Laura Dester Children's Center: *Playful Pup*
Montereau In Warren Woods: *Young in Spirit;* Come Unto Me*
Happy Hands School for the Deaf: *Set Free II*
Sherman Miller Museum of Jewish Art: *Noah II*
University of Tulsa Art Department: *A Study In Dignity*
Gilcrease Museum, fiftieth anniversary commemorative sculpture: *Peyote Bird**

*Commissioned

OPPOSITE
Rosalind with *Planting for the Future* at River Parks.
Photo by Don Kreutzweiser.

SCULPTURES IN PUBLIC PLACES AROUND THE WORLD

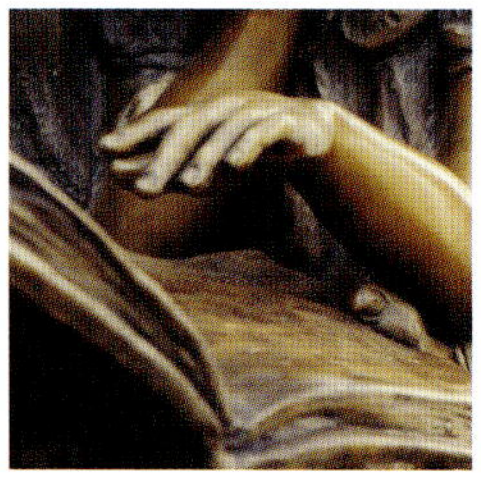 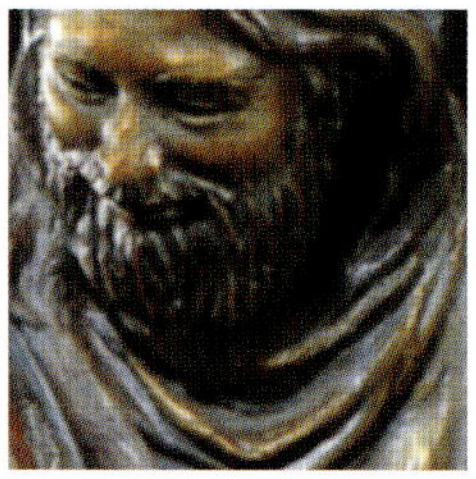 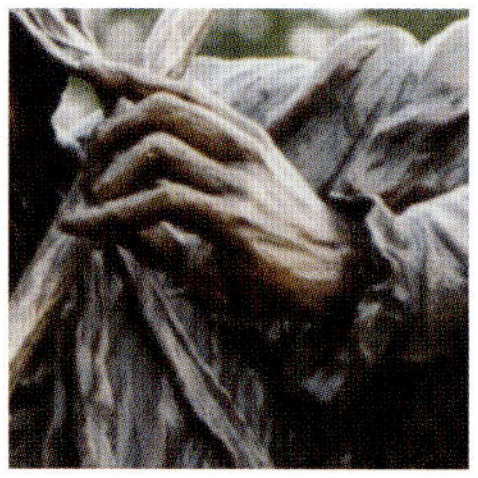 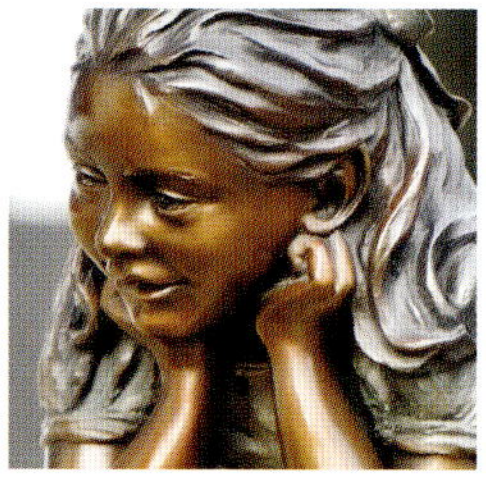

World Vision Headquarters, Federal Way, Washington: *Christ, The Bread of Life**

Compassion International Headquarters, Colorado Springs, Colorado: *Story Time for Three (East Indian Children);* Korean Mother and Son;* Come Unto Me;* Gift of Flowers;* African with Peruvian Children;* Set Free III**

Cleveland Heart Clinic, Cleveland, Ohio: *Welcome, Friends*

Na 'Aina Kai Botanical Gardens, Kauai, Hawaii: *Welcome, Friends; Turtle Boy; Turtle Dancer*

Kilohana Farms Plantation, Kauai, Hawaii: *Planting for the Future**

US Airways Center, Phoenix, Arizona: *Great Expectations*

Association of Baptists for World Evangelism Headquarters, Harrisburg, Pennsylvania: *Come Unto Me; Gift of Flowers; Prize Possession**

Benson Park, permanent sculpture collection, Loveland, Colorado: *Lillith*

City of Cerritos, Cerritos, California: *Legacy of Literature*

Texas City Parks, Texas City, Texas: *Turtle Boy*

Beatrice Public Library, Beatrice, Nebraska: *Lock and Lops and A Hare-y Carry*

St. Anthony Hospital, Oklahoma City, Oklahoma: *Welcome, Friends*

Innsbrook Resort, Innsbrook, Missouri: *Welcome, Friends*

St. Francis Catholic Church, Enid, Oklahoma: *Welcome, Friends*

Civic Center, Palm Desert, California: *Finders Keepers*

Hillside Village Complex, Sedona, Arizona: *Finders Keepers*

The Vatican, Rome, Italy: *Christ, The Bread of Life,* 18 inches high

Bethany Baptist Church, Puyallup, Washington: *Come Unto Me*

*Commissioned

ABOVE, LEFT TO RIGHT
Legacy of Literature (detail) / *Come Unto Me* (detail) / *Celebrating the Arts* (detail) / *Story Time for Three* (detail)

SCULPTURES IN PUBLIC PLACES AROUND THE WORLD

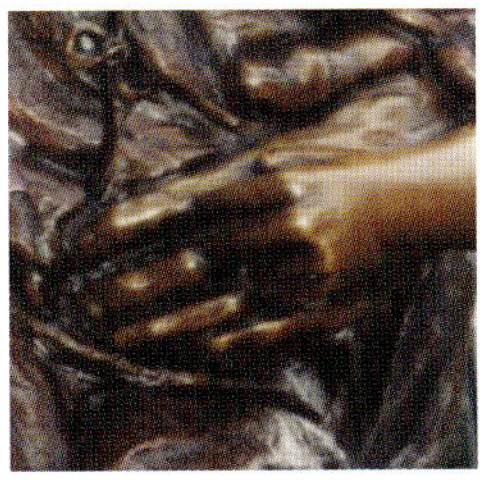
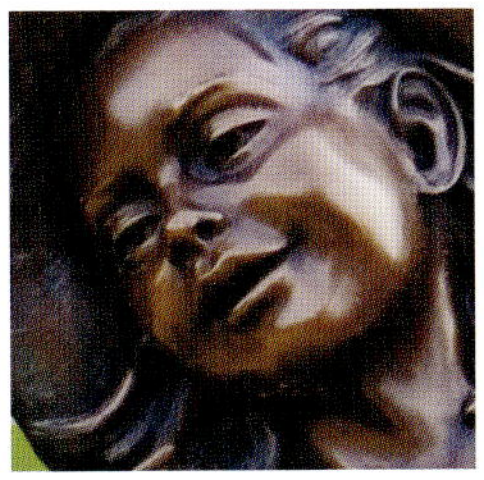
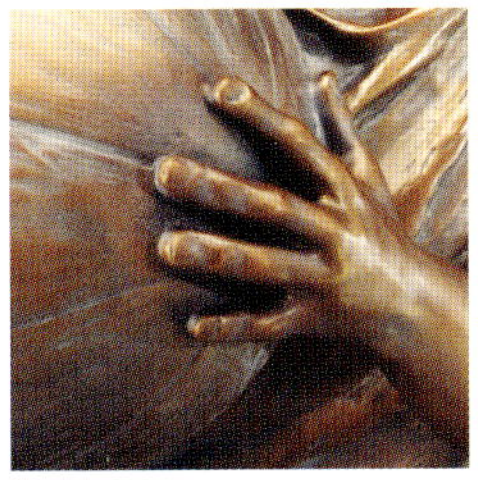
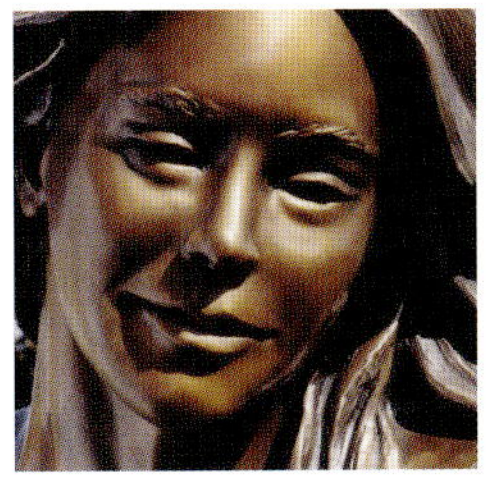

Casady Preparatory School, Oklahoma City, Oklahoma: *Welcome, Friends*
Sedgwick County Zoo, Wichita, Kansas: *Turtle Boy* and *Turtle Dancer*
Potter's Park Golf Course, Hamilton, Ohio: *Someday*
The City of Hamilton, Ohio: *Legacy of Literature*
Maple Knoll Village, Cincinnati, Ohio: *Summer Dancer**
University of South Alabama, Mobile, Alabama: *Celebrating the Arts*
Noel Art Museum, Odessa, Texas: *Turtle Rider; Playful Pup*
Hurst Public Library, Hurst, Texas: *Poems and Promises**
New Irving Library, Westminster, Colorado: *Legacy of Literature*
Cancer Treatment Centers of America, Atlanta, Georgia: *Celebrate Life**
Cancer Treatment Centers of America, Chicago, Illinois: *Celebrate Life**
Cancer Treatment Centers of America, Philadelphia, Pennsylvania: *Celebrate Life**
Cancer Treatment Centers of America, Phoenix, Arizona: *Celebrate Life**
Zelenograd Presbyterian Church, Zelenograd, Russia: *Christ, Our Good Shepherd*
Grand Island Public Library, Grand Island, Nebraska: *Legacy of Literature*
North Edmond High School, Edmond Oklahoma: *Story Time for Three*
Bristow Public Library, Bristow, Oklahoma: *Story Time for Three*
Mt. Crested Butte Wedding Garden, Crested Butte, Colorado: *Gratitude*
City of Crested Butte, Colorado: *Lillith*
Morningside Church, Blue Eye, Missouri: *Christ, Our Good Shepherd*
Oklahoma State Capitol, Oklahoma City, Oklahoma: *Soaring Spirit,**

*Commissioned

ABOVE, LEFT TO RIGHT
The Bread of Life (detail) / *Wendy*(detail) / *Great Expectations* (detail) / *Poems and Promises* (detail)

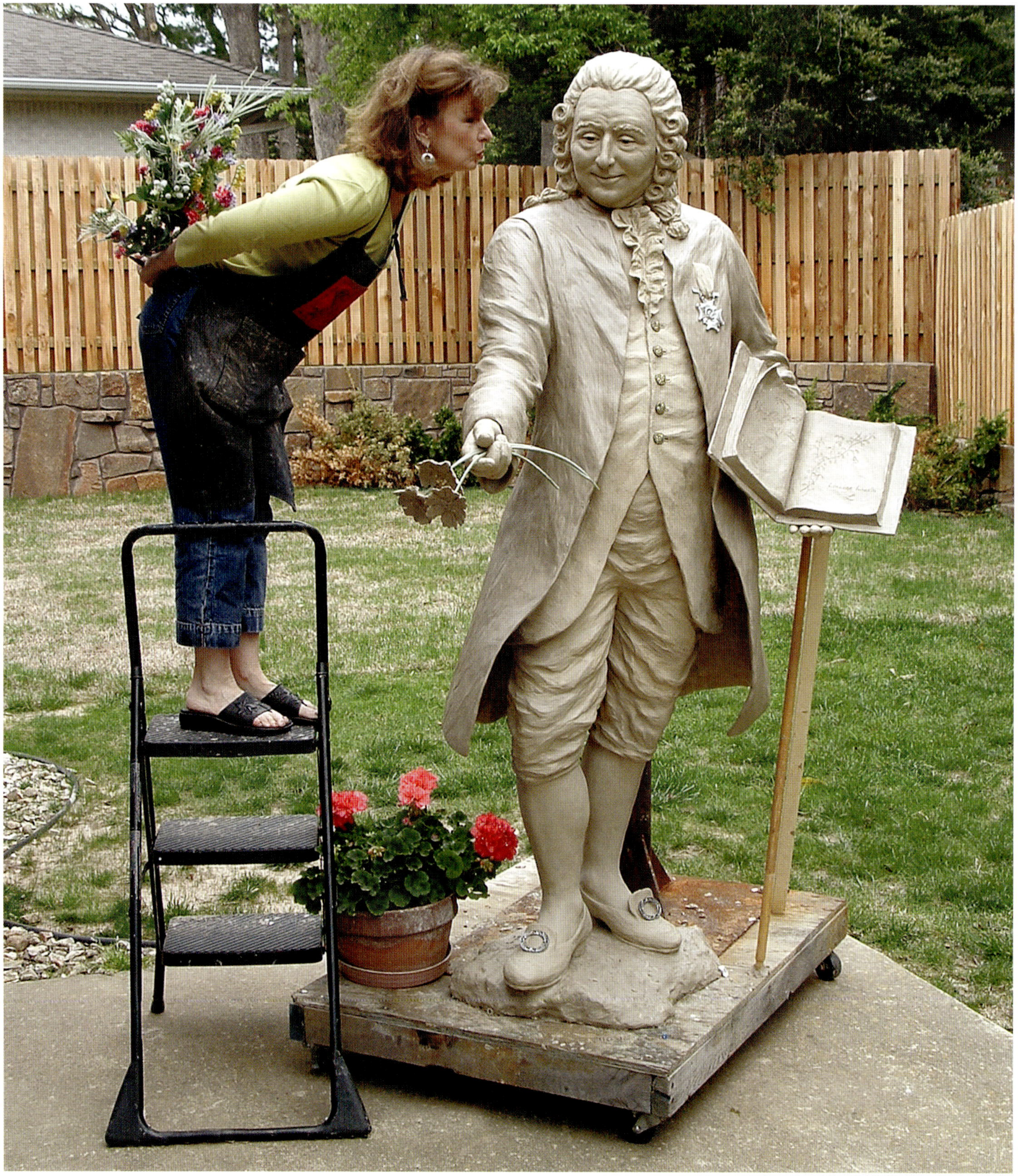

ACKNOWLEDGMENTS AND MANY THANKS

To the Good Lord, who is always faithful

To my Husband, **Hal Cook**, my dearest friend and supporter

To my Children, **Mark**, **Amy**, **and Clint**, who were always willing to lend me an ear, hand, or foot and who brought me the greatest joy

To my Editor, **John Brooks Walton**, who made me believe this book could actually exist, and who lent his knowledge, talents, and wisdom. We share a mutual admiration.

To my Graphic Designer, **Patricia Ridge Bradley**, who recognized my heart and brought this book into vibrant life through her many talents

To my Copy Editor, **Business/Office Manager**, **Melanie Sutton**, my dear friend who worked behind the scenes to make me successful

To my Foundries: The Bronze Horse and John Free Jr.; Art Castings of Colorado and Jeanne Toussaint and Tony Workman; Bronze Services of Loveland and Tom O'Gorman, Kim DeLyser, and Ginny Smith; Debbie Bakel

To my Studio Assistants: Denise Rinkovsky, the late Jim Pendergast, and Hal Cook

To my Photographers: Don Kreutzweiser, Mel Schockner, Andy Leithner, Jim Digby, Nathan Harmon, Bill Welch, Gary Hale, David Miller, and Dave Crenshaw

To the Galleries that represented my work through the years: Dodson Gallery, Gallery of the West, Breckenridge Gallery, Shaw Gallery, Pam Driscol Gallery, Pitzer's of Carmel, Trailside Gallery, Legacy Gallery, Mountain Trails Gallery, Danskin Gallery, Altermann Gallery, Downey Gallery, Westbrook Gallery, Cogswell Gallery, Greenhouse Gallery, Bronze Coast Gallery, Hilligoss Gallery, The Studio at Long Grove, The Master's Fine Art, and Caswell Galleries

To my Mentors and Teachers: the late Octavio Medellin, Claude Hixson, Glenna Goodacre, Lincoln Fox, Gary Hale, and the late Fritz White

To my Website Designer, Toni Moss and David Lawrence of T Moss Associates

To my Collectors: with special thanks to Walt and Peggy Helmerich, Dave and Clydella Hentschel, S.B. and Pamela Jucknies, Joe and Melanie Sutton, Bryan Close, Archie and Genelle Crenshaw, Bob Campana, Joyce Doty, Mike and Janie Brady, Steve and Deniece Linn, and James T. "Red" Hudson

To my Installation Supports: Aaron Rogers of CR Forma, Joe Howell of Howell & Vancuren, Mike Rives and team of Benchmark Monument Co., Chuck Hurt of Hurt's Stone Design, Molly Malone of Specialized Transportation Inc., Tom O'Gorman, and John Free

To my Cheerleaders: James Watts, art editor of the *Tulsa World*; our parents, Richard and Dorlene Wright and Laura B. Cook; my sister, Pamela Jucknies; my Tulsa friends; my Crested Butte friends; my models; those who have toured my studio; the organizations and churches that have invited me to speak; Gillies of Gilcrease Museum; my students at Philbrook Museum

To my Studio Dogs: the late Obie and present Aspen, who have been my constant companions

OPPOSITE
Rosalind with *Carolus Linnaeus*.

PAGE 144
Rosalind in the garden with *Windy*.

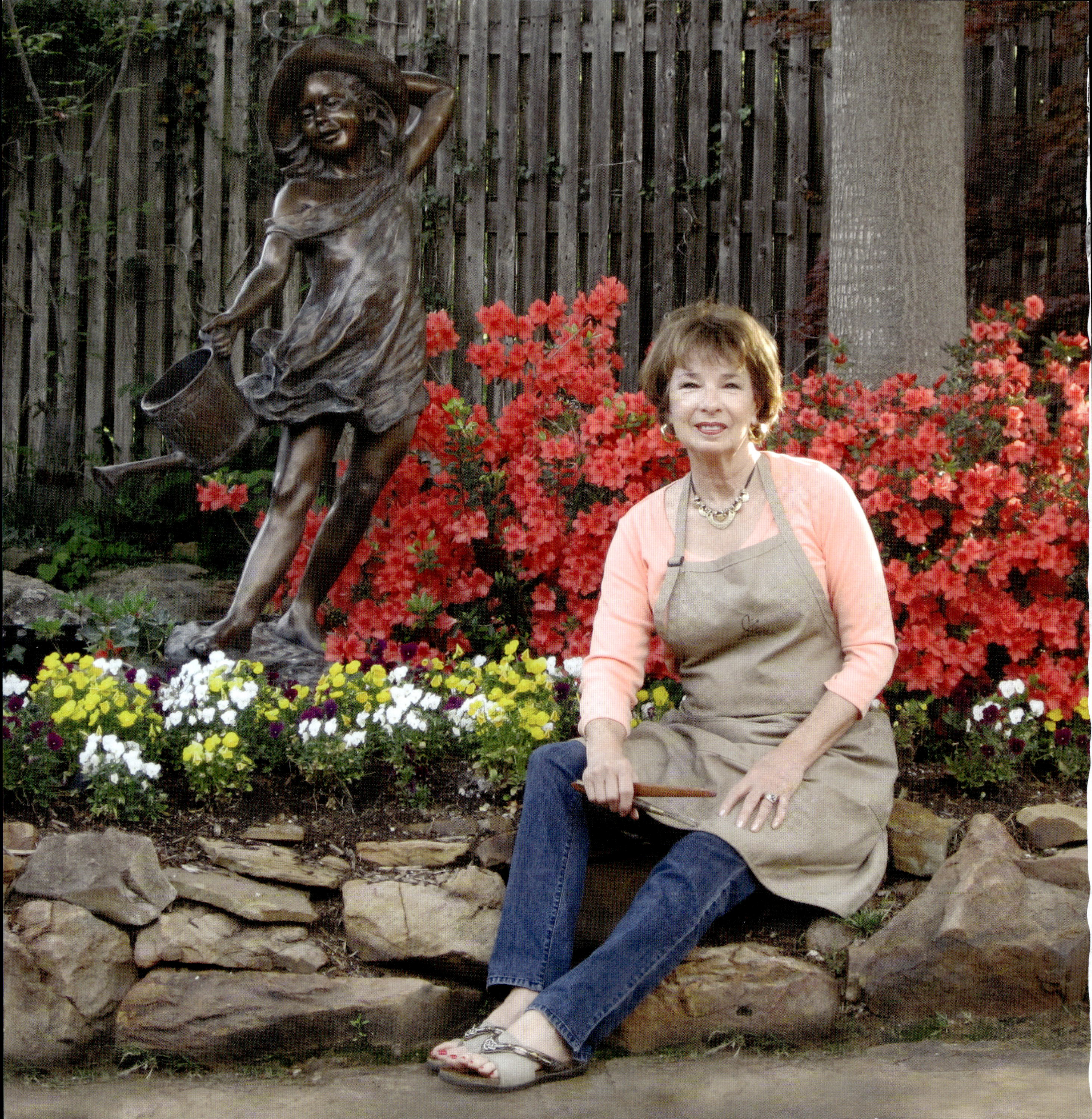

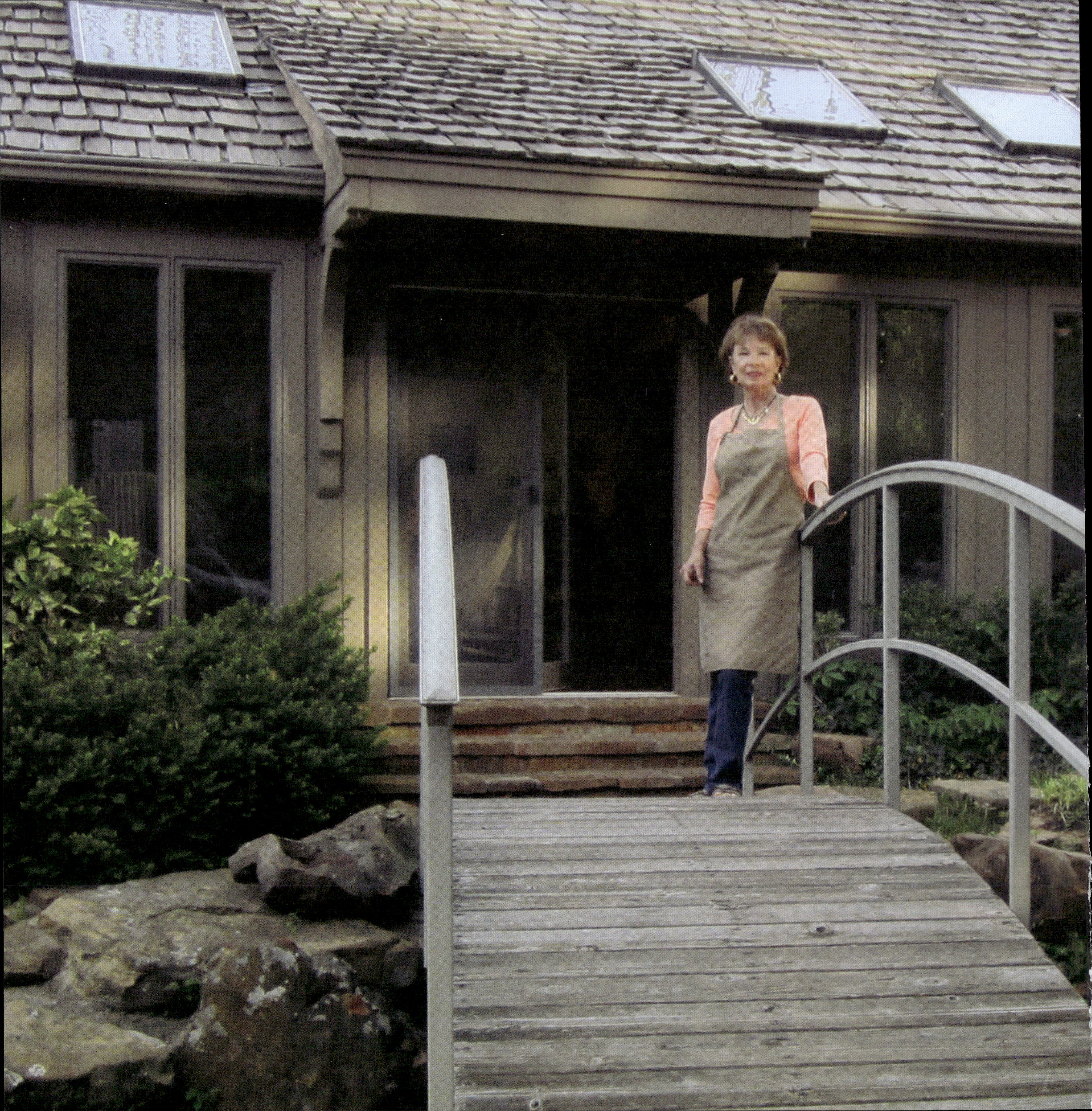